"Tom Bolin's *An Inspired Word in Season* is wise and learned and the book on biblical interpretation that we need in our polarized world. It should be essential reading for all serious Christians whether Catholic, Protestant, or other, as it surveys the history of biblical interpretation in a manner that invites everyone into the conversation. More than this, it is a book that covers complicated technical matters in a manner that is open to all serious readers, but not in a manner that excludes non-experts. Bolin calls for greater empathy and understanding in our biblical reading and greater personal engagement with those with whom we disagree. If every Catholic and every Christian were to read this book, and take it seriously, it could actually have a positive impact on biblical literacy, biblical interpretation, and reduce polarization in the Church and in the United States, for at its heart is a simple prescription: we need to read the Bible with each other guided by the rule of love."

— John W. Martens, professor of theology, St. Mark's College, Vancouver

"Polarization in the church begins with the divided ways in which we read the Bible—different interpretations but also different concepts of authority of Scripture. This book comes at a crucial time because it helps navigate the widening gap [of polarization] and to not abandon the Bible as a guide on current political issues."

— Massimo Faggioli, professor of historical theology, Villanova University

"As a guide for understanding how and why the Bible is used in so many different ways, this book could not be more timely. Deeply engaged in Christian and Catholic sources and tradition, Thomas Bolin uses wide-ranging examples (e.g., slavery, Church documents, Augustine, Huck Finn, Amelia Bedelia, and, of course, lots of biblical texts) to explain how we got here with the Bible and where we should go from here. His thought-provoking book is a perfect choice for a college course or parish discussion group or Bible study."

— Andrew R. Davis, professor of Old Testament, Boston College

I0805935

An Inspired Word in Season

Reading the Bible Responsibly in a Polarized World

Thomas M. Bolin

LP
A

LITURGICAL PRESS
ACADEMIC

Collegeville, Minnesota
litpress.org

Cover art courtesy of Shutterstock.
Cover design by David Drummond.

Library of Congress Cataloging-in-Publication Data

Names: Bolin, Thomas M. author
Title: An inspired word in season : reading the Bible responsibly in a polarized world / Thomas M. Bolin.
Description: Collegeville, Minnesota : Liturgical Press Academic, [2025] | Includes bibliographical references. | Summary: "Can Christians navigate the use of biblical texts that are quoted and used to support points across the political spectrum? What principles exist for interpreting those that support conflicting viewpoints? In An Inspired Word in Season, biblical scholar Thomas Bolin addresses these questions by equipping readers with an interpretive toolkit to use the Bible as a moral guide to inform their thinking as Christian citizens"—Provided by publisher.
Identifiers: LCCN 2024061696 (print) | LCCN 2024061697 (ebook) | ISBN 9780814688021 trade paperback | ISBN 9780814688274 epub | ISBN 9798400801884 pdf
Subjects: LCSH: Christianity and politics—Biblical teaching | Christianity and politics—Catholic Church | Christianity and politics—United States
Classification: LCC BS680.P45 B66 2025 (print) | LCC BS680.P45 (ebook) | DDC 220.8/32—dc23/eng/20250305
LC record available at https://lccn.loc.gov/2024061696
LC ebook record available at https://lccn.loc.gov/2024061697

For my students at St. Mary's University
and St. Norbert College, 1995–2025

Contents

Preface

In June 2018 it was reported that the US Border Patrol and the Immigration and Customs Enforcement (ICE) branch of the Department of Homeland Security was separating the children of Latin American refugees from their parents and detaining them. In some instances, infants as young as five months old were taken from their mothers and placed in detention facilities, which were often nothing more than a series of chain-link dog runs set up in large abandoned buildings. People across the country were justifiably horrified and outraged at this policy.

Clergy from all denominations condemned the treatment of these families as violations of biblical and Christian ethics. A delegation of Catholic bishops traveled to the border to visit these children. In response to this criticism, Jeff Sessions, US attorney general and a practicing United Methodist, defended his agency's action by appeal to a biblical text (Rom 13:1-7): "I would cite you to the Apostle Paul and his clear and wise command in Romans 13, to obey the laws of the government because God has ordained them for the purpose of order," Sessions said in a speech to law enforcement officers on June 14.[1] Numerous historians and theologians

[1] Richard Gonzales, "Sessions Cites the Bible to Justify Immigrant Family Separations," *National Public Radio*, June 14, 2018, https://www.npr.org/2018/06/14/620181177/sessions-cites-the-bible-to-justify-immigrant-family-separations. Here is the passage: "Let every person be subject to the governing authorities; for there is no authority except from God, and those authorities that exist have been instituted by God. [2] Therefore whoever resists authority resists what God has appointed, and those who resist will incur judgment. [3] For rulers are not a terror to good conduct, but to bad. Do you wish to have no fear of the authority? Then do what is good, and you will receive its approval; [4] for it is God's servant for your good. But if you do what is wrong, you should be afraid, for the authority

were quick to criticize Sessions's appeal to Romans 13.[2] Blase Cupich, the cardinal archbishop of Chicago, released a statement in which he bluntly said, "We are told this policy is supported by Scripture. That too is false."[3] The three Catholic bishops of Orange County, California, were much more detailed in their critique of the attorney general. In a published statement they said of Sessions's use of the Bible that: "When reading Romans 13 one must reckon with its historical misuse in the U.S. to support slavery and in Nazi Germany to support Adolf Hitler, to cite just two sad examples. All kinds of scripture can and have been used by people to justify atrocities and to whitewash the tombs (Matthew 23:27)."[4]

Like many Americans, I both was disgusted at this policy and felt powerless to make a difference. I contacted my congressional representatives, drew attention to the issue on social media, and took part in one of the many protest marches on June 30, 2018. But I wanted to do more, so I thought about how I could use my training as a biblical scholar and role as a Catholic professor at a Catholic college to help fellow Christians, fellow Catholics in particular, better understand how our government's mistreatment of refugees is an affront to the human dignity at the heart of the Christian faith. My mind kept returning to Jeff Sessions's use of Romans 13 to support an inhumane policy, and to the round of rebuttals that

---

does not bear the sword in vain! It is the servant of God to execute wrath on the wrongdoer. [5]Therefore one must be subject, not only because of wrath but also because of conscience. [6]For the same reason you also pay taxes, for the authorities are God's servants, busy with this very thing. [7]Pay to all what is due them—taxes to whom taxes are due, revenue to whom revenue is due, respect to whom respect is due, honor to whom honor is due."

[2] For example, Lincoln Mullen, "The Fight to Define Romans 13," *The Atlantic*, https://www.theatlantic.com/politics/archive/2018/06/romans-13/562916/; Casey Strine, "What the Bible's Romans 13 Says about Asylum—and What Jeff Sessions Omitted," *The Conversation*, https://theconversation.com/what-the-bibles-romans-13-says-about-asylum-and-what-jeff-sessions-omitted-98483.

[3] Cardinal Blase Cupich, "Statement of Cardinal Blase J. Cupich, Archbishop of Chicago, on the Administration's Family-Separation Policy," WTTW online, June 2018, https://chicagotonight.wttw.com/sites/default/files/article/file-attachments/Statement%20Version%20-%20English.pdf.

[4] Bishops Kevin Vann, Timothy Freyer, and Thanh Thai Nguyen, "On Taking Human Persons (and Holy Scripture) Out of Context," June 20, 2018, https://occatholic.com/diocese-of-orange-bishops-on-taking-human-persons-and-holy-scripture-out-of-context-2/.

followed. Both Sessions and those who disagreed with him were making claims about what the Bible said and how it could be applied to a modern ethical issue. Like many of Sessions's critics, I too believed his use of Romans 13 in this instance was a misappropriation of the biblical text, and I could articulate several reasons to support that evaluation. Thankfully, many other biblical scholars had already done this. Historians, too, noted the use of Romans 13 to support slavery.[5] But then I went on to consider all the other pressing contemporary social issues—with real-life stakes in the lives of many people—and how the Bible is used by believers on opposite sides to justify their positions in debating what ought to be done. I asked myself if there were a way to articulate some principles, or rules of thumb, that might help conscientious Christians use the Bible more responsibly in these situations. My answer to that question is this book. The COVID-19 pandemic greatly slowed down my progress, but as we reemerged into a very different kind of world, I found that the issues in 2018 that spurred this project had only become more pronounced and urgent. This is certainly the case as I write these words in the summer of 2024, in the midst of a presidential election campaign in which abortion and immigration remain as two contested issues.

Academics are often caricatured as insulated elites, nestled in "ivory towers" above the problems and stresses of "ordinary" (whatever that means) people. In reality, this is only true for a fraction of professors in America, and most of us are just as vulnerable to social and political shockwaves as our neighbors.[6] I acknowledge that academia can be a place where some scholars may be tempted to escape from the stresses of our current political climate by diving into research. This is especially true for biblical scholars. We have all sorts of old things to pass the time with: dead languages, inscriptions, artifacts, and the like. But reading the Bible is never a completely clinical act. The Bible's content repeatedly and in many ways engages its readers—puzzling, angering, challenging, and inspiring them. It has always been so, and it has been true

[5] Mullen, "The Fight to Define Romans 13," and Strine, "What the Bible's Romans 13 Says about Asylum."

[6] Indeed, a growing number of academics live at or below the poverty line as colleges and universities try to cut costs.

also for me. I could never have written this book without having spent my entire adult life with the biblical text. It has pricked my conscience time and again. May your reading of this book add to the range of ways the Bible speaks to you as either a Christian or a citizen.

I am grateful to the many friends and colleagues who read earlier drafts of chapters and offered helpful advice: Mara Brecht, Bridget Burke Ravizza, AnaMaria Seglie Clawson, Massimo Faggioli, Kathleen Gallagher Elkins, Rhiannon Graybill, Jennifer Hockenbery, Jim Keane, Mark Leuchter, Amy-Jill Levine, Jon Marks, Candida Moss, Eva Mroczek, Kaya Oakes, Andrew Tobolowsky, and Paul Wadell. As with my last book, special thanks go to Connie Hackl Muelemans of the interlibrary loan department at St. Norbert College, and to Mark Patel and his staff at Luna Café and Roastery in De Pere, Wisconsin. My spouse, Megan Wood Bolin, eagerly read each chapter as it was completed and offered needed encouragement. My thanks go also to my daughters: Elizabeth Bolin for reading the entire manuscript, and Margaret Bolin for patiently listening while this book took up so much space in my head. Richard M. Bullock Jr. provided a welcome and unforeseen gift at exactly the right moment that made the last few weeks of writing much easier than they otherwise would have been. Hans Christoffersen at Liturgical Press has been patient and supportive. I am happy to work with a publisher that is committed to producing books that are not priced beyond the reach of most readers.

For the past thirty years I have been a professor at Catholic colleges and have seen, literally, an entire generation of students come and go. While much about students has changed over that time, one constant is that those who are practicing Christians are aware of both the importance of the Bible as a contemporary moral guide and the difficulties in using it as one.[7] Much of this book is the result of thinking with my students on this question over the years, and I have rightfully dedicated this work to them.

[7] Let me hasten to add that I find distasteful the use of generational cohorts, e.g., millennials or Gen Z, to draw mostly negative generalizations about them.

Introduction

About This Book

This book is both descriptive and prescriptive. It is descriptive in that it looks at how the Bible is used by American Christians who argue from different and often opposing sides of a political issue. When someone uses the Bible to make the case for a political issue, there are a host of unstated assumptions and values at work that I will identify and make clear. For example: Do we look at the words of the Bible or the larger ethical norms that underlie them? How can we use biblical stories to arrive at relevant moral norms? How do we resolve the contradictions in the Bible concerning ethical behavior? The book is also prescriptive, because I make value judgments about these different ways of using the Bible and recommend some of those ways over others. These recommendations will be based on a set of guidelines for responsible use of the Bible that I have derived from the Christian tradition and modern biblical scholarship. My aim is to encourage and empower readers to arrive at a more thoughtful and, I think, "faithful" use of the Bible as we search for guidance on urgent issues—including our treatment of refugees and immigrants—in our country and in the church. Most importantly, the criteria I introduce are intended to be applicable to a wide variety of social issues, not just the ones that currently vex us. My hope is that readers will be equipped with an interpretive toolkit that does not tell them *what* to think about issues, but *how* to use the Bible in their moral reasoning about political and social issues. Just as importantly, this toolkit should help readers to understand others' use of the Bible in this regard too.

While this is a book for readers who are not necessarily trained academics, it is also a piece of scholarship that must carefully interact with and rely upon the work of other scholars. To keep the main text of the book as readable as possible, I have located most of this scholarly interaction in the footnotes, but I encourage every reader to give them a look. Almost all biblical translations are from the New Revised Standard Version Updated Edition (2021) but where I occasionally diverge from this translation, I indicate why.

With this book I am addressing a need that many other books written from a Catholic perspective do not directly address.[1] There are excellent books for Catholics that deal with the dangers of fundamentalism, the history of biblical interpretation, or the historical and literary background of the Bible.[2] Each of these topics is important, and what I'm writing about in this book will touch on each of them. There are also two recent volumes that deal with the Bible and American politics.[3] Both of these books, *The Bible in the Public Square* and *The Bible in Political Debate*, are collections of essays by biblical scholars that look at how the Bible is used in modern political and social conversations and describe the original social and cultural contexts of specific biblical texts and issues. Doing so highlights the vast differences that separate ancient Israel, early Judaism, early Christianity, and twenty-first-century North America. This kind of work is essential for anyone who wants to read the Bible competently, and I cover some of this ground here. Significantly, however, I also pay attention to how certain biblical texts have been read through time and, in some

[1] Protestant scholars and clergy are tackling these issues; see, e.g., Jonathan L. Walton, *A Lens of Love: Reading the Bible in Its World for Our World* (Louisville: Westminster John Knox, 2018); Sheri Faye Rosendahl, *Not Your White Jesus: Following a Radical, Refugee Messiah* (Louisville: Westminster John Knox, 2018).

[2] On fundamentalism, see Ronald J. Witherup, *Biblical Fundamentalism: What Every Catholic Should Know* (Collegeville, MN: Liturgical Press, 2001); on the history of biblical interpretation: George Montague, SM, *Understanding the Bible: A Basic Introduction to Biblical Interpretation*, rev. ed. (Mahwah, NJ: Paulist, 2007); Jaroslav Pelikan, *Whose Bible Is It? A Short History of the Scriptures* (New York: Penguin, 2006). On the historical and literary background of the Bible: Timothy Beal, *The Rise and Fall of the Bible: The Unexpected History of an Accidental Book* (New York: Houghton Mifflin, 2012).

[3] Mark Chancey, Carol Meyers, and Eric Meyers, eds., *The Bible in the Public Square: Its Enduring Influence in American Life* (Atlanta: Society of Biblical Literature, 2014); Frances Flannery and Rodney A. Werline, eds., *The Bible in Political Debate: What Does It Really Say?* (New York: Bloomsbury T&T Clark, 2016).

instances, I privilege these interpretations over those of the original biblical authors and readers. My ultimate goal is to help readers be more informed and thoughtful about how they and others use the Bible as a guide to forming reasoned opinions on current political issues. If people finish this book empowered (not disillusioned or discouraged) to examine carefully their assumptions about the Bible and its relevance to modern life, my time and efforts will have been worth it.

It is obvious that both American society in general and the American Catholic Church in particular suffer from a polarization of members around a number of pressing issues: abortion, race, same-sex marriage, gender identity, immigration, climate change, and the use of tax dollars for social safety nets such as welfare or health care. In a major survey completed in 2014, the Pew Research Center detailed that political polarization is at a twenty-year high, having essentially doubled in that time. The two political parties have moved even further apart, with 92 percent of Republicans moving to the right of the median Democrat, and 94 percent of Democrats to the left of the median Republican.[4] Results from the 2024 Vanderbilt Unity Index, an ongoing research project that "captures the amount of unity among Americans by collecting and analyzing data, including the public's ideological commitment, polarization in Congress and presidential disapproval" has shown a steady increase in these divides.[5]

This political polarization is mirrored among US Catholics, despite the fact that baptism makes all Catholics sisters and brothers to one another.[6] In a September 2015 report, the Pew Research

[4] Pew Research Center, "Political Polarization in the American Public: How Increasing Ideological Uniformity and Partisan Antipathy Affect Politics, Compromise and Everyday Life," June 12, 2014, https://www.pewresearch.org/politics/2014/06/12/political-polarization-in-the-american-public/.

[5] Vanderbilt Project on Unity and American Democracy, "Latest Vanderbilt Unity Index Shows the U.S. Continuing Its Trend toward Increased Political Polarization," February 14, 2024, https://news.vanderbilt.edu/2024/02/14/latest-vanderbilt-unity-index-shows-the-u-s-continuing-its-trend-toward-increased-political-polarization/.

[6] See the data and analysis in William D'Antonio, Michele Dillon, and Mary L. Gautier, *American Catholics in Transition* (Boston: Rowman & Littlefield, 2013); detailed discussion and analysis in Mary Ellen Konieczny, Charles C. Camosy,

Center noted that when it comes to specific political or social issues, American Catholics align more with their political party's positions than with the teachings of the church. For example, "nine-in-ten Catholic Democrats (91%) oppose substantially expanding the wall along the U.S. border with Mexico—while 81% of Catholic Republicans favor it."[7] Similar divides exist over government aid to the poor, climate change, and the legality of abortion, and have only grown more in the years since these data were collected.[8] In a recent book-length study on this issue, Aaron Wessman notes that "the Catholic Church appears well situated to be a microcosm of the macro-political scene in the United States."[9] If there is any hope of bridging these significant and often acrimonious divides, it lies only in a retrieval of a shared theological vision that prioritizes the bonds of ecclesial communion. Dialogue has been a hallmark of the pontificate of Pope Francis, and the 2023 Synod of Bishops has highlighted and modeled dialogue that is founded upon listening. In his encyclical On Fraternity and Social Friendship (*Fratelli Tutti*) Pope Francis offers a description of authentic dialogue of a vision for American Catholics to reach for:

> Together, we can seek the truth in dialogue, in relaxed conversation or in passionate debate. To do so calls for perseverance; it entails moments of silence and suffering, yet it can patiently embrace the broader experience of individuals and peoples. The flood of information at our fingertips does not make for greater wisdom. Wisdom is not born of quick searches on the

---

and Tricia C. Bruce, eds., *Polarization in the U.S. Catholic Church: Naming the Wounds, Beginning to Heal* (Collegeville, MN: Liturgical Press, 2016); Steven P. Millies, *Good Intentions: A History of Catholic Voters' Road from Roe to Trump* (Collegeville, MN: Liturgical Press, 2018); and the more recent data in Michael Lipka and Gregory A. Smith, "Like Americans Overall, U.S. Catholics Are Sharply Divided by Party," January 24, 2019, https://www.pewresearch.org/fact-tank/2019/01/24/like-americans-overall-u-s-catholics-are-sharply-divided-by-party/.

[7] Gregory A. Smith, Pew Research Center, "8 Facts about Catholics and Politics in the U.S.," September 15, 2020, https://www.pewresearch.org/fact-tank/2020/09/15/8-facts-about-catholics-and-politics-in-the-u-s/.

[8] Aleja Hertzler-McCain, "Survey: US Catholics More Polarized Than Ever over Pope Francis," *America*, April 12, 2024, https://www.americamagazine.org/politics-society/2024/04/12/pope-francis-polarization-us-catholics-247690.

[9] Aaron Wessman, *The Church's Mission in a Polarized World* (Hyde Park, NY: New City Press, 2023), 93.

> internet nor is it a mass of unverified data. That is not the way to mature in the encounter with truth. Conversations revolve only around the latest data; they become merely horizontal and cumulative. We fail to keep our attention focused, to penetrate to the heart of matters, and to recognize what is essential to give meaning to our lives . . . The process of building fraternity, be it local or universal, can only be undertaken by spirits that are free and open to authentic encounters.[10]

What I hope to do with this book is to help readers be able to, in the pope's words, "keep our attention focused" in terms of how we read biblical texts, why we read them differently, and how to "patiently embrace the broader experience of individuals and peoples."

Language Matters

"Sticks and stones may break my bones, but names will never hurt me." This nursery rhyme is often quoted by adults to children who have been teased or taunted by their peers.[11] The point of the saying seems to be that, because words are powerless to harm us (in comparison to weapons), we should disregard harmful words directed at us. However, the existence of the nursery rhyme itself may prove this very point to be false. The nursery rhyme functions as an act of protection against harmful words. This implies not only that there are words—such as name-calling—that can harm, but also that there are words with protective power—such as the nursery rhyme—that can shield us from harmful words. Indeed, children are known to respond to name-calling by reciting the nursery rhyme. This practice reveals that the saying's purpose isn't to declare that negative words are powerless. Instead, it is to deflect those negative words with more powerful words, rendering the attempt to harm meaningless.

[10] Pope Francis, *Fratelli Tutti* (Encyclical Letter on Fraternity and Social Friendship) 50, October 3, 2020, https://www.vatican.va/content/francesco/en/encyclicals/documents/papa-francesco_20201003_enciclica-fratelli-tutti.html.

[11] It appears in print at least as far back as 1872 in a story called "The Tailor's Cat," in Anna Jane Cupples (Mrs. George Cupples), *Tappy's Chicks: And Other Links Between Nature and Human Nature* (London: Strahan, 1872), 78.

Words have power, then, which we often overlook or take for granted. First and foremost, they give us the ability to make our internal thoughts, feelings, and desires available to others. They bring what is inside of us out into the open for others to know or share. Augustine of Hippo (354–430), someone we will encounter several times in the pages that follow, goes so far as to imply that we are not yet fully realized human beings without the capacity of speech. In the first book of his most famous work, the *Confessions,* he carefully describes the process by which children learn to speak and the corresponding freedom and power that comes with that ability. Indeed, the word *infant* comes from the Latin *infans*, which means literally "unable to speak."[12]

Words have power to change our lives and mark the changes in our lives. Every one of us can think of numerous times when we said something we wish we hadn't, or didn't say something we wish we had. In the penitential rite of the Mass, Catholics ask for forgiveness for the sins we have committed in our "thoughts and words" as well as in our actions. The Bible is full of advice regarding the power of the spoken word. Much of that advice centers on the need to know when to speak and when to be silent. For example, on the one hand, "To make an apt answer is a joy to anyone, and a word in season, how good it is!" (Prov 15:23); but likewise, "To watch over mouth and tongue is to keep out of trouble" (Prov 21:23). More succinctly, the author of Ecclesiastes says simply that "there is a time to keep silent and a time to speak" (Eccl 3:7). Significant life events are marked by words: oaths taken when assuming elected office or enlisting in the military, wedding vows, a child's first words, a loved one's dying wishes. Language is so powerful that it requires not only knowledge of what to say, but of when, how, and to whom it must be said.

All words have power, but all are not equally powerful. Oaths and the words of the sacraments carry more weight than that of the

[12] Writing about the lives of infants, Augustine relates, "Little by little I became aware of where I was, and I wanted to make my desires apparent to those who could satisfy them, but I could not: for my desires were inside me, whereas they were outside, and no sense of theirs could give them entry into my soul" (*Confessions* 1.6.8, in *Augustine: Confessions*, trans. Thomas Williams [Indianapolis: Hackett, 2019], 5).

nursery rhyme for most people. In many cases the source of the words, whether a speaker or a text or some combination of both, determines the weight given to those words. In other words (no pun intended) the *context* of words plays an important role in the authority those words are seen to have.

Using the Bible: Language, Content, and Context

I was once having a friendly but spirited debate about an ethical issue with a friend of mine. During the course of our conversation, my friend countered one of my statements by saying, "Well, it's just like it says in the Bible: 'To thine own self be true.'" "Um," I replied, "That's not the Bible; that's Shakespeare."[13] My friend's response came without hesitation: "It's the same thing!"

This isn't a case of somebody being "ignorant" of the Bible or Shakespeare. My friend is college-educated and attends church weekly. Their mistake isn't due to the fact that they haven't memorized the entire Bible or the complete works of Shakespeare. Such a feat is both unreasonable to expect of people and doesn't really get to the root of my friend's misquotation. What's really going on behind their mistake are some important issues that I want to spend a little time on as I introduce this book.

There are three important, overlapping concepts at work in my friend's confusion of Shakespeare with the Bible: *style*, *content*, and *context*. In terms of *style*, the quotation from Shakespeare sounds biblical because of its archaic language. And "biblical" language is seen to be archaic not only because the Bible is an old book, but more importantly because Americans, regardless of their religious tradition, most readily equate the language of the Bible with the King James Version (KJV) made in 1611 (which, in my friend's defense, was also during Shakespeare's lifetime). Although the biblical translation that the Puritans brought to New England in 1620 was the Geneva Bible, a version that the established Church of England thought too radical, by the time of American independence, the KJV was the dominant English Bible

[13] *Hamlet*, I.iii.

in America.[14] The founders were steeped in the KJV in every aspect of their lives from childhood on up. And even *they* found the language odd. As early as 1782 Benjamin Franklin was expressing concern about the archaic language of the KJV and calling for a new translation in contemporary language. His call went unheeded.[15] The first Bible printed in America, in 1782 by Philadelphia printer Robert Aitken, was the KJV. In the early 1800s a combination of rising literacy and technological advances in printing led to incredible growth in Bible printing.[16] The parade example of this is the foundation of the American Bible Society (ABS) in 1816. The mission of the ABS was to put a Bible in the hands of every American. This Bible was the KJV, and the founders of the ABS believed that it was essential to cement and safeguard the Protestant national identity of the young country.[17] Beginning in the nineteenth century and continuing well into the twentieth, children's educational primers, used to teach reading, relied on excerpts from the KJV. Political pamphlets used to attack opponents were written in King James style language to give them more punch.[18] Phrases from the KJV long ago entered English usage,

[14] Published in 1560 by English exiles in Geneva, the Geneva Bible was wildly popular in England, much to the consternation of the Anglican Church. The King James Bible, also called "The Authorized Version," i.e., authorized by the Crown as the official head of the Church of England, was intended to supplant the Geneva Bible's popularity among rank-and-file English Christians.

[15] Carl J. Richard, *The Founders and the Bible* (Boston: Rowman & Littlefield, 2016), 52.

[16] Paul C. Gutjahr, "Protestant English-Language Bible Publishing and Translation," in Paul C. Gutjahr, ed., *The Oxford Handbook of the Bible in America* (New York: Oxford University Press, 2018), 4–8. Of the almost 1,800 separate editions of the Bible published in the US between 1776 and 1865, over 90 percent were the KJV (Mark A. Noll, *America's God: From Jonathan Edwards to Abraham Lincoln* [New York: Oxford University Press, 2002], 372).

[17] John Fea, *The Bible Cause: A History of the American Bible Society* (New York: Oxford University Press, 2016), 19–29. Over two hundred years later, this is still a significant part of their mission: "We believe . . . THE BIBLE BRINGS HOPE TO OUR NATION. In 1816, American Bible Society was founded on a dream to share the Bible's values of faith, liberty, unity, justice, hope, and love with every American. Americans desperately need the Bible's foundation of truth. Christians need the teachings of Jesus. Lost people need the hope of the gospel" (https://www.americanbible.org/about).

[18] Eran Shalev, "'Written in the Style of Antiquity': Pseudo-Biblicism and the Early American Republic 1770–1830," *Church History* 79 (2010): 800–826.

and we still use them, often without knowing their origins: "Let there be light," "brother's keeper," "fly in the ointment," "how the mighty are fallen," "fire and brimstone," "out of the mouths of babes," "pride goeth before a fall," and many others discussed in David Crystal's delightful book, *Begat*.[19] There are today still a number of American Christians for whom the KJV is understood as the only legitimate translation of the Bible, and the English translators of the 1600s are believed by some to have been as inspired as the biblical authors themselves.[20]

While the Catholic Church has never used the King James Bible, its style of language is prevalent in American Catholicism. Catholics still use the archaic language of "thee," "thy," "thine," and "art" in the two most commonly known prayers, the Our Father and Hail Mary. In the same way that people have different pairs of shoes, or outfits, or plates for different occasions, so too do we use different kinds of language for different settings in life. Meaningful events or parts of life require a suitable language. Nowhere is this more apparent than in religion. The Ordinary of the Mass (the parts said every Sunday by the priest or people) has Catholics saying words they most likely never use elsewhere, like *consubstantial*, *grievous*, or *dewfall*, and this is by design. Special situations call for special language. So too with special writings, like the Bible: an important book ought to use important language; a unique book—the Word of God no less—should use unique language. For English speaking American Christians, that unique language is the KJV. So pervasive is its influence that people who have never read it still talk about the need to "Love thy neighbor," or describe something forbidden with the phrase, "Thou shalt not."

In terms of *content*, the Shakespearean quote, "To thine own self be true," is a direct piece of moral advice. It speaks right to the reader or listener, telling them to do something. Because most Christians understand the Bible as a moral rulebook that helps

[19] David Crystal, *Begat: The King James Bible and the English Language* (New York: Oxford University Press, 2010).

[20] This is nothing new. The third-century-BCE Jewish translation of the Torah from Hebrew into Greek, subsequently known as the Septuagint, was supported by a story of the translators' inspiration preserved in the ancient Jewish text known as *The Letter to Aristeas*.

them to live "good lives," they are inclined to assume that it contains mainly ethical teachings addressed directly to the reader. This is true of parts of the Bible. For example, there's an entire book of such teachings (Proverbs). Much more of the Bible, however, contains stories and poetry than teachings or rules. Our understanding of the Bible as mainly a book of rules is due in part both to how it's taught to us as children and also to the parts of the Bible that are most often quoted or visible in our culture, such as the Ten Commandments ("Thou shalt not," once again) or the Sermon on the Mount. Indeed, we are so accustomed to thinking of the Bible as mainly a moral rulebook that in the late 1990s almost 80 percent of Americans surveyed mistakenly identified the saying, "The Lord helps those who help themselves," as a biblical text.[21] And, of course, many people—and not just my friend—also misidentify "To thine own self be true" as biblical. These sayings, along with scores of other such pieces of advice, are part of our culture's collective wisdom.

Collective wisdom is that body of wise sayings or moral maxims that we learn because we have heard them used and then go on to use them ourselves. By its nature as a shared cultural tradition, this body of knowledge is often resistant to change in regard to wording. What does often change, however, is the source to which the words are attributed. A quote by Shakespeare may be thought to be from the Bible, or quotes from Shakespeare and the Bible can be thought of as "the same thing." Additionally, the meaning of the words can change over time as well. This is also the case with "To thine own self be true," which leads to the third concept under discussion here, *context*.

If location means everything in regard to real estate, it's almost as important in understanding written texts. When a portion of a written text is removed from its original context—its "neighborhood"—a new context must be supplied. This is exactly what happens with the quotation from Shakespeare that my friend thought was from the Bible. Its original setting is *Hamlet* (Act 1,

[21] The survey was conducted by the Barna Group and received quite a bit of attention from Evangelical clergy who, understandably, were dismayed. The saying entered American culture via Benjamin Franklin.

Scene 3) and it is spoken by Polonius as he sends his son Laertes off to university. Like any parent seeing a child off into the world alone, Polonius offers a great deal of advice to Laertes: Test the character of people before you befriend them. Don't be too free with your thoughts. Don't be ostentatious in your clothing. Don't lend or borrow money. This list of good behaviors leads up to the pinnacle of Polonius's wisdom: "This above all, to thine own self be true." It's all stirring stuff, and I must admit feeling a bit inspired as I reread this fatherly advice while writing this chapter. But context matters, because Shakespeare is here using this wisdom, and our quotation specifically, ironically by placing them in the mouth of a man who is a foolish, prying busybody. Polonius embodies the opposite of the virtues he rattles off to his son and, as befits a Shakespearean tragedy, he is dead by the end of Act 3, a victim of his own foolishness. By giving a stupid man a long speech on wisdom, Shakespeare could be making fun of Polonius (Here's a fellow who can't practice what he preaches!). Or he could be pointing out how useless it is to memorize moral proverbs (Even fools can quote this stuff.). Both of these things happen in the Bible too, most explicitly in the book of Job, where Job's three friends quote traditional wisdom to explain Job's suffering, all the while completely ignorant of its real cause. When God appears at the end, he bluntly tells the friends that they have "not spoken of me what is right" (Job 42:7).

In other words, taking a saying, story, rule (let's just call all of these "texts," for short) out of one context and putting it into another changes its meaning, sometimes drastically. Notice that I didn't say putting a text into a different context "misinterprets" it. That's a possibility, but it isn't a necessary outcome. I talk about this more later. For now, I want to state that a text that is part of a culture's collective wisdom is mobile. It moves from one context to another, often quite far from its "original" context. Importantly, one part of context is the author, and so when a text is attributed to a different author (such as when a line from Shakespeare is believed to be from the Bible), that can change a text's meaning, most often in regard to its authority. For Christians, the highest textual authority is, naturally, the Bible. As Charles Cosgrove notes, "Arguing from scripture is one of the public ways in which Christians test their moral judgments."[22] Therefore, when Christians refer to a biblical text (or think that they are) they broadcast the importance of the issue being discussed and the depth of their commitment to whatever side of that issue they are advocating for.

What This Text Will Do

I want to make clear that, from the standpoint of civil law, the Bible isn't, nor should it be, the authority by which we govern, although a significant number of Americans don't agree with me on this. Survey data compiled in 2022 by the Pew Research Center found that 45 percent of Americans say that the US "should be a Christian nation." In response to the question of whether the Bible should influence US laws, Pew found that

> nearly half of U.S. adults say they think the Bible should have a great deal of influence (23%) or some influence (24%) on the laws of the United States, while another half say it should have not much influence (16%) or none at all (36%). The Center asked this question once previously, in February 2020, and found broadly similar results then, though the share who say they Bible should have no influence at all on U.S. laws has ticked up slightly in the last two years (from 31% to 36%).[23]

Responding to the follow-up question of whether the Bible should take precedence over the will of the people if the two conflict, "27% of U.S. adults say that the Bible should have more influence on U.S. laws than the will of the people." What is significant about this 27 percent group is that it includes respondents who say that the US should *not* be a Christian nation. Indeed, one in five of those who do not want the US to be a Christian nation *also* want the Bible to influence US laws. Part of this must be due to our understanding of the Bible as a directly relevant text, specifi-

[22] Charles Cosgrove, *Appealing to Scripture in Moral Debate: Five Hermeneutical Rules* (Grand Rapids, MI: Eerdmans, 2002), 6.

[23] Pew Research Center, "45% of Americans Say U.S. Should Be a 'Christian Nation,'" October 27, 2022, https://www.pewresearch.org/religion/2022/10/27/45-of-americans-say-u-s-should-be-a-christian-nation/.

cally in terms of moral guidance, as we have been discussing in the introduction.

We rightfully have a "wall of separation" between church and state built into our system of government. This exists in tension, however, with the indisputable fact that the Bible has played a major role in American politics since the Puritans colonized Massachusetts four hundred years ago. Indeed, the first printed book in North America was the *Bay Psalm Book*, made in Cambridge, Massachusetts, twenty years after the landing at Plymouth Rock.[24] The governmental imposition of biblical morality (itself a deeply problematic concept) would be fraught with theological, social, and political upheavals, which would fundamentally and negatively change US democracy. It is reasonable for Christians, however, for whom the Bible is revealed truth, to look to the Bible for guidance for how to exercise their rights and duties as citizens. Assuming that, what are the different ways the Bible is used like this? Are these ways of using the Bible equally valid, or are some better than others? Can we discern any general principles for proper use of the Bible in contemporary American political and social debate? This book is my attempt to answer these questions.

The chapters are arranged to tell a story of how we got here and what we can do about it. The first four chapters, loosely speaking, tell the "How we got here" part.

Chapter 1 offers a brief historical overview of the Bible's role in significant American social and political debates, looking specifically at abolition and civil rights, before ending with the modern debate about abortion, using the *Catechism of the Catholic Church* as a test case. The chapter argues that the way the Bible was used in the fight over slavery has laid down the landscape that shapes subsequent uses of the Bible in American debate.

Chapter 2 is a careful description of what exactly happens when we read something and how all reading is a complex act of interpretation. This is a general overview into the act of interpretation, which is necessary before turning to the particular tasks involved in making sense of the Bible. It starts with what we might call

[24] Library of Congress, World Digital Library, https://www.loc.gov/item/71002405/.

"simple" communication and builds from there to describe longer and more complicated interpretive acts.

Chapter 3 is an overview that describes how the Bible had been read and thought about for the first 1,500 years of Christian history, before the watershed of the Reformation. Here I highlight what might be loosely called "premodern" ways of reading (although many people today still read the Bible in very similar ways). These ways include reading ancient texts as speaking directly to the reader's contemporary time or interpreting the elements of a text as symbols or allegories of something else. Reading the Bible in this way relies on the assumption that the text says more than what it appears to say; it contains hidden depths that must be revealed by skill or divine assistance. The Bible was understood, for the most part, as a vast treasury of sacred texts whose divine status gave it an aura of mystery and impenetrability.

Chapter 4 continues the story, but with a focus on the irrevocable changes the Reformation brought to how the Bible was understood and read. On the one hand, the Reformers' stress on the clarity and plain meaning of Scripture changed the view of the Bible for many Christians. No longer a collection of difficult oracles or symbolic meanings, the Bible became the clear teaching of God given to Christians for their salvation. Coinciding with and influenced by the advent of mechanical printing in the West, biblical texts were made widely available in vernacular languages and manageable formats. The Scriptures became *the* Bible: a single book one could hold in one's hand, which served as a concrete reminder that the biblical texts were, ultimately, the work of a single divine author.[25] At the same time, the Reformation also unleashed an intellectual trajectory that would result in the creation of biblical studies as an academic discipline in the modern university, an academic field that then proceeded on its own trajectory, for the most part separated from the lives of ecclesial communities.

[25] Which is to say that the technological development of mass-produced printing significantly changed how we interact with and understand the text. We are currently undergoing another significant shift in our view of the Bible with the advent of the digital Bible, which is in part a return to thinking about Scripture as an unbound collection.

Chapter 5 makes the argument that all meaningful biblical interpretation requires some external standard that is used to guide which texts are selected and how they are construed. It then examines the theological concept of the rule of faith, which has been one such standard for centuries, before turning to modern scholarly attempts to use the Bible in the articulation of theologically grounded ethical norms for modern Christians. The discussion from chapter 1 of the Catholic Church's use of the Bible in its teaching on life issues including abortion is revisited, along with recent church teaching on capital punishment, to show the complexity of how Bible is used by the magisterium in its moral teaching.

Chapter 6 begins with a retrieval of one of the oldest Christian works on biblical interpretation, Augustine of Hippo's *On Christian Teaching*. Augustine articulates a method of biblical interpretation that has come to be known as the rule of love, inspired by Jesus' teaching on the Great Commandment. Drawing on Augustine's thought and the Gospel texts of the Great Commandment, I articulate a particular standard of biblical interpretation that is sorely needed in this moment of deep polarization in the US church and society. My hope is that my suggestion offers a way to bridge the chasm that separates members of the church and American Christians in general from each other when they meet over the Bible.

This book has grown out of three decades of teaching and, in fidelity to that, it is structured using the pedagogical technique known as scaffolding. This means that simpler ideas are introduced that are then built upon to make more complex statements, all the while with a return to the beginning ideas as a reminder of the overall direction of the book's discussion. Readers will notice both an increase in complexity as they read and consistent references to earlier parts of the discussion.

Chapter 1

Where We Are and How We Got Here

The bulk of this chapter tells the story about how the Bible was used by Americans debating from both sides of what is arguably the most significant moral issue in the country's history—race. Once we get a grasp on how Americans in the past used the Bible to stake out positions on this fundamental social, political, and moral issue, we can begin to see how the same ways for reading the Bible are still at work in today's debates. Then, as now, the Bible's language, content, and context played major roles every step of the way in these debates, but not always in equal measure. In any particular situation, one of the three—language, content, or context—carried more weight than the other two. Focusing on the interaction between all three sheds light on how American Christians developed the interpretive strategies they use now.

The Bible and Racism in the United States

One of the more well-known scenes from the novel *Huckleberry Finn* occurs toward the end, when Huck has to decide whether or not to turn in his companion, the runaway slave Jim. Huck has a crisis of conscience; he thinks about how it was wrong to have accompanied a runaway, how we would never have done such a thing had he only gone to Sunday School. Anyone who does what Huck has done "goes to everlasting fire." He writes a letter to Jim's enslaver, telling her where Jim can be found. Afterward, he tries to pray and, seeing the letter, "I took it up, and held it in my hand. I was trembling because I'd got to decide, forever, betwixt two things, and I knowed it. I studied a minute, sort of holding my breath, and then says to myself: 'All right, then, I'll *go* to hell'—and tore it up."[1]

Both slavery and Christianity were essential parts of American society from its beginning. While most Americans learn in school that the "Pilgrims" landed on Plymouth Rock in 1620 in order to seek religious freedom in the New World, we are not taught that the year before, the first African slaves were brought to America in Jamestown, Virginia.[2] The beginnings of abolitionism in both England and the United States began in the late 1700s and had religious roots, with Quakers being among the first groups to call for an end to slavery. By 1840, chattel slavery (the practice of owning, buying, and selling human beings as property) had been abolished in the British Empire, French colonies, and the Papal States, but it would take another quarter century and the bloodiest war in its history for the United States to finally bring it to an end, although the Civil War did not end systemic racism and White privilege in America by any means. From the first part of the 1800s all the way up to the beginning of the war, clergy, politicians, and activists engaged in heated debate about the morality of slavery. Naturally, they used the Bible both to attack their opponents' position and to support their own. In his Second Inaugural Address, given toward the end of the Civil War, President Lincoln could note how both sides in the war "read the same Bible and pray to the same God." Lincoln read that Bible too and was a master at working its language and cadence into his own speech. Indeed, this section of the Second Inaugural Address is so rich in biblical quotations, allusions, and phrases that it's worth looking at more

[1] Mark Twain, *The Adventures of Huckleberry Finn: The Only Comprehensive Edition* (New York: Random House, 1996), 273. The book was originally published in 1885. For a more in-depth theological discussion of this scene in the novel, see Rachel Held Evans, "All Right Then, I'll Go to Hell," blog entry, May 23, 2012, https://rachelheldevans.com/blog/huck-finn-hell.

[2] In an attempt to address this, *The New York Times*, in conjunction with historians of American history, published *The 1619 Project* (https://www.nytimes.com/interactive/2019/08/14/magazine/1619-america-slavery.html). The political and social fallout from *The 1619 Project* has been prolonged and intense. It seems we are still not ready to fully learn this history.

closely. In the excerpt below, I have marked direct quotations in bold type, while allusions are underlined:

> Both read the same Bible, and pray to the same God; and each invokes His aid against the other. It may seem strange that any men should dare to ask a just God's assistance in <u>wringing their bread from the sweat of other men's faces</u>; but let us <u>judge not that we be not judged</u>. The prayers of both could not be answered; that of neither has been answered fully. The Almighty has His own purposes. **"Woe unto the world because of offences! for it must needs be that offences come; but woe to that man by whom the offence cometh!"** If we shall suppose that American Slavery is one of those offences which, in the providence of God, <u>must needs</u> come, but which, having continued through His appointed time, He now wills to remove, and that He gives to both North and South, this terrible war, as <u>the woe due to those by whom the offence came</u>, shall we discern therein any departure from those divine attributes which the believers in a Living God always ascribe to Him? Fondly do we hope—fervently do we pray—that this mighty scourge of war may speedily pass away. Yet, if God wills that it continue until all the wealth piled by the bond-man's two hundred and fifty years of unrequited toil shall be sunk, and until every drop of blood drawn with the lash, shall be paid by another drawn with the sword, as was said three thousand years ago, so still it must be said **"the judgments of the Lord, are true and righteous altogether."**[3]

First, let's deal with the two quotations, which are in bold type. The first is Matthew 18:7, the second Psalm 19:9. Both, of course, are from the KJV, for all the reasons I set forth in the introduction. The first is a saying of Jesus that both acknowledges that suffering occurs in life, but also condemns those who are the cause of suffering. For Lincoln, the cause of the war's great suffering are the Southern rebels. The second quotation, from the Psalms, closes out a stunning statement of Lincoln's that perhaps the South must pay back in both blood and resources the pain and labor they

[3] Text and images available at the National Archives, https://www.ourdocuments.gov/doc.php?flash=true&doc=38.

exploited from African slavery. The quotation, referring to the righteousness of God, gives Lincoln's claim a biblical context—perhaps this kind of reparation is what God requires.[4] Now for the allusions, which are underlined above:

> Lincoln: "wringing their bread from the sweat of other men's faces."
> KJV "In the sweat of thy face shalt thou eat bread." (Gen 3:19)
>
> Lincoln: "judge not that we be not judged."
> KJV "Judge not, that ye be not judged." (Matt 7:1)
>
> Lincoln: "the woe due to those by whom the offence came."
> KJV: "woe to that man by whom the offence cometh!" (Matt 18:7)

The first allusion refers to God's curse of the man in the Garden of Eden. According to established Christian theology, an essential aspect of existence after the Fall is the just punishment that human beings will have to work in order to live. Lincoln portrays slaveholders, whose livelihood is supplied by the work of their slaves, to be in direct violation of God's just punishment. Slavery, then, is a practice that goes against God's justice in that it attempts to avoid God's righteous penalty on people—we are supposed to earn our bread by our own labor and not by the forced work of others. After making this claim, Lincoln pulls back from it with the second allusion, from the Sermon on the Mount. This is an old rhetorical strategy: speculate something negative about your opponent and then step away from it. It plants the critical idea in the audience's mind without forcing them to pass judgment on a straightforward, unqualified assertion. It's a brilliant move by Lincoln, because in one swoop he implies that slavery violates God's justice, but also refrains from passing that judgment explicitly himself by quoting Jesus. Note how Lincoln changes the second-person command of Jesus ("lest *ye* be judged") into a first-person exhortation that includes himself ("lest *we* be judged"). The last

[4] For more on reparations, see Ta-Nehisi Coates, "The Case for Reparations," *The Atlantic* 313 (June 2014): 54–71. For a reading of a biblical text and its support of reparations, Thomas M. Bolin, "Job, White Privilege, and the Case for Reparations," *Ancient Jew Review*, February 2019, https://www.ancientjewreview.com/read/2018/12/9/job-white-privilege-and-the-case-for-reparations.

allusion is, of course, a restatement of Lincoln's first biblical quotation.

Now let's look at Lincoln's use of an already archaic (in 1865) phrase taken from the English of the KJV: "must needs" (also underlined above). Using this phrase, much like subliminal messaging, gives Lincoln's words a biblical rhythm (many people then knew the Bible by hearing it). This, alongside the quotations and allusions, gives Lincoln's words a weight, places them in a biblical context—a sacred neighborhood—that conveys to his audience his belief that the fight against slavery is in line with God's will. Here we see the confluence of language, content, and context, and not for the last time. Later in this chapter we'll see this combination again in Martin Luther King Jr.'s use of the Bible a century after Lincoln.

Biblical Arguments Surrounding Slavery

The arrival of the first enslaved Africans at Jamestown in 1619 raises the question of how Christianity did and did not speak to their condition in the American colonies. As Albert Raboteau details in his history of Christianity among enslaved Africans and their descendants, White Christians were not eager to evangelize the enslaved, because "the economic profitability of his slaves, not their Christianization, held top priority for the colonial planter."[5] However, the Second Great Awakening, which began in the late 1700s and continued throughout the first part of the 1800s, led to many of the enslaved becoming Christians, especially due to missionary efforts by Baptists and Methodists. The evangelical flavor of the Great Awakening meant that conversion was not about intellectual assent to a creed, but rather the result of an intense personal experience of the Almighty that left the person changed. Part of what appealed to the enslaved (and made slaveowners uncomfortable) was Evangelical Christianity's emphasis on the equality of believers before God. Before long, Southern states would pass laws outlawing Black ministers or Black literacy.

[5] See Albert J. Raboteau, *Slave Religion: The "Invisible Institution" in the Antebellum South*, rev. ed. (New York: Oxford University Press, 2004), 98.

Even the American Bible Society (discussed in the introduction) followed these rules and did not extend to the enslaved its mission of providing the Bible to every American family.[6]

White enslavers had reason to fear a biblically literate enslaved population. One of the Bible's core stories is the liberation of the Israelite slaves from Egypt and their arrival in a land promised them by God. The leader of one enslaved revolt of 1800, Gabriel Prosser, appealed to Leviticus 16:8 as biblical testimony of the revolt's rightness and success. Denmark Vesey's rebellion in 1822 was in part inspired by the Exodus story.[7] In particular, Vesey and others appealed to Exodus 21:16 to justify armed uprising against enslavers: "Whoever kidnaps a person, whether that person has been sold or is still held in possession, shall be put to death."[8] In addition to the legislative attempts to prevent the enslaved from having access to the Bible, White slaveowners arranged for White preachers to come to plantations and preach on "acceptable" biblical texts—mainly from the Pauline letters stressing the obedience of servants (more on this below).[9]

Naturally, the Bible that the enslaved encountered was the KJV and to this day it remains the translation of choice for many Black Christians in the US. Consequently, the KJV's vocabulary, ca-

[6] In a first-hand account, Samuel Ward notes how, in Louisiana in 1841, "Slaveholders and their abettors belong to and are officers of the American Bible Society and they control it." Quoted in Emerson B. Powery and Rodney S. Sadler Jr., *The Genesis of Liberation: Biblical Interpretation in the Antebellum Narratives of the Enslaved* (Louisville: Westminster John Knox, 2016), 49.

[7] "Five of you shall give chase to a hundred, and a hundred of you shall give chase to ten thousand; your enemies shall fall before you by the sword." Discussed in Raboteau, *Slave Religion*, 147. One of Vesey's co-conspirators testified that Vesey "read to us from the Bible, how the Children of Israel were delivered out of Egypt from bondage" (quoted in Allen Dwight Callahan, *The Talking Book: African Americans and the Bible* [New Haven: Yale University Press, 2006], 7).

[8] Jeremy Schipper, *Denmark Vesey's Bible: The Thwarted Revolt That Put Slavery and Scripture on Trial* (Princeton: Princeton University Press, 2022), 31. Elsewhere, Schipper notes that, "whereas Charleston's white elites often drew clear distinctions between the Old and New Testament texts in their proslavery arguments, for whatever reasons, Vesey and his associates did not make these distinctions as precisely, if at all . . . it simply did not matter to Vesey and his associates where in the Bible a text was located if the text proved useful for their cause" (Schipper, *Denmark Vesey's Bible*, 22).

[9] Raboteau, *Slave Religion*, 152–58.

dences, and phrases have formed and played a large part in Black American theology, literature, poetry, and music. As Alice Ogden Bellis notes, "Blacks revere the KJV for the same reason many Roman Catholics still are fond of the Latin/Vulgate Bible: the poetry and antiquitous tone associated with a spirituality of earlier times, even another world. That some of the text is 'mysterious,' i.e., not fully understood, is what makes it special, instantly beckoning one to prayer and active dialogue with God."[10]

Proslavery Christians looked to the Bible for support of both slavery as an institution in general and of the enslavement of Africans in particular. There was no shortage of evidence for slavery as a practice in the Bible. Sarah has a slave woman named Hagar who runs away from Sarah and is ordered by God to return (Gen 16; 21). Numerous laws given to Moses by God in the Torah, including the Ten Commandments, deal with the capture, release, punishment, and general treatment of slaves (Exod 20–21; Deut 15). Two New Testament letters bearing the Apostle Paul's name (Paul most likely didn't write Ephesians or Colossians) directly tell slaves to obey their masters (Eph 6:5-8; Col 3:22-25) and demonstrate that some of the early Christians owned slaves. Paul himself sent a runaway slave back to his owner, as recounted in the New Testament letter to Philemon. The cultural background of the Bible—both the Old and New Testaments—assumed slavery as a social "fact" of life. Proslavery Bible readers claimed they were reading the Bible literally and in its "plain sense."[11]

What was more difficult for proslavery Christians was finding biblical support for the enslavement of Africans. Slavery based on race is not found in the Bible and only began to appear in

[10] Alice Ogden Bellis, "The Bible in African American Perspectives," *Teaching Theology and Religion* 1 (1998): 162.

[11] But, as Wilda Gafney notes, the practice of racist chattel slavery in the modern world violated a number of biblical injunctions on the treatment of the enslaved. "Responsible exegesis of the scriptures of Israel requires abandoning racialized constructions of the ancient Israelites and naming those contexts in which contemporary racial constructions have been imposed on the text" ("Reading the Hebrew Bible Responsibly," in Hugh R. Page et al., eds., *The Africana Bible: Reading Israel's Scriptures from Africa and the African Diaspora* [Minneapolis: Fortress Press, 2010], 49).

Christianity around 1500.[12] In the Hebrew Bible, there are different rules for the treatment of Israelite and non-Israelite slaves, but there was no idea of biological "race" in antiquity. It's a product of Western European and North American thought in the late eighteenth and early nineteenth centuries.[13] Consequently, proslavery Bible readers turned to one of the Bible's more arcane stories to justify African slavery, the drunkenness of Noah in Genesis 9:

> 18The sons of Noah who went out of the ark were Shem, Ham,
> and Japheth. Ham was the father of Canaan. 19These three were
> the sons of Noah; and from these the whole earth was peopled.
> 20Noah, a man of the soil, was the first to plant a vineyard. 21He
> drank some of the wine and became drunk, and he lay uncov-
> ered in his tent. 22And Ham, the father of Canaan, saw the
> nakedness of his father, and told his two brothers outside.
> 23Then Shem and Japheth took a garment, laid it on both their
> shoulders, and walked backward and covered the nakedness
> of their father; their faces were turned away, and they did not
> see their father's nakedness. 24When Noah awoke from his wine
> and knew what his youngest son had done to him, 25he said,
>
> "Cursed be Canaan;
> lowest of slaves shall he be to his brothers."
> 26He also said, "Blessed by the LORD my God be Shem;
> and let Canaan be his slave.
> 27May God make space for Japheth,
> and let him live in the tents of Shem;
> and let Canaan be his slave." (Gen 9:18-27)[14]

Proslavery Bible readers made two important interpretive moves to see this text as justification for African slavery.

12 Stephen Haynes, *Noah's Curse: The Biblical Justification of American Slavery* (New York: Oxford University Press, 2002), 7. Haynes also notes that by the early 1700s, Bible dictionaries argued for the enslavement of Black Africans on the basis of Genesis 9 (Haynes, *Noah's Curse*, 32–40). For the larger historical narrative, see Nell Irvin Painter, *The History of White People* (New York: Norton, 2010).

13 Jonathan Marks, "Solving the Riddle of Race," *Studies in History and Philosophy of Biological and Biomedical Sciences* 59 (2016): 161–64.

14 I apologize if I've ruined the Noah's Ark story for anyone reading this. Despite the popularity of children's Bibles, it's not really a book for kids.

First, they read the statement in 9:19, which states that Noah's three sons were the ancestors of the world's people, alongside the list of their descendants in Genesis 10 that's known as the Table of Nations. There, Ham's sons are named as "Cush, Egypt, Put, and Canaan." Although it's difficult to connect ancient place names with modern locations, Cush has long been seen as reference to what is now Ethiopia and Put to modern day Libya. Putting these two alongside Egypt gives us three regions on or near the African continent (Canaan refers to the territory of the modern state of Israel and the Palestinian Authority). This made Ham the ancestor of Africans. This particular reading was not created by proslavery Americans but comes out of the early Christian tradition. Ambrose of Milan (d. 397) understood the curse of Ham to be the introduction of slavery into the world and the ninth-century Alexandrian patriarch, Eutychius, argued that the descendants of Ham are the Africans.[15] Neither of these ancient authors, however, argued for the enslavement of Black Africans on the basis of these texts; that practice would not appear until several centuries later.

Second, the proslavery Bible readers viewed the curse of Canaan in 9:25-27 as God's decree that *all* of Ham's descendants would be slaves to the other peoples of the Earth *for all time*. This made all Black Africans subject to a perpetual biblical punishment and their enslavement a fulfilling of God's will.

While modern Bible readers would agree that certain parts of the Bible contain some amount of historical information, this particular interpretation is strange to most of us because it rests on assumptions we aren't prepared to agree to: that Noah and his sons were historical people; that the biblical stories about them are factual; that Noah's three sons are the literal ancestors of all the peoples of the world; that Ham is the ancestor of Africans; that the curse of Canaan as punishment for his father's sin also extended to his three brothers, Cush, Egypt, and Put. Nevertheless, this reading has a long history of use by White Americans. Stephen Haynes details how proslavery readings of Genesis 9–10 also

[15] Pius Onyemechi Adiele, *The Popes, the Catholic Church and the Transatlantic Enslavement of Black Africans 1418–1839* (Hildesheim: Georg Olms Verlag, 2017), 181–82.

played into Southern fears of dishonor, sexual transgression, and a disordered society, which reappear in the debate around the Civil Rights movements in the 1950s and '60s.[16]

These assumptions all accept that the Bible is accurate in historical and scientific matters, in this case that there was a flood and that humankind is descended from three brothers. Modern historical and scientific study shows this view of the Bible to be wrong, but for proslavery readers, any part of secular knowledge that contradicted the Bible was a sign of infidelity to God and God's Word. This is still the case today for many regarding issues such as evolution or same-sex relationships. On the other hand, contemporary Catholic teaching on the historical nature of the Bible is more nuanced and is discussed elsewhere in this book.

To illustrate proslavery biblical interpretation with primary sources, let's look at a book written in 1864 by Ebenezer W. Warren, pastor of the First Baptist Church of Macon, Georgia. The book is subtitled, *Southern Slavery and the Bible: A Scriptural Refutation of the Principal Arguments Upon Which the Abolitionists Rely*,[17] and is a fictional dialogue between a Georgia enslaver and a Massachusetts minister who is his houseguest. Over the course of several days, the slaveholder and minister have conversations—debates, really—over the question of whether the Bible supports Southern enslavement of Africans. The outcome is never in doubt: the enslaver defeats the minister in every single encounter. The book is full of distortions and outright lies about the quality of life for Southern slaves and their treatment by Southern Whites, but I want to focus on Warren's use of the two biblical arguments I outlined above. In the first ten pages of the book, the very first biblical text Warren cites is Genesis 9: "the origin of slavery . . . comes directly from God through His servant Noah."[18] He repeats this appeal to the curse of Ham throughout the book, but most fully toward the end: "[Africans] were made slaves by the decree of heaven, and

[16] Haynes, *Noah's Curse*, 116–21.

[17] Ebenezer W. Warren, *Nellie Norton, Or, Southern Slavery and the Bible: A Scriptural Refutation of the Principal Arguments Upon Which the Abolitionists Rely* (Macon, GA: Burke, Boykin, 1864).

[18] Warren, *Nellie Norton*, 9.

the providence of God brought about the execution of that decree . . . the condition of the descendants of Ham is one of slavery under the Divine decree. . . . I have proved, by Divine authority, that God reduced one-third of the descendants of Noah to slavery by his own decree. It was not man that made the decree, it was the Creator. It was not man that reduced the free-man and made the first slave, it was the Almighty—the glorious Master and Supreme Ruler of the Universe."[19]

The enslaver also quotes the rules for slaves in the Hebrew Bible and the texts from the New Testament mentioned above (Ephesians and Philemon). Not content to rely on the Bible just as a support for slavery, Warren goes on to makes abolitionists out to be the enemies of God. The enslaver's claim is that the Bible must be taken "all or nothing." Therefore, to reject the Bible's acceptance of slavery necessarily means denying the validity of the entire Bible: "You will have, my dear sir, to admit slavery, or reject the Bible."[20] This is a powerful rhetorical move: if you disagree with my view of the Bible, then you are an enemy of the Bible. It assumes only one correct interpretation for a text and that the Bible has an answer for each and every modern situation and all the issues at work in it, be they scientific, historical, or moral.

How did abolitionists respond to the proslavery advocates' use of the Bible to support the practice? As Mark Noll describes, there was no way to escape the fact that the Bible accepted the practice of slavery in its own historical contexts.[21] Some abolitionists, including the Protestant minister Henry Ward Beecher, were ready to leave the Bible behind and write it off as a useless, out-of-date guide for modern morality. In one sermon, Beecher referred to the Gospel story of Jesus condemning the Temple when he drove out the money-changers and compared that to his own condemnation of the Bible being used to support slavery. In other words, two things meant to be sacred (the Temple and the Bible) were

[19] Warren, *Nellie Norton*, 150–52.

[20] Warren, *Nellie Norton*, 32. Elsewhere, "The Bible is a pro-slavery Bible, and God is a pro-slavery God, notwithstanding all you say to the contrary" (Warren, *Nellie Norton*, 185).

[21] Mark Noll, *America's God: From Jonathan Edwards to Abraham Lincoln* (New York: Oxford University Press, 2002), 367–401.

corrupted by evil people. The Temple was therefore destroyed. And the Bible? Well, for Beecher, perhaps it ought to be abandoned and left in the past too.[22]

But this radical approach wasn't the norm, and while Beecher's is an important voice in the history of abolition, I want to highlight and center the voices of the enslaved. Among the most well known of those voices is that of Frederick Douglass. Born into slavery in Maryland around 1818, Douglass surreptitiously taught himself to read with the King James Bible, whose pages he sometimes found in the street and picked up to read later.[23] He escaped to his freedom in 1838 and, until his death in 1895, he was one of the most inspiring and eloquent voices for equality in the United States. If slaveholders charged abolitionists with being against the Bible and true religion, Douglass made a sharp distinction between what he saw as true Christianity and the Christianity of the slaveholding South. His autobiography, published in 1845, contains an appendix that deals specifically with the religion of slavery. Noting that, as a slave, he was treated far worse by churchgoing Whites than he ever was by nonreligious ones, Douglass condemns in no uncertain terms what he sees as the diabolical corruption of Christian faith by all in the North or South who call themselves Chris-

[22] Here, in Beecher's own words: "If men can make the Bible teach me to disown childhood; if men can make the Bible teach me that it is lawful to buy and sell men, that marriage is impracticable between slaves, that laws cannot permit any custom which would hinder the easy sale of such property . . . if a man can take the Bible and lay it in the path over which men are attempting to walk from Calvary up to the gate of heaven;—then I declare that I will do by the Bible what Christ did by the Temple: I will take a whip of cords, and drive out of it every man that buys and sells men, women, and children; and if I cannot do that, I will let the Bible go, as God let the Temple go, to the desolating armies of its adversaries" (Henry Ward Beecher, "Our Blameworthiness," in *Patriotic Addresses in America and England, From 1850 to 1885, on Slavery, the Civil War, and the Development of Civil Liberty in the United States* [New York: Fords, Howard, and Hulbert, 1887], 262). The belief that the Jerusalem temple was destroyed because the Jewish community rejected Jesus is a long-held Christian teaching that, thankfully, is no longer held by the church.

[23] "I have gathered scattered pages of the Bible from the filthy street-gutters, and washed and dried them, that in moments of leisure I might get a word or two of wisdom from them" (Frederick Douglass, *The Life and Times of Frederick Douglass, Written by Himself* [London: Park Publishing, 1882], 111).

tian but do not oppose slavery. He writes, "For, between the Christianity of this land, and the Christianity of Christ, I recognize the widest, possible difference—so wide, that to receive the one as good, pure, and holy, is of necessity to reject the other as bad, corrupt, and wicked. To be the friend of the one, is of necessity to be the enemy of the other. I love the pure, peaceable, and impartial Christianity of Christ: I therefore hate the corrupt, slaveholding, women-whipping, cradle-plundering, partial and hypocritical Christianity of this land."[24]

Elsewhere, in his famous Fourth of July address, Douglass rails against his White Christian audience with the fervor of a biblical prophet: "A worship that can be conducted by persons who refuse to give shelter to the houseless, to give bread to the hungry, clothing to the naked, and who enjoin obedience to a law forbidding these acts of mercy is a curse, not a blessing to mankind."[25] For Douglass, the Bible's importance to Christian faith was its witness to the values that God endorsed, foremost among them liberty, which was also for Douglass the quintessential American ideal. Instead of relying on the citation of a verse or verses that directly illustrated this, Douglass looked to the larger sweep of stories in the Bible to demonstrate that God and his son, Jesus, were firmly on the side of human dignity that is expressed most fundamentally in freedom for all persons. In particular, he took the criticisms of ancient Israelite religious practice made by the biblical prophets—specifically Isaiah, Jeremiah, and Amos—and applied them to the White American Christianity of his day. Regarding the Bible's acceptance of slavery, Douglass brilliantly saw that the Bible was old and written by a group of men in different circumstances than its readers. In this regard, it was much like the Constitution, another authoritative document in American life which was also fought over by proslavery and abolitionist readers. Douglass would draw comparisons between the need for nonliteral, nuanced

[24] Frederick Douglass, *Narrative of the Life of Frederick Douglass, An American Slave* (Boston: Anti-Slavery Office, 1845), 118.

[25] Frederick Douglass, "What to the Slave Is the Fourth of July?," July 5, 1852, https://teachingamericanhistory.org/library/document/what-to-the-slave-is-the-fourth-of-july/.

interpretation of both the Bible and the Constitution when discussing the legitimacy of slavery.[26]

Besides well-known voices like that of Douglass, we also are fortunate to possess the testimony of the enslaved in firsthand accounts published before the Civil War by escapees from slavery as well as interviews with formerly enslaved individuals after the war. In their analysis of these narratives, Emerson B. Powery and Rodney S. Sadler Jr., show that for the enslaved, the Exodus narrative revealed God to be on the side of the suffering and that the person of Jesus ("sold to the highest bidder") was God's own participation and vindication in their unjust suffering: "To put it more precisely, the formerly enslaved never hesitated to take Jesus as a metatext, something beyond—though loosely connected to—the written letters on the page. In Jesus, they discovered a reconciler, a redeemer, a fellow sufferer, a companion, and a confidante who understood their deepest sorrows as they faced extraordinary trials on Southern plantations."[27] Or, in the words of Allen Dwight Callahan, enslaved Africans and their descendants found in the Bible a book that "privileges those without privilege and honors those without honor," and that offered them "a warrant for justice in this world."[28]

I want to pause here and discuss the underlying principles at work in the use of the Bible by both sides in the debate over slavery because, as will soon be made clear, they are the same principles still at work today. Douglass's analogy between biblical and con-

[26] Frederick Douglass, "The Dred Scott Decision: An Address Delivered in Part, In New York, New York," in John W. Blassingame, ed., *The Frederick Douglass Papers, Series 1, Vol. 3: Speeches, Debates, and Interviews, 1855–1863* (New Haven: Yale University Press, 1979), 181–83, https://frederickdouglasspapersproject.com/item/8829. See also the discussion in J. Albert Harrill, "The Use of the New Testament in the American Slave Controversy: A Case History in the Hermeneutical Tension between Biblical Criticism and Christian Moral Debate," *Religion and American Culture* 10 (2000): 160–61.

[27] Powery and Sadler, *Genesis of Liberation*, 146. Raboteau notes that "the appropriation of the Exodus story was for the slaves a way of articulating their sense of historical identity as a people," and that the "Exodus functioned as an archetypal event for the slaves" (Raboteau, *Slave Religion*, 311).

[28] Allen Dwight Callahan, *The Talking Book: African Americans and the Bible* (New Haven: Yale University Press, 2006), xiii–xiv.

stitutional interpretation is insightful, and we will see it again. The judicial interpretation of the Constitution (and all laws) is bounded by two poles, strict and loose constructionism. For strict constructionists, the plain meaning of the Constitution's text is the ultimate arbiter in judging between interpretations. No readings beyond the ordinary meaning of the words are allowed. Closely related to strict constructionism are the interpretive principles of textualism (which rules out any external evidence in interpreting the text) and originalism (which gives priority to the intentions of the text's authors), both of which also limit interpretation to as few potential meanings as possible. Loose constructionism, as its name implies, acknowledges that there are contextual, linguistic, and historical ranges of meaning that may be validly applied in interpreting the Constitution or other legal text.

There is a similar phenomenon at work in how pro- and antislavery Christians read the Bible. As seen above, proslavery Christians appealed to the plain text of the Bible, which contained laws about owning slaves and direct commands for slaves to obey their masters. In this way they resemble the strict constructionists in the American legal tradition. However, the reading of the Bible for its plain sense meaning in American Protestantism was born out of the Reformation in the sixteenth century and not American jurisprudence. In Ebenezer Warren's biblical defense of slavery, the Southern slaveholder tells the Northern minister that, as a Christian, the minister is "required . . . to believe . . . what God has spoken in plain language."[29] On the other hand, as seen from Douglass's speeches above, antislavery Christians were faced with the challenge of constructing interpretations of the Bible that had to draw on more than the plain sense of the words. In response they appealed to larger ideals or values from biblical stories that revealed insights into the nature of God. One of the most important of these biblical stories was the Exodus, which illustrated freedom for captives to be a biblical value. Both in the writings of abolitionists and in the spirituals sung by the enslaved, God's liberation of the Israelites from slavery showed that God was on the side of the

[29] Warren, *Nellie Norton*, 52–53.

enslaved, biblical laws notwithstanding.[30] Even though both pro- and antislavery Christians saw the Bible as divine revelation, their understanding of what exactly was being revealed were very different. For the proslavery readers, the Bible's commands on slavery were what matter. To see the Bible's importance in that it contains rules or commandments is to understand the Bible as a form of *communication*: this book tells us things that God wants us to do or not to do. For antislavery readers who argued not on the basis of specific commandments but on more abstract biblical themes and values (often illustrated in specific passages), the Bible's revelation was understood as a form of *disclosure*: this book tells us what God is like and obligates us to pattern our lives on the values revealed in God's qualities.

This isn't to say that antislavery readers *never* appealed to specific Bible verses, because they did. However, these specific verses were often not understood as commandments, but rather as illustrations of qualities of the divine nature or of God's values. In particular, abolitionists appealed to Acts 17:26 ("From one ancestor he made all peoples to inhabit the whole earth") and its message of humankind's common ancestry to show that the Bible did not acknowledge racial inferiority.[31] This also doesn't mean that proslavery readers *never* appealed to larger values that they saw at work in the Bible, because they did. But on the whole, antislavery readers tended to see the Bible as a book of divine disclosure, and on the whole, proslavery readers tended to see it as a book of divine commands. These two views of the Bible should be imagined as two poles on a spectrum, with a range of combinations between them, but as poles they mark two fundamental approaches to biblical interpretation that have characterized how Americans have used the Bible to inform political and social struggles ever

[30] Raboteau, *Slave Religion*, 311–12; Keith D. Miller, "Second Isaiah Lands in Washington, DC: Martin Luther King, Jr.'s 'I Have a Dream' as Biblical Narrative and Biblical Hermeneutic," *Rhetoric Review* 26 (2007): 405–24, at 406–7; Harrill, "Use of the New Testament," 162; and Richard Newton, "The African American Bible: Bound in a Christian Nation," *JBL* 136 (2017): 224–25.

[31] See Powery and Sadler, *Genesis of Liberation*, 140–42. The database available at https://americaspublicbible.org/ shows that this text from Acts was one of the biblical passages most widely quoted in regard to slavery in Northern newspapers leading up to the Civil War.

since. That's why I've taken the time and space to discuss the Bible and slavery in this chapter explaining "How We Got Here."

After Slavery: Racism, Civil Rights, and the Bible

While the Emancipation Proclamation, Civil War, and Thirteenth Amendment put an end to chattel slavery in the United States, they did not eradicate racism, White supremacy, and discrimination, all of which we are still contending with now, although the use of the Bible to support White privilege and whiteness is less pronounced than in the past.[32] With the 1954 Supreme Court decision against segregation, the racist readings of the curse of Ham in Genesis 11, in Stephen Haynes's words, "reemerged with a vengeance." West Virginia Senator Robert Byrd even read the passage out on the Senate floor (from the KJV, of course) during his 1964 filibuster of the Civil Rights Act.[33] In response to the revival by segregationists of the proslavery readings of the Bible, the Civil Rights Movement drew upon and made new the biblical interpretation of antislavery Americans. The obvious examples that first come to mind are, of course, from the speeches and writings of Martin Luther King Jr. Although King was trained in the methods of modern biblical scholarship, he drew more from the African-American interpretive tradition in his speeches and sermons than from his graduate study.[34] King's most well-known speech, "I Have A Dream," delivered on August 28 at the Lincoln Memorial during the 1963 march on Washington is a masterpiece of subtle biblical allusion and sophisticated biblical interpretation.[35] Keith Miller has analyzed how King brilliantly used a part

[32] See Bryan Massingale, *Racial Justice and the Catholic Church* (Maryknoll, NY: Orbis, 2010). Most recently, modern White supremacists have appealed to a distorted view of ancient Greece and Rome for historical support for their racist ideologies, as discussed in Donna Zuckerberg, *Not All Dead White Men: Classics and Misogyny in the Digital Age* (Cambridge, MA: Harvard University Press, 2018).

[33] Haynes, *Noah's Curse*, 116.

[34] Richard Lischer, *The Preacher King: Martin Luther King, Jr. and the Word That Moved America* (New York: Oxford University Press, 1995), 198–205.

[35] See the book-length treatment in Drew Hanson, *The Dream: Martin Luther King, Jr. and the Speech That Inspired a Nation* (New York: Ecco, 2003).

of the Bible that itself reinterprets an earlier biblical tradition.[36] Chapters 40–55 in Isaiah (which biblical scholars call "Second Isaiah") refer to the defeat of Babylon by Cyrus of Persia and the subsequent return from Babylon to Jerusalem of those exiled by Nebuchadnezzar. But Second Isaiah does this by seeing the return from Babylonian exile as a new Exodus; these chapters use Exodus imagery to interpret the significance of the return as another manifestation of power by the God who values freedom over captivity. Here are the well-known opening lines:

> A voice cries out:
> "In the wilderness prepare the way of the LORD,
> make straight in the desert a highway for our God.
> Every valley shall be lifted up,
> and every mountain and hill be made low;
> the uneven ground shall become level,
> and the rough places a plain.
> Then the glory of the LORD shall be revealed,
> and all people shall see it together,
> for the mouth of the LORD has spoken." (Isa 40:3-5)

The paths in the desert wilderness evoke the Israelite trek through the desert after being freed from Egyptian slavery and refer also to the paths walked back to Jerusalem by the returning exiles from Babylon. Christian readers may also recognize these lines from Advent readings or from the Gospel of Mark, which begin with Isaiah 40:1 in reference to John the Baptist.[37] Placing himself in this chain of interpretation, King, in a brilliant, indeed virtuoso, recontextualization of this language, brings the imagery—along with the God it describes—to the steps of the Lincoln Memorial

[36] Miller, "Second Isaiah Lands in Washington, DC," 405–24. See also Marc Zvi Brettler, "I Have a Dream: Martin Luther King Jr.'s Biblical Prophetic Speech," *The Torah* online, https://www.thetorah.com/article/i-have-a-dream-martin-luther-king-jrs-biblical-prophetic-speech.

[37] "As it is written in the prophet Isaiah, 'See, I am sending my messenger ahead of you, who will prepare your way; the voice of one crying out in the wilderness: "Prepare the way of the Lord, make his paths straight,"' so John the baptizer appeared in the wilderness, proclaiming a baptism of repentance for the forgiveness of sins" (Mark 1:2-4).

and the history of Black oppression in the United States. And, as with Lincoln's Second Inaugural Address above, here I put King's biblical quotation in bold type (note that King, like Lincoln, cites the KJV):

> I have a dream that one day **every valley shall be exalted, every hill and mountain shall be made low, the rough places will be made plain, and the crooked places will be made straight, and the glory of the Lord shall be revealed, and all flesh shall see it together.**[38]

Notice that King uses direct quotation rather than allusion and, most importantly, he omits the beginning of the passage, "A voice crying in the wilderness," and replaces it with "I have a dream that one day." This is important for two reasons. First is that King situates his dream for America alongside the voice of the prophet in Isaiah 40 and that of John the Baptist in Mark's Gospel. This gives King's voice authority by placing it alongside the voices of Isaiah and John the Baptist. This is similar to how Lincoln used the KJV's language in his Second Inaugural Address to connect his words with those of the well-known biblical text. Second, King recasts the biblical text and places it into an indefinite future—in other words, giving it a different context. Both Second Isaiah and Mark use these words to describe something that has already happened or is happening (the return of the exiles to Jerusalem, the preaching of John the Baptist). In contrast, King places this vision of a harsh world made livable into an unknown later time—a time that he can but only see as a dream. As I discussed above with the quote from Shakespeare, a text's context (or neighborhood) makes a difference in how to make sense of it. Polonius is for Shakespeare a buffoon, but his fatherly advice is reused as tried-and-true wisdom. The same phenomenon is at work here. Many of King's listeners would have known the biblical language of Second Isaiah to refer to things that had already happened, or to refer to something to come, but in a way and at a time they

[38] Martin Luther King Jr., "I Have a Dream" speech, https://www.archives.gov/files/social-media/transcripts/transcript-march-pt3-of-3-2602934.pdf.

could not perceive. But also, in their new context, the words are a challenge to King's audience: What must be done to work alongside the God of liberation to make the rough places smooth, and the crooked ways straight?

This recontextualization of biblical passages of liberation to the contemporary struggles of African Americans wasn't limited to public figures like King. African American spirituals, sung in Black churches for over a century, were reinterpreted to address their singers' struggle for equal rights. For example, reference in the hymn "Jacob's Ladder" to "traveling through an unfriendly land" serves to connect the wandering patriarchs in the book of Genesis to the societal homelessness of Black Americans in Jim Crow America. More directly, the singer Cleo Kennedy changed the hymn "I'm On My Way to Canaan Land" to "I'm On My Way To Freedom Land."[39]

This way of reading the Bible continues today in the continuing struggle for racial equality in the US. On June 27, 2015, Bree Newsome, an activist and artist, climbed the flagpole of the South Carolina statehouse and removed the Confederate battle flag that flew from it. When law enforcement shouted at her to come down, she replied, "You come against me with hatred, oppression, and violence. I come against you in the name of God!" This is a slightly adapted version of what David says in response to Goliath's taunts in 1 Samuel 17:45.[40] As she descended into the waiting arms of the police, she recited the opening verse of Psalm 27 ("The Lord is my light and my salvation; whom shall I fear?" The Lord is the stronghold of my life; of whom shall I be afraid?") and, as they led her away in handcuffs, she spoke the first verse of Psalm 23 ("The

[39] Both examples in Keith D. Miller, "City Called Freedom: Biblical Metaphor in Spirituals, Gospel Lyrics, and the Civil Rights Movement," in Vincent Wimbush, ed., *African Americans and the Bible* (London: Continuum, 2000), 546–57, at 553–54. See also James H. Cone, *The Spirituals and the Blues* (Maryknoll, NY: Orbis, 1972; repr., 1991), and more recently, James H. Cone, "God and Black Suffering: Calling the Oppressors to Account," *Anglican Theological Review* 90, no. 4 (Fall 2008): 701–12.

[40] "And David said to the Philistine, 'You come to me with sword and spear and javelin, but I come to you in the name of the Lord of hosts!'" Bree Newsome's removal of the Confederate flag can be seen at https://youtu.be/gr-mt1P94cQ. It is discussed in Newton, "The African American Bible," 227.

LORD is my shepherd; I shall not want."). Both of these psalms are prayers to God expressing hope and confidence in divine protection.[41] Newsome's use of the Bible situates her act of dramatic civil disobedience and bravery in a theological world where God sides with the weak against the powerful (David rather than Goliath) and is founded on hope that God protects those who do the work of justice from their oppressors (Psalms 23 and 27). These reconfigurations of biblical texts aren't just citations. They are different from reference to a biblical rule as justification for a contemporary social practice. They require us to use our imaginations to see both what the biblical texts say about God and then about what that understanding of God says to us about how we are to act in the here and now. They make the text alive. In Catholic teaching, this is a process known as actualization, which is discussed later in this book.

Looking back at our discussion, we see that the use of the Bible by US Christians in debates over slavery shows a trend in which proslavery readers read biblical texts in what they believed to be the texts' plain meaning. These texts were understood as rules for behavior; they communicated God's commands for how to live. For the most part, antislavery Christians looked to larger narratives and themes in the Bible (mainly the Exodus, but also the prophets) and not to specific passages, although Acts 17:26 was one passage used. They saw in these stories insight to what God was like and what God valued. For them the Bible didn't communicate God's commands so much as disclose, or reveal, a part of God's nature. A century later and continuing to this day (as Bree Newsome's action shows) these kinds of readings were adopted between the respective descendants of the proslavery and antislavery readers. This shouldn't be surprising, given how the racism present in the US today is the persistence of the racism that fueled African slavery. However, the same dichotomy of reading the Bible as divine communication or divine disclosure is at work when Christians appeal to the biblical text in discussing other pressing moral issues today. The final section of this chapter wants to touch on this before taking it up more in-depth later in this book.

[41] Newsome appears to cite the NRSV translation of these texts.

The Bible in Contemporary American Catholic Debate

Some readers might wonder how Catholicism fits into the story I've been telling here of the Bible and race in America. Lest anyone think the preceding pages are an indictment of only White Protestant Christians, I want to offer a brief historical overview of Catholicism and slavery to introduce this section. A sober look at the facts reveals that the church played an important role in the enslavement of Black Africans from the beginning. The careful documentary work of Pius Onyemechi Adiele demonstrates that, as early as 1418, the church gave its blessing to Black slavery in part because of Rome's deep political ties with Portugal, whose kings were engaging in political and economic expansion along the western coast of Africa in what most Western civilization courses in the US benignly call "The Age of Exploration." Throughout the 1400s, popes would issue decrees supporting the conquest, subjugation, and enslavement of Africans and portraying it as a Crusade. These decrees would explicitly mention and approve of enslavement. In 1452, Pope Nicholas V issued the papal decree, *Dum Diversas*, to Portugal's King Alphonse, which allowed the king "to invade, conquer, fight, and subjugate," Muslims and all other non-Christians, "and to lead their persons into perpetual servitude."[42] With the colonization of the New World by the Spanish, French, and Portuguese, race-based enslavement of Africans and Indigenous peoples in the Americas was widespread in Catholic areas, and while the church sometimes spoke out against the enslavement of Indigenous peoples, it was consistent in its support of Black African slavery until the early nineteenth century.

In the United States, the picture isn't any better. John Carroll, the first American bishop and brother of one of the signers of the Constitution, reported to Rome in 1785 that the Catholic population in Maryland—almost sixteen thousand people—also owned over three thousand enslaved Africans.[43] John Hughes, archbishop

[42] Translations of all papal decrees and analysis in Adiele, *Popes, Catholic Church and Transatlantic Enslavement*.

[43] Raboteau, *Slave Religion*, 112.

of New York from 1842 to 1864, and arguably the most important Catholic prelate in the country, could at best only hope for a slow, gradual emancipation of American slaves. Hughes believed that Blacks were better off enslaved than in their so-called "primitive" state of freedom. Like the proslavery Bible readers discussed above, Hughes pointed to the presence of slavery in the Old Testament as support for its continued practice. He was also a staunch opponent of the abolitionists. And while he occasionally would express hope for the end of slavery in America, "instead of abrasive cries for action, Hughes offered prayers, gave promises and urged good will."[44] The "thoughts and prayers" rhetoric of inaction goes back a long way in the American psyche. Religious orders and Catholic institutions such as universities, schools, and hospitals were built by and maintained by slaves. As Bryan N. Massingale details in his essential book, *Racial Justice and the Catholic Church*, the US bishops began to issue significant statements on racism only in the wake of the 1954 Supreme Court case *Brown v. Board of Education of Topeka*, which ordered the desegregation of public schools.[45] As the US Catholic bishops acknowledge in their 2018 pastoral letter against racism, "The truth is that the sons and daughters of the Catholic Church have been complicit in the evil of racism." They continue:

> Therefore we, the Catholic bishops in the United States, acknowledge the many times when the Church has failed to live as Christ taught—to love our brothers and sisters. Acts of racism have been committed by leaders and members of the Catholic Church—by bishops, clergy, religious, and laity—and her institutions. We express deep sorrow and regret for them. We also acknowledge those instances when we have not done enough or stood by silently when grave acts of injustice were committed. We ask for forgiveness from all who have been harmed by these sins committed in the past or in the present.[46]

[44] Walter G. Sharrow, "John Hughes and a Catholic Response to Slavery in Antebellum America," *Journal of African American History* 57 (1972): 265.

[45] Massingale, *Racial Justice and the Catholic Church*, 43–61.

[46] United States Conference of Catholic Bishops, *Open Wide Our Hearts: A Pastoral Letter Against Racism* (2018), 20–21.

The point I want to make in the rest of this section is the culmination of this chapter: namely, that the interpretive strategies used by Bible readers in the debate over slavery and civil rights are the same that are used in debates between Catholics over pressing social issues, most notably, abortion. In his recent book, *Good Intentions*, Steven Millies traces how American Catholics, once liberated from their immigrant ethnic "ghetto" after the Second World War, became open to and influenced by the all-or-nothing rhetoric and dynamics of the Cold War, which aligned with the church's strong anti-communist stance. With the legalization of abortion in 1973 and the fall of the Soviet Union in 1989, Evangelical Christians and many Catholics took their uncompromising approach to communism and brought it to bear on the so-called culture wars of the 1990s, most specifically, abortion.[47] This is also not to say that the church was against the decriminalization of abortion by the 1973 *Roe v. Wade* decision from the beginning, because it was. But in a slow process that built through the 1980s and coincided with the growing influence of the religious right, much of the US Catholic Church became politically aligned with White Evangelical Christianity. Sixteen years of two Democratic presidential administrations (Bill Clinton and Barack Obama) further solidified the anti-abortion movement and, correspondingly, their opponents who support the maintenance and expansion of abortion rights. The overturning of *Roe v. Wade* in 2022 has not cooled down this debate but rather shifted it to the state level as activists on both sides of the issue continue their efforts to mobilize their respective bases and influence policy. As I did above with the issue of slavery, here I want to examine some representative examples of how Christians on both sides of the abortion debate use the Bible to support their positions and refute those of their opponents.

For this analysis I look at the *Catechism of the Catholic Church* (CCC). Significantly, the moral teachings of the church are arranged in the *Catechism* according to the version of the Ten Commandments in Exodus 20.[48] Abortion is placed under the fifth commandment

[47] Steven Millies, *Good Intentions: A History of Catholic Voters' Road from Roe to Trump* (Collegeville, MN: Liturgical Press, 2018), 29–61.

[48] Beginning in CCC 2052. Official English translation available at https://www.vatican.va/archive/ENG0015/_INDEX.HTM. There are two versions of

("You shall not kill" [Exod 20:13]) alongside capital punishment, intentional homicide, euthanasia, and suicide. We need to look at how the *Catechism* discusses the fifth commandment at the beginning of this section before looking at its specific teachings on abortion.

First off, the commandment is cited alongside Jesus' expansion of it in Matthew 5:21-22 to include anger and insult. Significantly, the commandment to not kill is interpreted to teach that "no one can under any circumstance claim for himself the right directly to destroy an innocent human being" (*CCC* 2258). The introductory section of the *Catechism*'s teachings of this commandment and its relation to contemporary forms of killing begins with a section entitled, "The Witness of Sacred History" (*CCC* 2259–2262). This is a series of biblical references deemed relevant to Catholic moral teaching.

The opening biblical text in this series is the Bible's first murder—that of Abel by his brother Cain (Gen 4)—understood to be the result of original sin, and the *Catechism* quotes God's words to Cain after the murder: "The voice of your brother's blood cries out to me."[49] Next follows quotation of Genesis 6:5-6, where God tells Noah that the penalty for killing a human being is death ("The one who sheds a person's blood, by a person will their own blood be shed"). Reference to "blood" in these two texts from Genesis (Cain and Abel, Noah and the Flood) segues into the observation that blood is a sign of life in the Old Testament, with citation of a dietary commandment in Leviticus 17:14 ("Because the life of all flesh is in its blood"). The *Catechism* cites this text and goes on to observe that "this teaching remains necessary for all time" (*CCC* 2260). It then returns to the book of Exodus (where

---

the Ten Commandments in the Hebrew Bible. The more well known is in Exodus 20, and the other is in Deuteronomy 5. The biblical translations in this discussion are those found in the CCC.

[49] "In the account of Abel's murder by his brother Cain, Scripture reveals the presence of anger and envy in man, consequences of original sin, from the beginning of human history. Man has become the enemy of his fellow man. God declares the wickedness of this fratricide: 'What have you done? The voice of your brother's blood is crying to me from the ground. And now you are cursed from the ground, which has opened its mouth to receive your brother's blood from your hand'" (*CCC* 2259).

the fifth commandment occurs in 20:13) to cite 23:7: "Do not kill the innocent or the just." The *Catechism* states that this rule in Exodus 23 "specifies the prohibition contained in the fifth commandment" (*CCC* 2261). In other words, the general commandment, "Don't kill," is here narrowed to "Don't kill innocent or just people." Finally, this introductory section ends with the example of Jesus and cites once again the Sermon on the Mount, where Jesus expands the scope of the fifth commandment to include anger and insult (Matt 5:21-23), commanding the love of enemies and the turning of the other cheek. Here, in contrast to the narrowing of the commandment, Jesus expands it. I want to underscore the process at work here: the very same commandment in Exodus 20 is both narrowed and expanded in its use in contemporary Catholic moral teaching. Finally, the introductory discussion in the *Catechism* ends with Jesus' command to Peter in the Passion not to defend Jesus during his arrest in the Garden of Gethsemane (Matt 26:52; cited in *CCC* 2262).

This little section of the *Catechism* is a good example to illustrate how complex the use of the Bible can be in making contemporary theological arguments, and I want to sit with it a bit longer and unpack some of what it is doing. Remember that use of the Bible to argue for moral positions in the US views the Bible either as a communication of God's desires to us or as a disclosure of God's identity to us. The table on the following page shows an outline of the section's biblical references and how they are used.

The table shows that there are eight biblical references—five of them quotations—in the *Catechism*'s introduction to the church's teaching on killing. Of these eight references to biblical texts, six use the Bible as a source for communicating commands and two point us to texts that reveal the character of God. Notice too how the placement of the dietary rule against eating blood from Leviticus 17 alongside God's commandment about not shedding blood in Genesis 9 gives the rule from Leviticus a different meaning, or—to bring back the image I used above when discussing the quotation from Shakespeare—how it places the text from Leviticus in a different neighborhood.

When we get to the section from the *Catechism* that directly discusses abortion (*CCC* 2270–75) the use of the Bible is less com-

CCC Section	Biblical Reference (* = quotation)	How Used (Communication/Disclosure)
III.2.ii.5	Exod 20:13* Matt 5:21-22*	Communication (Don't kill; don't be angry; don't insult.)
Paragraph 2259	Gen 4:8-12*	Disclosure (God hears the cry of victims.)
Paragraph 2260	Gen 9:5-6* Lev 17:14	Communication (Those who shed blood will have their blood shed; blood is life.)
Paragraph 2261	Exod 23:7*	Communication (Don't kill the innocent or just.)
Paragraph 2262	Matt 5:22-39, 44 Matt 26:52	Communication (Don't give in to anger or insult). Disclosure (Jesus did not defend himself when attacked.)

plicated, but no less interesting. Two direct quotations are offered (*CCC* 2270) to support the church's stance that human life is sacred from the moment of conception:

> Before I formed you in the womb, I knew you. Before you came out of the womb, I had consecrated you. (Jer 1:5)

> My frame was not hidden from you, when I was being made in secret, intricately woven in the depths of the earth. (Ps 139:15)

In their new neighborhood, these two quotations are mirror images of each other. In the first, God is speaking to a person, while in the second the speaker is a person addressing God. Both quotations are used to disclose something about God—that God individually knows and creates each person before their birth. Significantly, this isn't what the quotation from Jeremiah means in its original context. There, God's statement is in direct reference to the prophet Jeremiah, and occurs as part of his call to prophetic ministry. When placed alongside the quotation from Psalm 139, however, the reference to a specific individual (Jeremiah) can be read as a universal description of every person.

Notice that in the *Catechism*'s section on abortion there are no uses of the Bible as a book that communicates something that God requires of us. There are no biblical rules cited here. That's because nowhere does the Bible say anything directly about abortion, for or against. This places those who would argue against abortion in a similar position as antislavery American Christians, who also read the Bible as disclosing something about God's values and identity in regard to slavery. For antislavery readers, the Bible showed God to value freedom over slavery and liberty over oppression. For the authors of the *Catechism*, the Bible shows God to value each individual human life even before it is born.

Of course, the fact that the Bible makes no reference to abortion means that those Christians who believe that there are moral grounds for allowing abortion in some circumstances are in the same position as their sisters and brothers on the other side of the issue regarding the Bible and abortion. This also means that these Christians look to the Bible as disclosing something about God's values that in turn supports their moral evaluation of abortion. In her book, *Pro-Choice and Christian*, Kira Schlesinger reads the Bible as a book of liberation, in the tradition of the abolitionists and civil rights activists. She situates God's privileging of liberation as part of the larger divine value of life—here understood to be more than the biological state of being alive. For Schlesinger, the Bible is a "pro-life story . . . a testimony to the pro-life character of God. . . . God is for life over death, for freedom over slavery, and for human flourishing over all kinds of oppression—social, legal, political, economic, and religious."[50] Schlesinger's understanding of the "life" part of "pro-life" is based in part on her expansive reading of "life" based on her reading of the Bible, which includes the "social, legal, political, economic, and religious" dimensions of life. The Bible describes a God who consistently values and is concerned with these aspects of human life. The understanding of "life" in this approach by necessity must embrace more than the literal fact of being alive, and here we see a biblical approach that relies on reading the text as disclosure rather than communication.

[50] Kira Schlesinger, *Pro-Choice and Christian: Reconciling Faith, Justice, and Politics* (Louisville: Westminster John Knox, 2017), 62.

A Brief Conclusion

In this book's introduction I used a story about quoting Shakespeare to begin a discussion about style, content, and context in our use of culturally authoritative texts. A look at how the Bible is used by both sides in the debates about race in the United States showed how the content of the biblical texts was viewed differently by readers. Does the text tell us what God wants from us, or what God is like? How does the text's new context—its placement in new contexts or neighborhoods—help support moral positions that weren't directly addressed by the biblical text? In general, proslavery and later pro-segregationist readers, based on the tradition of reading the scriptural text for its "plain meaning," saw the Bible as communicating God's expectations for human behavior, while antislavery and later civil rights readers saw the Bible as disclosing God's nature as a deity for whom liberation and freedom were essential values. Turning to contemporary debates about abortion, we see the same reading strategies at work, but without the somewhat neat distinction between strategies and sides of the debate as was the case in the debates over racial equality. My aim in this chapter is to describe these reading strategies and not evaluate their effectiveness. In later chapters I will offer evaluations and recommendations for how to use the Bible for guidance in contemporary moral issues, but there is more descriptive work to do. Our discussion above of the complex ways the *Catechism* used biblical references in its opening section on the church's teaching about life brings to light the variety of ways that we interact with texts—how we make sense of them. The next chapter offers a more detailed examination of what happens when we interpret a text.

Chapter 2

Making Sense

In chapter 1, we took a brief look at how the Bible has been used in the conflict over the morality of slavery in America. We saw that the interpretive strategies employed there laid down a landscape of Bible reading that not only shaped ongoing struggles against systemic racism in America, but also inform contemporary debates about abortion. Those strategies involved engaging with different levels of the biblical text, which were in turn determined by what kind of text readers see the Bible to be—a relatively straightforward communication of moral imperatives, or a divine self-disclosure. The heart of this book is about interpretation, and this chapter introduces the complexity involved in any attempt at understanding human communication before the following chapters focus specifically on biblical interpretation and the issues at work in the different ways that the Bible is read.

Misunderstanding and Meaning

A well-known series of children's books are the Amelia Bedelia stories, which follow the misadventures of the main character, Amelia Bedelia, who is a maid for the Rogers family.[1] The premise of every book is the same: Amelia is given instructions by someone (usually her employers), but she misinterprets them and hilarity ensues. While adults might soon tire of what is essentially the

[1] The character was created by Peggy Parish (1927–1988) in 1963, and new stories are now written by her nephew, Herman Parish.

repetition of the same gag, many children find each new situation of misunderstanding funny.

Looking at the kinds of interpretive mistakes Amelia makes is a helpful way to begin a discussion of interpretation. Her errors fall into two broad categories. First, faced with a word that has multiple meanings, Amelia invariably chooses the wrong one. When asked to "put out the lights," Amelia hangs them from the trees outside. Told to "pitch" the tent during a camping trip, she throws it into the brush. Second, where instructions are not explicit, and assume that Amelia will also do what isn't explicitly said along with what is said, she doesn't. When Mr. Rogers asks for "toast and an egg" for his breakfast, Amelia brings him a piece of toast and a raw egg. Because she wasn't specifically asked to cook the egg, she didn't. These errors on Amelia's part don't so much reveal her own limitations as much as they show us the limitations of language, particularly the facts that words can mean more than one thing and that phrases often contain implied rather than explicit meaning.

Children not only enjoy these absurd situations, but they also learn from them that language is ambiguous. We must strive to understand others and to make others understand us. They also learn that the ambiguity of language is fun (think here of knock-knock jokes, which are often based on the interplay between similar-sounding words). Language's ambiguity can also be exploited and used to deceive. When we deliberately take advantage of two different meanings of a word in order to trick another person, this is called equivocation. It's the reverse of the situation in Amelia Bedelia, where the people giving her instructions want her to understand them. In the case of equivocation, the interpreter is deliberately led to misunderstand. For example, the term "cookies" refers both to the baked goods and to a feature of internet browsing that accumulates in a user's computer. If I know that Grandma is both a great baker and has trouble with technology, I can ask if she needs help clearing her cookies, with the intention of getting her to think that I want to help her with her internet problems. If she agrees, then the next time I go to visit, I'll help myself to the latest batch of oatmeal peanut butter cookies on her kitchen counter. Equivocation is a particularly underhanded form of deception because the person who commits it can blame the victim for the "misunderstanding," when all along misunderstanding was the goal. When people striving for clarity say that they are speaking "unequivocally," they are making explicit that there is no intended secondary meaning to their words—or at least wanting us to think that.

A less nefarious use of language's ambiguity is the pun, which is the deliberate use of two meanings of the same word at once, or of two different words that sound alike. Derided as the lowest form of humor, a good pun demonstrates a mastery of language and can often convey a dangerous or subversive message. The Hebrew Bible is full of puns that are lost in translation. Many of them occur in naming stories of characters of places. For example, when Pharaoh's daughter rescues the Hebrew baby from the Nile, we are told, "She named him Moses, 'because,' she said, 'I drew him out of the water' " (Exod 2:10). The explanation makes no sense in English. You have to know that the name, "Moses" in Hebrew (*Mosheh*) sounds like the Hebrew verb "to draw out" (*mashah*) in order to understand her statement. Here's the whole phrase in Hebrew, with the two words in bold: *vattiqra shemo* ***mosheh*** *vattomer ki min-hammayim* ***meshitihu***. Once you see the pun, you can now think about why the author chose to make it—and this is clearly an author's invention, because we wouldn't expect an Egyptian princess to make puns in biblical Hebrew.

A weightier example is in the Adam and Eve story (Genesis 2–3). The first part of the story is propelled by a dynamic of problem posed, problem solved:

> Problem: God plants a garden, but there's nobody to care for it.
>
> Solution: God makes a human being to tend the garden.
>
> Problem: The human being needs a companion.
>
> Solution: After making the animals and finding no companion, God makes the woman to be the first person's companion. The first person finds the woman to be the perfect companion. They dwell in the garden together.

When this second problem is solved, the scene ends with the observation that "the man and his wife were both naked and were not ashamed" (Gen 2:25), which is immediately followed by the observation that the serpent "was more crafty than any other wild animal" made by God (Gen 3:1). Think of everything the story leaves out here at this point: Why do we need to know that the man and woman are naked? Why did God make the serpent so crafty? Do the man and the woman know that the serpent is like this? Why are these two statements right next to each other, one an observation about the first couple (they were naked) and another about the first serpent (it was crafty)? The answer, like that with the naming of Moses, is found in a Hebrew pun. The word for naked in Gen 2:25 (*arummim*) and the word for crafty in Gen 3:1 (*arum*) are practically identical, and they're put here right next to each other. Why? Because the author is setting up the reader for an exquisite pun in Gen 3:10. There, in response to God's asking for his whereabouts, the man replies, "I heard the sound of you in the garden, and I was afraid, because I was naked, and I hid myself." When the man says that he's hidden himself "because I was naked" (*erom*) the reader also picks up the similar sounding word for "crafty" (*arum*) as well, because of the author's juxtaposition of the two words earlier in the story. And so, when the man, attempting to lie about his hiding, offers the excuse that he was naked, unbeknownst to him, he reveals his deceit because he has also confessed to his cunning. It's a brilliant play on words.

The model of communication assumed in these situations is often depicted by the three-part diagram of sender–message–receiver. In the same way that we are using the word "texts" as a shorthand to denote a variety of human expression, let's call the sender of any such expression an "author" and the recipient a "reader." With all of these examples—from Amelia Bedelia to the author of Genesis 2–3—the primary factor involved is the intention of the author. Either the author is misunderstood, or they try to lead the reader to misunderstanding, or they deliberately want the reader to see more than one meaning at play in their words. Underlying this is the realization that words mean more than what their authors intend to, and consequently that authors may take actions to lead their readers to the "correct," that is, their intended, meaning.[2]

[2] Of course, an author may also intend to show readers how a text can have more than one viable interpretation and thus invite the reader to become invested in their reading of the text beyond the goal of wanting to understand what the author meant.

But what if authors are unavailable to help readers arrive at their intended meaning, or their attempts to clarify aren't successful? This happens more than we might realize—certainly with almost everything we read that isn't a live chat or text conversation. What do we do then? When left to our own devices to make sense of a text, we turn to bodies of knowledge we can access in the absence of an author to clarify. Because coming to know something is, in many ways, a movement from what we already know into the unknown, we draw on these bodies of knowledge to give us a foothold from which we can connect with and make sense of a puzzling text. When used to interpret a text, these bodies of knowledge are called context—from the Latin *con* + *texere* (to join together)—because we are bringing together different kinds of knowledge and placing them alongside a text in order to interpret it. As mentioned earlier, we are putting the text in neighborhood that will help us to make sense of its meaning. Context both expands and limits what we see with the text. It expands by allowing us to see multiple possible meanings and to judge among them for the most likely. It limits by helping us to discard by process of elimination what something can't possibly mean. The remainder of this chapter explores several of those different contexts, why they're important, and what goes into our use of them.

Hearing, Seeing, Saying, Writing

When confronted with a puzzling written text, we might read it out loud, which brings our knowledge of what words sound like to bear on what we're seeing. I've often done this with puzzling instructions that are important for me to follow clearly. This is an often-overlooked interpretive strategy. Being taught to read as a child, or learning a new language as an adult, involves reading things out loud. It's an important part of correct interpretation because it engages other senses along with sight in the work of making sense. As we gain competence in a language, we learn to read silently, but that doesn't preclude us from reverting to reading out loud when necessary. And it is necessary, because our writing system doesn't always adequately convey our spoken language. We speak in syllables, but we write in phonemes, the smallest unit of linguistic sound which the letters of the alphabet express. At the end of the day, writing systems are imperfect means to express a spoken language fully and easily, because to have a distinct character or letter for each distinct sound might make the writing system too cumbersome to learn. Cuneiform, one the world's earliest writing systems, had different characters for each possible syllable in the Babylonian language. Consequently, the cuneiform writing system had hundreds of signs. At twenty-six characters, our alphabet does its best to convey all the necessary sounds needed to properly interpret written language, but we are all aware of shortcomings. Here are just a few: long, short, and silent vowels use the same written characters, and a person must learn which vowel is being represented (the *a* in *cat* and *cake*),[3] or that *gh* can be pronounced like *f* (rough). In the nineteenth century (and picked up by James Joyce) it was pointed out that the word *fish* can also be spelled *ghoti*: the *gh* as in *rough*, the *o* as in *women*, and the *ti* as in *nation*. And in some cases, pronunciation helps determine meaning. Take for example, the word *permit*. How is it pronounced? It depends on what part of speech it is. As a verb the second syllable is stressed: "Per*mit* me, please, to come through." As a noun the first syllable is stressed: "Yes, I have a *per*mit for my dog." But they are written identically.[4] Other languages that use the same alphabet also use accents to distinguish between two different pronunciations of the same letter. For example, in Italian, one writes the word *and* like this: *e*, but the verb "it/he/she is" like this: *è*. Written English doesn't yet allow for *pérmit* as a noun and *permít* as a verb, but perhaps one day it will.

I'm emphasizing these seemingly obvious and rudimentary aspects of how we read and write because, while most of us do them without second thought, they are in fact rather complex. We usually don't stop to think about how we understand things until

[3] Children are taught that the silent *e* on the end of *cake* makes the *a* long, but then they have to negotiate the fact that *e* can be either sounded or silent, not to mention anomalies such as the fact that *brake* and *break* are pronounced identically.

[4] Another example is the word *appropriate*. As an adjective, the *a* in the word's final syllable is short ("That was an appropriate response to the situation."). As verb, the *a* is long ("He decided to appropriate the resources for himself."). Nothing in our writing system denotes that. We learn to make the distinction by context.

we have a problem trying to interpret something. I want to think about how we make sense of any text as a necessary first step to thinking about how we make sense of the Bible. To that end, it bears mentioning that the question of how to properly express and interpret spoken language in writing are issues in the cultures that produced the Bible. Ancient Hebrew and Aramaic (the languages of the Jewish Scriptures) were written in an alphabet that, with very few exceptions, only expressed the consonant sounds of the language. Vowels were supplied by the reader, based on their knowledge of the language and the reading tradition of the text. The correct vowels were essential to correct interpretation, since supplying different vowels yields a different meaning.[5] For example, there is the common Hebrew root, שׁמר, written *shmr* in our alphabet.[6] This is one of the first root words that beginning Hebrew students learn, but it has different meanings and different grammatical functions depending on its vowels. This table offers a quick glimpse at how the unwritten vowels impact meaning. In each of the biblical examples, the consonants of the written word are identical and, in our earliest biblical manuscripts would therefore look identical:

Word with vowels	Meaning	Example (word in bold)
shamar	he guarded, kept, watched	"So his brothers were jealous of him, but his father **kept** the matter in mind." (Gen 37:11)
shomer	guarding, keeping, guard, keeper	"Am I my brother's **keeper**?" (Gen 4:9)
shemor	keep! guard!	"**Be careful** to obey all these words that I command you." (Deut 12:28)

[5] Modern Hebrew is also written without vowels, and its daily use by many people in Israel demonstrates that correct interpretation is possible without written vowels.

[6] Note that one Hebrew letter conveys a sound that in English requires two (*sh*).

Ensuring that the proper vowels (and hence, proper meaning) were expressed required reading aloud in many instances. Indeed, in biblical Hebrew, there is no specific verb to express the act of reading. Rather, the verb *qārā'* (to call aloud) is used.

Over the span of a thousand years, give or take, there was concern among Jewish scholars that the proper vowel sounds of the biblical text might be forgotten or changed if only preserved in oral reading traditions. Jewish scholars in the period from roughly the sixth to the tenth centuries CE known as the Masoretes devised a system of signs consisting of dots and small lines that they placed above, below, and inside the consonantal letters of the Hebrew Bible to represent the vowel sounds and preserve the traditional meaning. Looking at the examples above, adding the vowel marks to the root, שׁמר, to have it read *shamar* ("he guarded") would look like this: שָׁמַר. Some of these traditional meanings, however, preserve difficult or problematic interpretations that modern biblical scholars are able to correct by replacing the traditional vowels with others that yield more sense. Coming from the other direction, similar sounding words often affected the spelling of the Hebrew consonants. An influential example is the opening line of Psalm 29, which in Hebrew directs the "sons of gods" (Hebrew: *benei elim*) to praise the Lord. The word *gods* is pronounced the same as the word for *rams* (*elim*), although the two words are spelled differently in Hebrew letters. This led to the psalm being read and translated as a command to the "children of rams" to offer praise to the Lord, and it was this translation that was used in Catholic morning prayer for centuries.[7]

The New Testament is written in Greek and the Greek alphabet has characters that not only denote short and long vowels (such as ε and η for short and long *e*, respectively) but also characters that express combined phonemes such as θ for *th*. While this means that Greek doesn't present the same interpretive problems as read-

[7] This was a two-step process: The Hebrew text was translated into Greek with "sons of sheep," which was then translated into Latin and made part of the Vulgate, from where it was taken up into the Roman Breviary. Until the liturgical changes of the Second Vatican Council (1962–1965), priests, monks, and nuns chanted one morning a week: *Adverte Domino filios arietum* ("Give to the Lord, children of rams").

ing ancient Hebrew did, it was not without its challenges. In antiquity, Greek was written in all capital letters, with no punctuation or division between words. ITWOULDHAVELOOKEDSOME THINGLIKETHIS. For most of us, the only time we do this kind of reading might be online with hashtags, and there, in the case of a long hashtag, we might find ourselves sounding out the words. And sometimes this way of writing presents us with more significant interpretive problems. Here's one that has made the rounds of youth retreats and the internet: GODISNOWHERE. One can divide the words in this string of letters to read either "God is nowhere" or "God is now here," which express opposing viewpoints.

Because ancient Greek texts were written without word spaces, readers sometimes (but by no means always) read aloud as they sounded out the words in order to separate them aurally and make up for their lack of visual separation on the page.[8] This explains the story in Acts 8:26-35 of the apostle Philip's encounter with the Ethiopian eunuch on the road away from Jerusalem:

> Then an angel of the Lord said to Philip, "Get up and go toward the south to the road that goes down from Jerusalem to Gaza." (This is a wilderness road.) [27] So he got up and went. Now there was an Ethiopian eunuch, a court official of Candace, queen of the Ethiopians, in charge of her entire treasury. He had come to Jerusalem to worship [28] and was returning home; seated in his chariot, he was reading the prophet Isaiah. [29] Then the Spirit said to Philip, "Go over to this chariot and join it." [30] So Philip ran up to it and heard him reading the prophet Isaiah. He asked, "Do you understand what you are reading?" [31] He replied, "How can I, unless someone guides me?" And he invited Philip to get in and sit beside him.

The eunuch was "seated in his chariot . . . reading the prophet Isaiah" (v. 28), and we are told that Philip, travelling on foot, "*heard* him reading the prophet Isaiah" (v. 30). That's because the eunuch

[8] It was once erroneously thought that all reading in antiquity was done out loud, but see the evidence against this in A. K. Gavrilov, "Techniques of Reading in Classical Antiquity," *Classical Quarterly* 47 (1997): 65–73.

was reading aloud. When Philip asks him if he understands what he is reading, the eunuch's exclamation is not a request to help make out the words on the page. The eunuch is already doing that. Rather, he wants Philip to explain something more than what the words say. That something more requires looking at texts from large-scale contexts.

Large-Scale Meaning: Genre

In the same way that we use strategies based on our prior knowledge to understand specific words and phrases, we also bring knowledge of different kinds of writing to make sense of entire works. In other words, when we read a text, we decide on its genre and, depending on that choice, read with different sets of expectations and interpretive strategies. This is another way we seek to give a text a context. Of course, "the Bible" is itself a genre designation and we come to it with certain expectations that I touched on in this book's introduction when talking about my friend's confusion of Shakespeare with the Bible. I look at how the Bible functions as its own genre in chapters 3–4. For now, I just want to talk about genre in general. Genre is both something guessed at by the reader and chosen by authors, whose genre selection helps in part to shape the style, organization, and content of their texts. When this works, both the author and the reader share the same understanding of genres and what is distinctive about each one. In this way, understanding a text in the absence of the author is more likely to occur.[9]

Take, for example, a mystery novel. Before someone even begins reading, they bring expectations from past reading about what is and isn't part of the kind of writing known as a "mystery": a narrative that contains an unexplained and puzzling event with several viable explanations; a main character whom the reader

[9] Detailed discussion of the kinds of small- and large-scale genre guessing readers of the Bible engage in is found in Karolien Vermeulen and Elizabeth R. Hayes, *How We Read the Bible: A Guide to Scripture's Style and Meaning* (Grand Rapids, MI: Eerdmans, 2022), and Mark Reasoner, *Five Models of Scripture* (Grand Rapids, MI: Eerdmans, 2021).

accompanies in the search for the cause of the event; a steady, but not too revealing, string of data ("clues") that leads to a solution; characters and events that offer tantalizing, but false, leads; a resolution of the story which reveals the cause of the event and the motives behind it. Readers of a mystery bring to the text a set of expectations similar to these and use them both to predict what happens next in the text and to evaluate how well the text functions as an example of a mystery. When we read mysteries (or other genres) that we wind up disliking, it is usually because they have failed to meet our expectations of what a text in that genre ought to be like.

I want to make clear that we do this with every text we encounter, and not just novels or pleasure reading. When I see a street sign that reads, "Fine for Parking Here," I know from my prior experience that, because street signs usually describe prohibited behavior, this sign isn't telling me that it's fine (legal) to park next to it, but rather that I face a fine (monetary penalty) for parking next to it. Reading instructions or recipes can often be frustrating because we expect clarity and there is only so much that can be conveyed by words. That's why many instructions also include illustrations.

When we encounter a text of an unknown genre, we revert to the categories that we know in an attempt to make sense of it. In my introductory classes, when first-year students are asked to read a nonfiction book on a religious or theological topic that advances a particular thesis (as this book does) they often call it a "novel."[10] This is because most US students who graduate from high school have read only two different genres of books: the textbook, and the novel. Textbooks, of course, have lots of specific qualities that allow readers to correctly identify them: specific vocabulary highlighted or in bold print, a glossary, boxes with important points alongside the main text, questions or exercises. My students know that the books we read in my class are not textbooks because they have none of these features. Therefore, they choose the other genre that they have been exposed to and

[10] For example, Timothy Beal, *The Rise and Fall of the Bible: The Unexpected History of an Accidental Book* (New York: Houghton Mifflin, 2012).

call these books novels. To reiterate, this category mistake is not the students' fault. They are doing what all readers do—making a genre designation based on their background knowledge.

In the case of my students, this genre mistake doesn't impact them negatively, because they are in a group with their peers and me, and we learn together how to interpret the genre of a nonfiction work of scholarship. But that's not always the case. An important example is the reception of the 2003 novel *The Da Vinci Code* by Dan Brown. On the first page of the novel, Brown had a statement prefaced by the large type word, "FACT," which stated that two of the organizations in the novel are real groups and that "all of the artwork, architecture, secret documents, and rituals in this novel are accurate."[11] The book was a worldwide bestseller, and many of its readers mistakenly assumed that the specific plot of the novel—that Jesus and Mary Magdalene had been married, had a child whose descendant still lived, and whose life was protected by a secret society against the machinations of an evil Vatican—was also factual. What's more, other historical claims Brown made in the book, for instance about the development of the Bible, were also factually incorrect. In the years immediately following publication of the book, more than a few students and their parents would approach me to talk about their belief that the entire book was factual and that consequently it had changed their understanding of Christianity. This widespread genre mistake—seeing a novel as a nonfiction historical work—led to a small industry in books from scholars of religion trying to clarify the matter.[12] Moreover, it occurred despite the fact that the "FACT" page notes that the book is a novel.[13]

[11] Dan Brown, *The Da Vinci Code: A Novel* (New York: Anchor Books, 2003).

[12] Here is a representative sample: Bart D. Ehrman, *Truth and Fiction in The Da Vinci Code* (New York: Oxford University Press, 2004); Hank Hanegraaff and Paul Maier, *Da Vinci Code: Fact or Fiction?* (Carol Stream, IL: Tyndale House, 2004); Carl E. Olson and Sandra Miesel, *The Da Vinci Hoax: Exposing the Errors in the Da Vinci Code* (San Francisco: Ignatius Press, 2004). Respectively, these three volumes are written by secular, Protestant, and Catholic scholars.

[13] Note that this is the inverse of the genre mistake my students sometimes make (thinking a work of nonfiction is a novel). Here, readers of *The Da Vinci Code* think that a novel is a work of nonfiction.

Let's return to Philip and the Ethiopian eunuch in Acts 8, sitting in the chariot and puzzling over Isaiah, picking up where the story left off:

> 32 Now the passage of the scripture that he was reading was this:
> "Like a sheep he was led to the slaughter,
> and like a lamb silent before its shearer,
> so he does not open his mouth.
> 33 In his humiliation justice was denied him.
> Who can describe his generation?
> For his life is taken away from the earth."
> 34 The eunuch asked Philip, "About whom, may I ask you, does
> the prophet say this, about himself or about someone else?"
> 35 Then Philip began to speak, and starting with this scripture, he
> proclaimed to him the good news about Jesus.

Notice the eunuch's question: "Does the prophet say this about himself or about someone else?" There is genre interpretation happening here. A book written by a prophet means that it is a book of prophecy. That's a genre designation which brings its own set of interpretive strategies to it, specifically the fact that prophecy is understood as predictive, and therefore that the exact thing being predicted must be determined.

Once again, when understood as a single book, the Bible has a genre designation that I discuss in detail in the next two chapters. But as a collection of various writings, the Bible also contains a number of different smaller genres. Some of these genres were already known in the ancient world. For example, the core of the book of Deuteronomy bears striking similarity in language and structure to the treaties established between great ancient Near Eastern powers and their vassal states, particularly but not exclusively those that date from the Neo-Assyrian empire (eighth–seventh centuries BCE, which may be roughly the same time as the composition of Deuteronomy). Paul's letters follow the structure and format of Greco-Roman letter writing from the first century CE. The Bible itself also mentions different genres. Numerous poems in the Hebrew Bible are described by the term *qinah* (lament, lamentation; 2 Sam 1:17; Jer 9:10; Ezek 19). There are different types of psalms that have different names, such as *shir* (song), and some of these names still resist translation, like *mizmor*, or *shiggayon*. The most well-known biblical genre is probably the parable and, although the Bible is full of parables, those of Jesus are what come to the minds of most readers.[14]

Other genres were attributed to the biblical texts by later Jews and Christians, such as the term *Torah*. The term itself can mean "law, instruction, teaching," and refers to different bodies of written teaching in the Hebrew Bible: the tablets Moses brings down from Sinai (Exod 24:12), particular ritual rubrics (Lev 6:1, 14:57; Num 6:13), the rules in Deuteronomy (Deut 1:5). It is also at times specifically referred to as a "book" (Deut 28:61; 2 Kgs 22–23). By the fifth–fourth centuries BCE, we see references to a specific set of writings called "The Torah," or, "The Book of the Torah," "The Torah of Moses" or "of the LORD" (Ezra 7:6; Neh 9:3), although the exact contents of this Book of the Torah are unclear.[15] So while the Hebrew Bible refers to a written Torah many times, it isn't until the second century BCE that the "Torah of Moses" refers to the first five books of the Hebrew Bible, a designation that has lasted to this day.[16] A similar phenomenon occurs in the New Testament with the term "gospel." In the earliest known Christian writings, which are the letters of Paul, gospel doesn't refer to any written document. Rather, gospel (which translates the Greek word, *evangelion*, meaning "good news") denotes short, varied, oral expressions of the heart of the Christian faith. For example, Paul begins his letter to the Romans describing "the gospel" of God's Son thus:

> [he] was descended from David according to the flesh and was declared to be Son of God with power according to the spirit of holiness by resurrection from the dead, Jesus Christ our Lord. (Rom 1:3-4).[17]

[14] Amy-Jill Levine, *Short Stories by Jesus: The Enigmatic Parables of a Controversial Rabbi* (San Francisco: HarperCollins, 2014).

[15] See the discussion in Thomas M. Bolin, *Ezra-Nehemiah* (Collegeville, MN: Liturgical Press, 2012).

[16] In rabbinic Judaism, *Torah* has come to denote not only the biblical texts, but the entirety of the Mishnah, Talmud, and other commentaries on the text as well as the process of studying these texts. Torah has moved from instruction or teaching to now encompass the act of learning.

[17] See also 1 Cor 15:1-5: "Now I want you to understand, brothers and sisters, of the good news that I proclaimed to you, which you in turn received, in which

By the middle of the second century CE, however, Christian intellectuals were arguing about which writings constitute sacred Scripture, and it is in these debates that we begin to see written biographies of Jesus referred to as "Gospels."[18] By the end of that century as shown in the writings of Irenaeus of Lyons (ca. 180), we have our first clear references to the four written Gospels of Matthew, Mark, Luke, and John.[19]

Finally, there are other genre designations for biblical texts that aren't mentioned in the Bible but instead have been identified and named by modern scholars. One is the *call narrative*. This is a small genre (often called a type-scene) which often introduces the story of a prophet and usually consists of four elements:

1. *Theophany*: A visual or vocal manifestation of God.
2. *Commission*: A particular task articulated by God to the chosen person.
3. *Protest*: An attempt by the chosen person to delay or avoid God's commission.
4. *Reassurance*: A response by God to the person's reluctance which further urges them to fulfill the divine request.

---

also you stand, through which also you are being saved, if you hold firmly to the message that I proclaimed to you—unless you have come to believe in vain. For I handed on to you as of first importance what I in turn had received: that Christ died for our sins in accordance with the scriptures, and that he was buried, and that he was raised on the third day in accordance with the scriptures, and that he appeared to Cephas, then to the twelve."

[18] Much of this activity centered around the thought of the second-century Christian Marcion, who argued, among other things, that the Jewish scriptures should not be part of Christian sacred literature and that only Luke's Gospel—from which Marcion removed large portions—was inspired. See Judith Lieu, *Marcion and the Making of a Heretic: God and Scripture in the Second Century* (Cambridge, UK: Cambridge University Press, 2015).

[19] While Mark's Gospel begins with the phrase, "The beginning of the good news [gospel] of Jesus Christ," most scholars don't read this as a genre designation. For two distinct ways of approaching the question, see C. E. Hill, *Who Chose the Gospels? Probing the Great Gospel Conspiracy* (New York: Oxford University Press, 2010), and Matthew D. C. Larsen, *Gospels Before the Book* (New York: Oxford University Press, 2018).

Elements of a call narrative can be amplified or rearranged. In the call of Moses, which covers all of Exodus 3 and extends halfway into Exodus 4, the protest and reassurance elements are multiplied:

Call Narrative Elements	Call of Moses (Exod 3–4)
Theophany	"There the angel of the LORD appeared to him in a flame of fire out of a bush; he looked, and the bush was blazing, yet it was not consumed" (Exod 3:2).
Commission	"Now go, I am sending you to Pharaoh to bring my people, the Israelites, out of Egypt" (Exod 3:10).
Protest	"Who am I that I should go to Pharaoh and bring the Israelites out of Egypt?" (Exod 3:11); "But look, they may not believe me or listen to me, but say, 'The LORD did not appear to you' " (Exod 4:1); "O my Lord, I have never been eloquent, neither in the past nor even now that you have spoken to your servant; but I am slow of speech and slow of tongue" (Exod 4:10).
Reassurance	"I will be with you" (Exod 3:12); "The LORD said to him, 'What is that in your hand?' He said, 'A staff.' And he said, 'Throw it on the ground.' So he threw the staff on the ground, and it became a snake" (Exod 4:2-3); "What of your brother Aaron, the Levite? I know that he can speak well; even now he is coming out to meet you, and when he sees you his heart will be glad" (Exod 4:14).

In Isaiah's call from chapter 6 of the book of Isaiah, the commissioning element is placed at the very end, after the protest and reassurance:

Call Narrative Elements	Call of Isaiah (Isa 6)
Theophany	"In the year that King Uzziah died, I saw the Lord sitting on a throne, high and lofty; and the hem of his robe filled the temple" (Isa 6:1).
Protest	"And I said: 'Woe is me! I am lost, for I am a man of unclean lips, and I live among a people of unclean lips, yet my eyes have seen the King, the LORD of hosts!' (Isa 6:5).
Reassurance	"Then one of the seraphs flew to me, holding a live coal that had been taken from the altar with a pair of tongs. The seraph touched my mouth with it and said, 'Now that this has touched your lips, your guilt has departed and your sin is blotted out' " (Isa 6:6-7).
Commission	"Then I heard the voice of the Lord saying, 'Whom shall I send, and who will go for us?' " (Isa 6:8).

Many, if not most, of the genres identified by modern scholars are of small literary units like the call narrative. In the Hebrew Bible another such small genre is the *place-naming etiology*, which is a story that explains how a place got its name. The ancestor stories in Genesis 12–37 contain many of these. In the New Testament, *conflict* or *controversy stories* are those antagonistic encounters in the Gospels that Jesus has with religious and civil authorities.[20]

[20] These stories are themselves based on a Greco-Roman genre known as the *chreia*, many of which were written about ancient Greek philosophers and collected by, among others, Plutarch (46–119 CE). Ronald F. Hock and Edward N. O'Neil, *The Chreia in Ancient Rhetoric*, vol. 1 (Atlanta: Scholars Press, 1986); Ronald F. Hock and Edward N. O'Neil, *The Chreia in Ancient Rhetoric*, vol. 2 (Atlanta: Society of Biblical Literature, 2002); and Ronald F. Hock, *The Chreia in Ancient Rhetoric*, vol. 3 (Atlanta: Society of Biblical Literature, 2012).

It is important to notice that biblical genres come both from the authors who composed them in antiquity and from readers interpreting those same texts centuries later. Given that genre identification can be important in how well one interprets a text, we need to know as much as we can about the genre choices available to authors. This is relatively easy when reading a text that comes from our time, but the Bible is a collection of ancient texts written in foreign languages. These two features require readers to bring other contexts into play when reading biblical texts.

Meaning Across Time and Space

This chapter began with a description of seemingly simple interpretive problems in the Amelia Bedelia books. There, one person (Mr. or Mrs. Rogers) gives a direct message to another person (Amelia Bedelia) in their shared native language. That example was used to point out that all interpretation—even the simplest—involves complex mental processes, many of which we take for granted because we have so much practice at using them. However, the chapter has moved steadily from that relatively simple act of interpretation into the more difficult task of interpreting written texts, which is more complicated because the authors may be unavailable to clarify or point out misinterpretations. And, in the case of the Bible, not only is the author of any given biblical text unavailable, but all the biblical authors lived in different cultural and historical contexts centuries ago and wrote in what are foreign languages to modern readers. This section explores what is involved in interpreting ancient, foreign texts like the Bible.

We saw in chapter 1 that the common practice of slavery in ancient Israel and the Greco-Roman world[21] and its acceptance in the Bible played a role in the debates over race-based slavery in the US. The Bible demonstrates belief in and acceptance of a number of things which the majority of modern people no longer do. It contains social norms such as how to treat women and girls, behavior in warfare, and capital punishment, along with numer-

[21] The phrase "biblical times" is too vague and broad to be useful. The texts of the Hebrew Bible date anywhere from the ninth to the second century BCE. Those of the New Testament come from ca. 50–110 CE. That's a nine-century span.

ous beliefs concerning the natural world that we now know to be incorrect. The reason I am writing a book to help readers to interpret the Bible in a meaningful way for the twenty-first century is precisely because it comes from vastly different times and places.

Knowledge of the ancient social and linguistic contexts is essential for interpreting biblical texts as fully as possible. Returning to the story of Philip and the Ethiopian eunuch in Acts 8, it's important to know why Luke mentions that the man is a eunuch. The dictionary definition of the term is a boy or man who has been castrated. However, the term's use in the Bible, while it includes this aspect at times, is broader. In both Hebrew and Greek, the term can also refer to highly placed officials in royal courts, regardless of whether they have their reproductive organs.[22] Potiphar, the man who buys Joseph in Genesis 39, is called by the Hebrew term for "eunuch" (*seris*) but the context implies that he is not castrated (he is married) and so the NRSVue translates the term as "officer." In Acts 8:27, notice that the man is called both a eunuch and "a court official" (Greek: *dynastēs*). This double identification is probably to alert us that the man is both a highly placed person in the court of the Ethiopian queen and castrated. This also helps us to understand the remark of Jesus in Matthew 19:12: "There are eunuchs who have been so from birth, and there are eunuchs who have been made eunuchs by others, and there are eunuchs who have made themselves eunuchs for the sake of the kingdom of heaven." The last kind of eunuch, those who have chosen to be so for the kingdom builds on the term's meaning of a physically castrated person and of highly placed person in a court. Jesus is saying that those self-made eunuchs will be highly placed in the kingdom, God's heavenly court. In Acts 8, the conversion of the Ethiopian eunuch is part of Luke's main theme in the book concerning the worldwide, inevitable, God-driven spread of the Gospel. In this case, the Ethiopian eunuch represents the margins both geographically, because Ethiopia was understood to be the southern edge of the world, and socially, because physically castrated males were denied offspring who could care for them and carry on their memories.

[22] See the survey in F. P. Retief, J. F. G. Cilliers, and S. P. J. K. Riekert, "Eunuchs in the Bible," *Acta Theologica Supplementum* 7 (2005): 247–58.

Another example of the necessity of knowing a text's social and cultural contexts for interpretation is the prophecy against Babylon in Isaiah 46. It begins with the naming of two major Babylonian gods (46:1: "Bel bows down; Nebo stoops"). Bel is another name for the main Babylonian god, Marduk, celebrated as the creator of the cosmos and ruler of the storm. Nebo is the Babylonian god of wisdom, Nabū. Here the book of Isaiah asserts these two gods as nothing more than empty idols—statues made of wood and covered in precious metals, which is exactly how divine statues were made in the ancient Near East. Isaiah 46 continues, describing how the statues of Bel/Marduk and Nebo/Nabū are loaded onto beasts. The image here is twofold: first, there is the carrying off of the Babylonian gods by the invading army of Cyrus the Persian.[23] Second, the carrying of the two gods calls to mind major Babylonian religious festivals, where divine statues would be processed and paraded around and through the great city of Babylon. These were displays of the gods' power. Isaiah 46 inverts this in two ways: now the helpless gods are being carried away by the Persians, and, in contrast to the false gods of the Babylonians, the God of Israel affirms:

> Listen to me, O house of Jacob,
> all the remnant of the house of Israel,
> who have been borne by me from your birth,
> carried from the womb;
> even to your old age I am he;
> even when you turn gray I will carry you.
> I have made, and I will bear;
> I will carry and will save. (Isa 46:3-4)

The author of this particular oracle in Isaiah, drawing upon his or others' experience as exiles in Babylon, makes a powerful point in his use of vivid imagery that a modern reader might overlook without sufficient knowledge of the ancient Near Eastern cultural context.

[23] Cyrus the Persian conquered Babylon in 539 BCE, but according to texts written by Babylonian scribes, he did not take the gods of Babylon into captivity.

Turning to the need for linguistic context now, the three ancient languages which were used to write the biblical texts, Classical Hebrew, Aramaic, and Koine Greek, are known to various degrees. Of the three, Classical Hebrew has the smallest body of writings available, which often poses problems for translators, because the more written examples of a non-spoken language available, the larger context one has to help understand the meanings of certain words. Consequently, in the text of the Hebrew Bible there are some words we do not yet know. Here are two: In Jonah 4, after the prophet has preached to Nineveh at God's command, Jonah goes outside the city and builds a hut for himself. Then God provides Jonah "a bush" (Jonah 4:6) for shade and shelter. The word for Jonah's bush, *qiqayon*, occurs only here in the Bible and its exact meaning has stumped interpreters for centuries. Indeed, two Doctors of the Church, Augustine and Jerome, got into a heated argument over this very word and exchanged harsh letters about it.[24] Many of the Classical Hebrew terms used to describe plants or animals are as yet unknown. A more substantial example is the Hebrew term, *nefesh*, which has a range of meanings including "neck," "appetite," "breath," "inner being," "individual," and "corpse," depending on the context.[25] Scholars look at the range of usage of a term in a wide body of texts and, in cases where there aren't that many texts, also look at writings in related languages. For example, most scholars of Classical Hebrew are also able to work with other the other ancient Semitic languages of Aramaic, Ugaritic, and Akkadian, which often shed light on Hebrew words whose meaning we might not otherwise know. This broad cultural and linguistic expertise aims to supply the missing interpretive contexts that time and distance have taken away. It seeks to, in the words of Pope Pius XII, "go back wholly in spirit to those remote centuries" in order to "accurately determine what modes of writing, so to speak, the authors of that ancient period would

[24] Thomas M. Bolin, *Freedom Beyond Forgiveness: The Book of Jonah Re-Examined* (London: Bloomsbury, 1997), 25–28.

[25] Matthew J. Suriano, *A History of Death in the Hebrew Bible* (New York: Oxford University Press, 2018), 133–53. In most modern English translations, *nefesh* is translated as "soul," which in many cases reads Greek philosophical concepts about the human person into the Hebrew text.

be likely to use, and in fact did use."[26] The pope's lyrical language notwithstanding, this process of "going back" in time will always be ongoing and at best only partial.

A Meaning of One's Own

So far in this chapter, when we have discussed correct interpretation, we have understood it to mean that one has captured the intention of the author. To arrive somewhere other than the author's intended meaning is to misunderstand. We moved beyond the examples of Amelia Bedelia getting her employers' instructions wrong and looked at more complicated examples of interpretation and the strategies we employ to arrive at a correct interpretation when authors are absent: reading aloud, making educated guesses about genre, and, for ancient or foreign texts, gaining as thorough a knowledge as possible of their language and culture. Again, the implicit aim of these strategies is to arrive at the author's intended meaning of a text. Of course, with ancient and anonymous texts, the exact author's intended meaning is an ideal rather than an achievable goal, and most scholars speak of arriving at the meaning a text would have had to its "first readers." But the goal is the same: to somehow, as Pius XII so poetically put it, "go back" in time and encounter a text as its author intended it to be encountered. There is an entire tradition of biblical scholarship known collectively as the historical-critical method that has spent the past two centuries working to achieve this goal.[27] My biblical examples in this chapter are all results of this scholarly approach. I and many other biblical scholars underwent graduate school training in the historical-critical method—learning to read ancient languages, becoming familiar with the social, political, and religious aspects of numerous ancient cultures, studying the

[26] Pope Pius XII, *Divino Afflante Spiritu* (Encyclical Letter on Promoting Biblical Studies) 35, September 30, 1943, https://www.vatican.va/content/pius-xii/en/encyclicals/documents/hf_p-xii_enc_30091943_divino-afflante-spiritu.html.

[27] For an overview of the historical-critical method, see the lengthy discussion in the 1993 document of the Pontifical Biblical Commission, *On the Interpretation of the Bible in the Church*, and the relevant sections in John Barton, *The Nature of Biblical Criticism* (Louisville: Westminster John Knox, 2007); Corrine Carvalho, *Primer on Biblical Methods* (Winona, MN: Anselm Publishing, 2009).

archeological findings of the many relevant excavated sites—all to be put to use in the attempt to uncover original or intended meanings of biblical texts. But striving to find out what the biblical authors intended to say isn't the only possible or legitimate interpretive goal when it comes to reading a variety of different texts, including the Bible.

Let's think about Amelia Bedelia one last time. The source of her mishaps lies not in her limitations, but in the fact that words can mean more that what a speaker intends them to. This is the nature of language and, while we've been looking at its shortcomings in this chapter, for the most part it's a bonus and not a drawback. Language's inherent surplus meaning—the capacity for words to mean more than what their speaker intends—is not to be looked at exclusively, or even primarily, as a limitation. On the contrary, it is one of language's strengths. In fact, the ability of language to express more than what its users mean or what its hearers understand is one of the main reasons we read certain ancient texts. Indeed, if the meaning of the biblical texts were limited only to what their authors intended and first readers interpreted, then there would be no point in our reading these texts for any purpose other than historical curiosity. While it is essential to try and grasp the authorial intention of an ancient text, it's not enough for modern readers. Ancient texts need to speak to us in some way, and not only function as windows into the past. The very fact that we still read certain ancient texts is proof that they have something to say to us. We see this in the conversation of Philip and the Ethiopian eunuch. The eunuch has been reading Isaiah 53:7-8:

> Like a sheep he was led to the slaughter,
> and like a lamb silent before its shearer,
> so he does not open his mouth.
> In his humiliation justice was denied him.
> Who can describe his generation?
> For his life is taken away from the earth. (Isa 53:7-8 as quoted in Acts 8:32-33)[28]

[28] Luke's quotation of Isaiah is slightly different from what we find in the book of Isaiah, owing to the variety of biblical manuscript traditions and the way that ancient authors remembered and cited texts.

Hearing the eunuch read this passage, Philip asks him outright, "Do you understand what you are reading?" The eunuch not only responds that he doesn't, but asks Philip the question that is driving his search for understanding: "About whom, may I ask you, does the prophet say this, about himself or about someone else?" If the answer to the eunuch's question is an attempt to discover Isaiah's original context, centuries before the setting in Acts, then reading Isaiah becomes for the eunuch an exercise in understanding the past. But if it means something besides what Isaiah had intended centuries before, then it can mean something more to the eunuch than only what Isaiah wanted to say.

When we realize that a text's meaning embraces more than what an author intends for it, we arrive at a significant conclusion. The surplus meaning of language doesn't automatically lead to misunderstanding; it leads to multiplicity. The experience of "misunderstanding" occurs when the author or another reader offers a different interpretation of a text alongside one that someone has already put forward. This juxtaposition of different interpretations allows for their relative strengths and weaknesses to come to light. It's not a case of understanding versus misunderstanding, but rather of determining which is the better interpretation, with "better" being a criterion that itself is influenced by different readers (Better for whom?) and their contexts (Better for what purpose?).

Interpretation: An Art and Not a Science

What we've been thinking carefully about in this chapter is what in academia is called "hermeneutics," the study of how we interpret texts. In the last two hundred years especially, the question of whether interpretation of ancient texts involved more than reconstructing their original or intended meanings has come to dominate discussions among historians, classicists, theologians, and legal scholars. And while this isn't the place to give a detailed overview of hermeneutics as a field of study, I want to highlight two different approaches that are best used as complementary, rather than exclusive, ways to make sense of texts.[29]

[29] An accessible overview of hermeneutics is Alexander Jensen, *Theological Hermeneutics* (London: SCM Press, 2007).

The first was articulated by Friedrich Schleiermacher (1768–1834), a German Protestant theologian. Correct interpretation for Schleiermacher is aimed at arriving at the intended meaning of the author. Any other interpretations are misunderstandings to be avoided by means of a thorough knowledge of the author's language and culture. "The success of the art of interpretation depends on one's linguistic competence and one's ability for knowing people."[30] Any text is an expression in a particular language and, therefore, "can be understood only in the context of the totality of the language."[31] This is what I've been describing in this chapter and what the historical-critical method is founded upon.

What this approach often overlooks (although Schleiermacher himself wasn't guilty of this) is the inescapable fact that people engaged in the historical-critical method are themselves inextricably embedded in a particular historical and cultural context which cannot be bracketed or otherwise set aside when they attempt to read an ancient text "on its own terms." We cannot extricate ourselves from our own limited vantage point to look at ancient texts from a bird's eye viewpoint nor can we fully embed ourselves into the worldview of ancient authors. Consequently, the German philosopher Hans-Georg Gadamer (1900–2002) argued convincingly that interpretation is an active exercise of human creativity which is influenced by our own historical and cultural conditions.[32] In other words, when we read a text, we bring the contexts of our own lives—broadly understood as our individual, cultural, social, and political histories—to that text, and use those contexts to make sense of that text, *whether we are aware of that or not*. This means that we do not *receive* meaning from a text; we *create* it. Texts are where we experience and create understanding, which may be different from an author's intended meaning. Understanding is the production of meaning by the reader and not just the reproduction of the author's intended meaning. With Amelia Bedelia

[30] In Kurt Mueller-Vollmer, *The Hermeneutics Reader* (London: Continuum, 2006), 76.

[31] Mueller-Vollmer, *Hermeneutics Reader*, 75.

[32] Hans-Georg Gadamer's fullest expression of this position is his book, *Truth and Method*, 2nd rev. ed. (London: Continuum, 2004), first published in 1960. For an accessible introduction to the philosophical background of Gadamer's thought, see Sarah Bakewell, *At the Existentialist Café* (New York: Other Press, 2016).

and the opening sections of this chapter, we discussed interpretation as a model that looks something like this: sender/author → message/text → receiver/reader. This is a transactional model of communication. Something is being handed on by someone to someone else, and if anything happens to "break" the arrows in the model, then misunderstanding occurs. But Gadamer points out that this isn't the only thing that can happen in the interpretative process. Understanding isn't only a transaction; it's an experience in which the author, text, and reader each plays a significant role. The text is a site of transformation, and not of transaction.

Gadamer uses the horizon as a metaphor to describe how interpretation occurs. In the same way that a horizon is the limit of what one can see based upon their location, so too is every person's view of reality conditioned by historical contingency, along with any texts we read that come from another historical era. Unlike Schleiermacher, Gadamer does not consider the act of acknowledging a text's historical difference to be genuine interpretation. For Gadamer, only what makes sense can be understood, and what we call "historical understanding" is limited to those things that don't make sense *to us*. Understanding can only occur when the two horizons of the text and the reader come together. This encounter, what Gadamer calls "the fusing of horizons," is a creative act out of which come new meanings. This happens in part because, for Gadamer, understanding demands that we move from what we know into the unknown, which we undertake by projecting probable meanings onto a text and then assessing those expectations with our experience of reading the text.[33] Our projections of meaning are either confirmed, revised, or rejected. There is no objectivity that exists independently of this confirmation or disconfirmation of our projections.

Our ability to project expected meanings, in short, our horizon of meaning, is shaped by our own culture and tradition. These in turn are formed in part by certain influential and authoritative texts. Gadamer calls these texts "classic," by which he means texts that a culture understands to be normative and that constitute a

[33] "A person who is understanding a text is always projecting" (Gadamer, *Truth and Method*, 267).

part of that culture's tradition—the values, imagery, and stories that the culture preserves and retells to reproduce its identity through time from one generation to the next.[34] In other words, to say that a text is normative for one's culture, or a part of a cultural tradition, is to make a genre designation about it that assumes that text to be able to speak to readers across time whom the authors may never have considered. Gadamer states that the power of such works "to speak directly is fundamentally unlimited."[35] We have already seen the Bible as an example of a cultural classic in the introduction to this book when we discussed the importance of a culture's collective wisdom and how that functions as a new "neighborhood" for texts that are included in that body of material. In this chapter, we saw how the book of Isaiah functioned as a classic text for both the Ethiopian eunuch and Philip in Acts 8. As should be obvious now, for Christians the Bible is the classic text par excellence.

Practically speaking, the inexhaustible nature of texts doesn't necessarily mean that readers can extract any meaning from them precisely because readers are not fully independent agents in the process of interpretation. Readers are shaped and limited by the very culture of which classic texts are part, not to mention the impact that a reader's particular social location and individual life experiences have on their interpretation. But those social locations and experiences can and do allow potential meanings of a text to be actualized even if they had never been so before.[36] When Thomas Jefferson wrote the words "all men are created equal" in the summer of 1776, his intended meaning was that all White, male, property holders were created equal. Certainly, the more than six hundred human beings that Jefferson owned over his adult life were not included in this sentence, nor were any of the

[34] To be more specific, such texts are part of what a culture would call "classical," in the sense that they are normative and constitutive for that culture; see Gadamer, *Truth and Method*, 277–91. Gadamer also articulates an understanding of cultural tradition, which is considered below alongside discussion of the idea of tradition in the Vatican II document *Dei Verbum*, which I discuss in chap. 3.

[35] Gadamer, *Truth and Method*, 290.

[36] The actualization of potential meanings is discussed in more detail in chap. 3.

women whom he knew.[37] It was only the later readers of this text, bringing their own values and experience to it who unlocked a more expansive—and truer—meaning of those words. Jefferson's words meant more than what he had intended, and in the encounter of Americans whose lived experience did not coincide with Jefferson's words, both the words and the readers' worlds were transformed for the better. Additionally, this limiting feature works on the other side of the reader-text equation. That is to say that, although a text can mean more than what its author intends, a text cannot simply mean anything because language is both empowered and limited by its potential. The French philosopher Gilles Deleuze speaks of a text's "virtual multiplicity," by which he means the potential meanings inherent in a text that are either activated or not by readers approaching the text from many different standpoints,[38] as did enslaved Africans and their descendants with the Exodus.

This chapter has covered quite a bit of ground and I have tried to be as concise as possible without leaving out anything significant. From this point, the discussion will focus exclusively on the Bible, beginning with the next chapter, which explores through an historical framework in more detail the interpretative strategies used when the Bible is understood as a classic text.

[37] For information on Jefferson's history of slave owning, see the page dedicated to the topic at the Monticello website (https://www.monticello.org/slavery/slavery-faqs/). Of the over six hundred people Jefferson owned, he only freed seven. In his *Notes on the State of Virginia*, published in 1785, Jefferson claims to be against slavery, but also states that Africans are inherently inferior to Europeans (p. 141; https://tile.loc.gov/storage-services/service/gdc/lhbcb/04902/04902.pdf).

[38] Gilles Deleuze, *Bergsonism* (Princeton: Princeton University Press, 1991). For an extensive consideration of how to use Deleuze's thought in biblical studies, see Brennan W. Breed, *Nomadic Text: A Theory of Biblical Reception History* (Bloomington: Indiana University Press, 2014). I have also discussed and engaged with Breed's work in Thomas M. Bolin, *Ecclesiastes and the Riddle of Authorship* (London: Routledge, 2017).

Chapter 3

The Divine Library

The last chapter offered a slowed-down examination of the steps we take, often quickly and unconsciously, when we go about interpreting texts, whether they be verbal interactions, written instructions, jokes, or writings considered to be important or timeless. It highlighted the fact that a text's meaning isn't limited to what its author intended, but rather that what we call "meaning" is the outcome of a complex interaction between the author, the reader, and the text—itself a thing that exists independently of its author. In this way, we can think of the text as a site of human creativity not only on the part of its author, but of its readers who, based on their own experiences and understandings of reality, bring their imaginations to bear in the generation of new meanings. This is dynamic interpretive process has been traditionally described as a circle in which meaning occurs in the movement between reader and text.[1] We also saw that genre is an important interpretive key, and that there are many kinds of genres that make up the collected writings of the Bible. These genres are identified in part by clues in the text. We also use textual clues to create an image of the author as we read. But there are other places we go for interpretative clues to help us make sense: our past experience of reading and interpreting are brought to the text in front of us. This also informs our guesses of a text's genre. But everyone's reading and interpretive histories are different—not wildly so in most cases, but different nonetheless. We therefore make sense differently. These differences often break along cultural, religious,

[1] There are different understandings of the parts of the hermeneutic circle. My use of it here relies mainly on the work of Hans-Georg Gadamer discussed in the last chapter.

economic, gender, or ethnic lines and, more particularly, along the lines of our own distinctive histories and potentialities. All of these factors are magnified when the Bible is read as Scripture, which is a particular—even unique—genre designation for a text.

This chapter further explores some of the interpretive strategies at work with the Bible in particular and specifically when readers subsume the different genres of biblical texts under the larger category of sacred or inspired writing. On the one hand, this genre designation works like others, insofar as it shapes the reader's expectations about what a biblical text is about or how it communicates. However, in the case of an authoritative text, as briefly noted in the last chapter with the Declaration of Independence, the assumption of timelessness leads readers to have much greater expectations of what the text can mean. In other words, if interpretation is about the reader's making of meaning from a combination of the author's intention and the text's inherent interpretive power, then in the case of an inspired text, that text's power comes to overshadow the author's intent or cultural horizon. This is certainly case with much biblical interpretation. I want to frame this chapter with two stories that describe encounters with the Bible. The stories are centuries and miles apart, but both illustrate the point that our prior ideas about the Bible's importance determine how we interpret it.

The first comes from the 1772 autobiography of an enslaved African, James Albert Ukawsaw Gronniosaw. Recounting his capture in Africa and subsequent voyage on a Dutch ship, Gronniosaw describes how his enslaver

> used to read prayers in public to the ship's crew every Sabbath day; and when first I saw him read, I was never so surprised in my whole life as when I saw the book talk to my master; for I thought it did, as I observed him to look upon it, and move his lips. I wished it would do so to me. As soon as my master had done reading, I followed him to the place where he put the book, being mightily delighted with it, and when nobody saw me, I opened it and put my ear down close upon it, in great hope that it would say something to me.[2]

[2] James Albert Ukawsaw Gronniosaw, *A Narrative of the Most Remarkable Particulars in the Life of James Albert Ukawsaw Gronniosaw, An African Prince, as*

Gronniosaw's encounter with what he later learned was a Bible is echoed by the accounts of other enslaved Africans who recounted their unsuccessful attempts to listen to this special book talk to them. The literary critic Henry Louis Gates Jr. grouped these narratives under a literary motif he called the "talking book," which he included as part of his influential analysis of African American literature.[3] While this image of a talking book that does not talk to everyone underscores the enslaved Africans' status as marginalized in the world of their enslavers, this alienation was not to last. As Allen Dwight Callahan notes in his important study on African American biblical interpretation:

> American slaves did not read the Bible through, or even over and against, the traditions they brought with them from West Africa: they read the Bible as a text into which these traditions were woven. The characters and events of the Bible became the functional equivalent of the ancestors and heroes long celebrated in West Africa. The many ancestral and natural spirits were subsumed in the Holy Spirit, and the mighty acts of God supplanted ancient tales of martial valor. Biblical patriarchs and heroes now sat on the stools of the esteemed ancestors of ages past.[4]

Callahan's description of this interpretive process is a good example of what Hans-Georg Gadamer calls the fusion of horizons, which occurs in the interaction between a reader and a classic text. Recall that for Gadamer, a classic text is normative and practically inexhaustible in its ability to speak to people. As we saw in chapter 1, enslaved Africans and their descendants were able to bring their experiences to the biblical text that was presented to them

---

Related by Himself (Bath: W. Gye, 1772), 10, https://docsouth.unc.edu/neh/gronniosaw/gronnios.html.

[3] Henry Louis Gates Jr., *The Signifying Monkey: A Theory of African-American Literary Criticism* (1988; repr., New York: Oxford University Press, 2014). See the discussion of this passage and others in Allen Dwight Callahan, *The Talking Book: African Americans and the Bible* (New Haven: Yale University Press, 2006), 13–14, and Henry Louis Gates Jr. and William L. Andrews, eds., *Pioneers of the Black Atlantic: Five Slave Narratives from the Enlightenment, 1772–1815* (New York: Civitas, 1998).

[4] Callahan, *Talking Book*, xii.

as normative and find in it a meaning that not only spoke to their experiences but also challenged the authority of their enslavers.

This chapter doesn't intend to be a comprehensive history of biblical interpretation; there are several fine books that already offer such a narrative.[5] Rather, I want to highlight some of the interpretive strategies at work when readers of the Bible read it with the assumption that it is a sacred text, and to explore how that assumption informs those ways of reading.

The Changing Nature of Prophecy

In the previous chapter, we saw the Ethiopian eunuch in Acts 8 reading from a prophetic book (Isaiah) and puzzling over to whom or what a specific passage referred. This is because readers most usually understand the genre of prophetic texts as speaking about an otherwise hidden future that has been revealed to the prophet by God. Correct interpretation therefore depends upon discovering the specific future being described. In other words, for people to read ancient prophetic texts as predictive or relevant to them requires that they already think of those texts as relevant, as possessing knowledge that transcends the time of their writing.

But it was not always so. What we know from a variety of prophetic texts that come from both ancient Israel and neighboring cultures is that the overwhelming number these writings dealt with the immediate, or at the very most proximate, futures of their authors and first readers.[6] Among the thousands of clay tablets written in cuneiform from the ancient Assyrian and Babylonian

[5] E.g., George Montague, SM, *Understanding the Bible: A Basic Introduction to Biblical Interpretation*, rev. ed. (Mahwah, NJ: Paulist, 2007); Jaroslav Pelikan, *Whose Bible Is It? A Short History of the Scriptures* (New York: Penguin, 2006); Alexander Jensen, *Theological Hermeneutics* (London: SCM Press, 2007).

[6] For the cultural continuities between ancient Israelite prophecy and the prophetic practices in Assyria and Babylon, see Victor H. Matthews, *The Hebrew Prophets and Their Social World* (Grand Rapids, MI: Baker, 2012); Esther Hamori, *Women's Divination in Biblical Literature: Prophecy, Necromancy, and Other Arts of Knowledge* (New Haven: Yale University Press, 2015). For a wide range of prophetic texts in translation, see Martti Nissinen, C. L. Seow, and Robert K. Ritner, *Prophets and Prophecy in the Ancient Near East* (Atlanta: Society of Biblical Literature, 2003).

kingdoms are manuals of divination, and prophetic messages sent to kings, either in response to specific queries or unbidden warnings and blessings. For example, in 650 BCE, a woman prophet named Dunnasha-amur sent a message of comfort and protection to the Assyrian king Ashurbanipal (ruled 669–631 BCE) in the names of the goddesses Inlil and Ishtar. Through their spokeswoman, these deities (speaking together in the singular) assure the king, "I have ordained life for you in the assembly of all the gods. My arms are strong, they shall not forsake you before the gods. My shoulders are alert, they will keep carrying you. . . . I will rise and slaughter your enemy."[7]

Prophets in ancient Israel in the pre-exilic period (ca. 900–586 BCE), like their counterparts in neighboring cultures, offered answers or gave oracles from supernatural beings in response to immediate or pressing concerns in the lives of their contemporaries. Indeed, the book of Deuteronomy states that the way to determine a false prophet is if "a prophet speaks in the name of the Lord but the thing does not take place or prove true" (Deut 18:22). This implies a relevance in the near future from the time of the prophecy. In this scenario one cannot wait decades or centuries to prove the truth of a prophecy. Note also the similarities between the immediate relevance of the Assyrian oracle and this prophecy of comfort from Isaiah to King Hezekiah of Judah during the Assyrian siege of Jerusalem in 701 BCE: "Therefore, thus says the Lord concerning the king of Assyria: He shall not come into this city, shoot an arrow there, come before it with a shield, or cast up a siege ramp against it. By the way that he came, by the same he shall return; he shall not come into this city, says the Lord. For I will defend this city to save it, for my own sake and for the sake of my servant David" (Isa 37:33-35). As a final example, there is a Hebrew letter written on a pottery shard in 589 BCE from a Judahite soldier to his commander in Lachish, a city near Jerusalem that was fortified in response to the invading Babylonians

[7] Text and translation in Simo Parpola, *Assyrian Prophecies* (Helsinki: Helsinki University Press, 1997), 40–41; available online https://oracc.museum.upenn.edu/saao/corpus. Compare with King Josiah's representatives consulting the woman prophet Huldah in 2 Kgs 22:14-20.

who would soon besiege and destroy Jerusalem. At the end of the letter, which details military matters, the soldier mentions that he has forwarded a letter to his commander from an unnamed prophet that reads simply, "Beware!"[8]

This understanding of prophecy as focused on the immediate future of the prophet's original audience changed in the centuries after 539 BCE with the return of the exiles from Babylon to Jerusalem, a change that has long been referred to as the "death of prophecy."[9] Only three prophetic books, Haggai, Zechariah, and Malachi, date to the postexilic period.[10] Haggai and Zechariah, as is the case with preexilic prophets, are concerned with their immediate futures, particularly the royal aspirations of Zerubbabel, a little-known figure who appears in postexilic writings and is sometimes portrayed as having Davidic ancestry. Of more relevance to the changing understanding of prophecy in the postexilic period is the book of Malachi, which concludes with the prediction that the great prophet Elijah, taken up into heaven by God in 2 Kings 2, will return to usher in the end of the era. Here we have a prophetic text speaking, perhaps, of a coming event in an indeterminate future.

This change in the understanding of prophecy was caused in part by the fact that there was no longer a local monarchy, and hence no king who needed to consult prophets about issues of military or political strategy. After the exile, what was once the kingdom of Judah became a province of the vast Persian empire and was overseen by a local governor. As the books of Ezra and Nehemiah show, authority was shared between the Persian-

[8] Lachish Letter 3. Text and translation James M. Lindenberger, *Ancient Aramaic and Hebrew Letters* (Atlanta: Scholars Press, 1994), 111–12.

[9] Numerous rabbinic texts make this claim, e.g., "From the death of the latter prophets, Haggai, Zechariah, and Malachi, the spirit of holiness has departed from Israel" (b.Sanhedrin, 11a). "Death of prophecy" is a rather dramatic phrase for, as Frederick E. Greenspahn demonstrates, there were prophets in postexilic and early Judaism, but their authoritative role as religious elites was greatly diminished as the authority of scribes and teachers grew ("Why Prophecy Ceased," *JBL* 108 [1989]: 37–49).

[10] While the book of Jonah is also a postexilic book counted among the prophetic writings, I don't include it in this discussion because it's a story about a prophet, rather than a collection of oracles. See Thomas M. Bolin, *Freedom Beyond Forgiveness: The Book of Jonah Re-Examined* (London: Bloomsbury, 1997).

appointed governor and the priests of the rebuilt temple, who were seen to be scholars of the Torah. These textual scholars were supported by the Persian administration, which sought to use indigenous elites and traditions as much as possible to govern their vast imperial holdings. Ezra and Nehemiah were, respectively, the scribe and governor appointed by the Persians to establish order in postexilic Jerusalem. This results in a shift to texts, instead of specific individuals, as means of prophetic knowledge and divination. Prophetic texts replace prophets when these texts begin to be read by audiences that the writers and collectors of those texts did not envision. Those audiences generated new meanings that those writers and collectors had not (and could not) have thought of.

We can see this phenomenon in and among the biblical books themselves, perhaps most famously in Daniel 9, which dates to the first half of the second century BCE. There, Daniel recounts his realization that a prophecy written in the book of Jeremiah actually applies to Daniel's own situation, some four centuries after the time of Jeremiah. The truth of Daniel's insight is then confirmed by a heavenly messenger. "I, Daniel, perceived in the books the number of years that, according to the word of the Lord to the prophet Jeremiah, must be fulfilled for the devastation of Jerusalem, namely, seventy years" (Dan 9:2). This is most likely a reference to Jeremiah 25:11-13: "This whole land shall become a ruin and a waste, and these nations shall serve the king of Babylon seventy years. Then after seventy years are completed, I will punish the king of Babylon and that nation, the land of the Chaldeans, for their iniquity, says the Lord, making the land an everlasting waste. I will bring upon that land all the words that I have uttered against it, everything written in this book, which Jeremiah prophesied against all the nations." Jeremiah's oracle, coming from the sixth century BCE, is directed to that immediate context, namely the Babylonian destruction of Jerusalem and deportation of its inhabitants. However, four centuries later, the author of Daniel comes across this text and, on the assumption that the prophecy must be relevant to his own time, prays for understanding. In response, the angel Gabriel comes to Daniel and gives the meaning of the prophecy: "Daniel, I have now come out to give you wisdom and understanding. At the beginning of your supplications a word went out, and I have come to declare it, for you are greatly beloved. So, consider the word and understand the vision: Seventy weeks are decreed for your people and your holy city" (Dan 9:22-24).

There is much to untangle here. First are the references to books in these two passages. Daniel refers to a plural collection ("the books," Dan 9:2) in which he finds the prophecy of Jeremiah. While not a reference to anything like a closed canon of Scriptures, which would not exist for at least another two centuries and only then for some Jewish and Christian groups,[11] Daniel seems to have access to a collection of writings that he consults for knowledge and which include at the very least this portion of Jeremiah.[12] Notice also that the oracle in Jeremiah refers to a single book: "I will bring upon that land all the words that I have uttered against it, everything written *in this book,* which Jeremiah prophesied against all the nations" (Jer 25:13). Already in the text of Jeremiah, the prophet's words are referred to as being written in a book. In other words, the book of Jeremiah is both a book about a prophet and his oracles *and also* a book about itself— the book of prophecies attributed to Jeremiah. This is part of a larger role that the written words of Jeremiah play in the written book of Jeremiah. For example, in Jeremiah 36, Baruch the scribe writes down on a scroll "all the words" that God has spoken to Jeremiah (v. 2). This scroll is subsequently burned by King Jehoiakim, but Baruch rewrites it at Jeremiah's dictation and adds an oracle directed against the king for having burned the scroll. There is also the text of the letter in Jeremiah 29 that the prophet is said to have sent to the

[11] Among the many books that discuss this, see John Barton, *Oracles of God: Perceptions of Prophecy in Israel after the Exile* (New York: Oxford University Press, 1986), and Malka Simkovich, *Discovering Second Temple Literature* (Melrose Park, PA: Jewish Publication Society, 2018).

[12] I hesitate to speculate on the nature of the text of Jeremiah that is referred to in Daniel. We know that there were at least two distinct versions of the book, witnessed by the Septuagint and Qumran scrolls. Nathan Mastnjak has recently undertaken a study of the material process of scroll production in ancient Israel and how that technology can shed light on the growth and arrangement of biblical books, including Jeremiah (*Before the Scrolls: A Material Approach to Israel's Prophetic Library* [New York: Oxford University Press, 2023], 149–84).

exiles in Babylon, which also prophesies the seventy-year length of the exile. The reading and rereading of prophetic texts in the Hebrew Bible doesn't only occur between Jeremiah and Daniel, but it also is present within the prophetic books, especially the Major Prophets, Isaiah, Jeremiah, and Ezekiel.

A key feature of Daniel's rereading of Jeremiah requires attention—namely, the multiple uses of the Hebrew root *bnh*, which broadly encompasses the act of perception, understanding, or insight. Daniel "perceives" (*binoti*, 9:2) but doesn't understand. A long prayer, accompanied by fasting, sackcloth, and ashes, ensues (vv. 3-19) with references to the "written law of Moses" (vv. 11, 13). In response, Gabriel appears to Daniel with the express purpose of giving Daniel the correct interpretation of the text, which is described as "wisdom and *understanding*" (*binah*, v. 22). Gabriel prefaces his revelation of the text's meaning to Daniel with two uses of *bnh* in rapid succession (noted here in italics): "So *consider* the word and *understand* the vision" (*uvin . . . vehaven*, v. 23).

Note carefully what has happened here. Jeremiah the prophet—by definition someone given a divine message—becomes the author of a text that is now itself a divine message. Centuries later a reader (Daniel) is given a divine message to help interpret that same text. To properly interpret an inspired text, to read it "with wisdom and understanding" (Dan 9:22), itself requires inspiration on the part of the reader. Another clear example of this type of reading in early Judaism occurs in the hundreds of texts found near the ancient site of Qumran. Among these texts are a genre known as *pesharim*, which take a prophetic text and, verse by verse, show its correct interpretation (Hebrew: *pesher*) in the time of the commentator. The explanation of each verse is introduced with the phrase, "this is its meaning" (Hebrew: *pishro hu*). While the most well known of these texts is the Pesher Habakkuk (1QpHab) there are also *pesharim* on the books of Isaiah, Hosea, Micah, Zephaniah, and the Psalms.[13] This ancient way of reading is still practiced. As we saw in chapter 1, Martin Luther King Jr. reinterpreted the

[13] 1QpHab can be accessed at http://dss.collections.imj.org.il/habakkuk and the fragments of other *pesharim* at https://www.deadseascrolls.org.il/explore-the-archive/search#q='Pesher'.

prophecies of Isaiah 40 to apply to a hoped-for future of a post-racist America.

This understanding of texts as a place where inspiration might occur for readers led also to the generation of a vast amount of literature in early Judaism—problematically classified as "inter-testamental" or "extracanonical"—that were attributed to figures in earlier texts, figures such as Enoch or Adam, whose reputations both enhanced these texts but were also enhanced by them.[14] The early Jewish text known as 1 Enoch explicitly states this at the outset. In the introductory section, most likely added to the first portion of this long book, the narrator says directly, "Not for this generation do I expound, but concerning one that is distant I speak."[15] The author of the text, writing for his own time around the third century BCE, but setting it in the distant past of the figure of Enoch mentioned in Genesis 5, makes clear that this putatively ancient revelation is meant for the time and place of his readers. In other words, because ancient texts were read as talking about the time of their later readers, contemporary texts were written as if they had come from the distant past. What's more, for early Jewish readers—including the first Christians—almost all the texts that would eventually wind up in the Bible were understood as being "prophetic" in the sense that they spoke directly to the situation of their readers and hence required a particular interpretive skill to correctly understand them.[16] A significant Christian example of this kind of reading can be seen in the Emmaus story in Luke 24, where Jesus, "beginning with Moses and all the prophets interpreted to them the things about himself in the scriptures" (Luke 24:27). Notice that, apart from the Pentateuch ("Moses"), the remainder of the biblical books are understood to be prophetic.

[14] Eva Mroczek, *The Literary Imagination in Jewish Antiquity* (New York: Oxford University Press, 2016).

[15] George W. E. Nickelsburg and James C. VanderKam, *1 Enoch: The Hermeneia Translation* (Minneapolis: Fortress Press, 2012), 19.

[16] Quite thoroughly argued in Barton, *Oracles of God*. See also the collection of review essays edited by Ehud Ben Zvi, "Rereading *Oracles of God*: Twenty Years After John Barton, *Oracles of God: Perceptions of Prophecy in Israel after the Exile* (London: Darton, Longman and Todd, 1986)," *Journal of Hebrew Scriptures* 7 (2007), https://doi.org/10.5508/jhs.2007.v7.a14.

Everything Is Inside of It

The premise driving this widespread reinterpretation of ancient texts deemed to be prophetic is that, because their message comes from the past but is really intended for "us," the words cannot be taken at face value. They must mean other than what they say at first or even second glance.[17] This way of reading texts wasn't devised by or limited to early Jewish and Christian readers. In classical Greece, as early as the fifth century BCE, a way of reading the myths about the gods and heroes in Homer and Hesiod was used which was based upon the idea that the words of these poets meant something other than their ordinary meaning. This type of reading was called allegory (*allēgoría*) from a verb that can be translated as "meaning something other than what it says."[18] As with the biblical texts in Judaism, this reading presupposed that the Homeric poems were normative in some way and that, therefore, they were not only relevant to readers centuries after their writing, but relevant in important ways. Additionally, allegorical reading served to reinterpret the often-unflattering portrayals of the gods and heroes in Homer and Hesiod. In the first century CE, Heraclitus the Grammarian wrote an allegorical commentary on Homer in order to defend the poet against his alleged "disrespect for the divine." In the opening sentences, Heraclitus acknowledges the necessity of reading Homer's *Iliad* and *Odyssey* allegorically, for "if he [Homer] meant nothing allegorically, he was impious through and through, and sacrilegious fables loaded with blasphemous folly, run riot through both epics."[19]

[17] See also the discussion in Mark Reasoner, *Five Models of Scripture* (Grand Rapids, MI: Eerdmans, 2021), 151–73.

[18] In Book 2 of *The Republic*, Plato famously banned both poets and allegorical reading in his ideal city: "Things that we must not admit into our city either wrought in allegory or without allegory. For the young are not able to distinguish what is and what is not allegory," *Rep.* 378d (Plato, *The Republic*, trans. Paul Shorey [Cambridge, MA: Harvard University Press; London: William Heinemann, 1969]). Plato uses the term *hyponoia* (ὑπονοία) to describe allegory. The term also carries the meaning of "suspicion, conjecture, guess."

[19] Donald A. Russell and David Konstan, eds. and trans., *Heraclitus: Homeric Problems* (Atlanta: SBL Press, 2005), 3.

Heraclitus then demonstrates how every problematic thing that Homer says about the ethical behavior of the gods or heroes is really saying something quite the opposite. The story of the Olympian gods' rebellion and imprisonment of Zeus (*Il* 1.399–404) is, in fact, "a theological account of . . . the origin of all things. Homer is the sole originator of the scientific doctrine of the elements."[20] Or when discussing the great trickster Odysseus, whom Homer repeatedly describes with the Greek term *polymetis,* which implies a high degree of wisdom and cunning, Heraclitus asserts that the hero is "a sort of instrument of every virtue" because the poet "hated the vices which ravage human life."[21]

I dwell on Heraclitus's allegorical readings because I want both to highlight how odd they might seem to modern readers and to point out that this is a widely used approach found in a variety of early Christian writings, including those in the New Testament. Christian allegorical reading is indebted to its presence in Jewish writings, most notably those of the first-century-CE philosopher Philo of Alexandria (ca. 20 BCE–ca. 50 CE). Philo lived in the intellectual center of his day, the site of the world's largest library at the time and the center of Homeric scholarship.[22] He produced a large corpus of literature, most of which is allegorical readings of stories from the Jewish Bible. Philo's aim in these allegorical interpretations is apologetic: he seeks to demonstrate that the Jewish "epic" or normative texts are sure guides to truth and virtue in the same way that Greek intellectuals, such as Heraclitus, used allegory to read the writings of Homer. For example, Philo discusses the deaths of Aaron's sons, Nadab and Abihu, as recounted in Leviticus 10. There, the text states that the two brothers offered "strange" (Hebrew: *zarah,* NRSVue: "unholy") fire before the ark and that God burned them alive for their transgression (Lev 10:2). For Philo, the deaths of these two priests represent the ascent of those pure souls to God who have stripped themselves of irrational thoughts

[20] Russell and Konstan, *Heraclitus: Homeric Problems,* 41.

[21] Russell and Konstan, *Heraclitus: Homeric Problems,* 113.

[22] See also Dennis R. MacDonald, "Alexandria and Allegory," *Bible Odyssey,* https://www.bibleodyssey.org/places/related-articles/alexandria-and-allegory/.

and mortal glory. They "had drawn nigh to God and . . . become partakers of the life immortal."[23] For Philo, a puzzling text about an irrevocable divine punishment of two people for blasphemy becomes instead a story of spiritual ascent with the two characters functioning as positive role models worthy of emulation.

Again, modern readers might find this kind of reading odd, and even see it as an attempt to airbrush authoritative texts in order to remove from them otherwise awkward or embarrassing features. It might be better to look at it the other way around: it's not that an embarrassing or problematic aspect in an authoritative text must be covered up, but rather that authoritative texts are already assumed to mean more than they say. The words are but the surface of hidden depths that await to reveal profound truths to the reader who knows to look for them. Consequently, anything in a text that appears odd or "embarrassing" is simply what appears on the surface, and once the inner meaning is revealed, these problems disappear. So prevalent was this approach to normative texts in antiquity that often one way to tell if a reader views a text as normative and relevant is if they read it allegorically.[24] In the rabbinic literature as well we see this kind of reading for deeper meanings (alongside many others). Rabbinic texts distinguish between *peshat* and *derash*. *Peshat*, from the same root as *pesher*, discussed above, is often used to refer to the meaning of a text in its literary and historical context. *Derash* often describes readings that go beyond—sometimes way beyond—the literary and historical contexts of a text and engage in a variety of expansive

[23] οἱ ἐγγίσαντες θεῷ καὶ τὸν μὲν θνητὸν βίον καταλιπόντες, τοῦ δ' ἀθανάτου μεταλαχόντες (Philo, *Alleg Int* II.57-58, in Philo, *On the Creation: Allegorical Interpretation of Genesis 2 and 3*, trans. F. H. Colson and G. H. Whitaker [Cambridge, MA: Harvard University Press, 1929], 258).

[24] This is not limited to Jewish and Christian texts. In India, the ritual texts of the Vedas were read symbolically in the Upanishads to describe the journey of the mind toward contemplation of the true nature of reality. T. Lubin, "The Virtuosic Exegesis of the Brahmavadin and the Rabbi," *Numen* 49 (2002): 427–49; H. Goodman, ed., *Between Jerusalem and Benares: Comparative Studies in Judaism and Hinduism* (Albany: SUNY Press, 1984); and Thomas M. Bolin, "Out of the Wilderness? Some Suggestions for the Future of Pentateuchal Research," in Ingrid Hjelm and Thomas L. Thompson, eds., *History, Archaeology and the Bible Forty Years after "Historicity"* (New York: Routledge, 2016), 47–59.

interpretations. Again, this was based on the presupposition that the biblical text[25] contained an inexhaustible surplus of meaning, or, in the words of the rabbinic scholar Ben Bag Bag, "Turn it over and turn it over again, because everything is in it" (*Pirke Avot* 5:22).

As mentioned above, allegorical reading comes into Christianity via the sacred texts of Judaism; that is to say, Christian use of allegory wasn't a secondary development that the early Christians brought to their reading of the Jewish Scriptures. Paul explicitly uses the term in Galatians 4:24 ("Now this is an allegory," *allēgoroumena*) to introduce his reading of the Sarah and Hagar story from Genesis. Practically the entire letter to the Hebrews is a tour de force of allegorical readings of the entire Old Testament (more on Galatians and Hebrews below). By far the most influential proponent of this reading in early Christianity is the third-century thinker Origen of Alexandria (ca. 185-ca. 253 CE). Space here cannot do justice to Origen as a person, the breadth of his intellect, or his influence on the development of early Christian theology.[26] Trained in Neoplatonic philosophy and possessing some knowledge of Hebrew and rabbinic biblical interpretation, Origen's extant biblical commentaries (most famously on the Song of Songs and John's Gospel) and homilies combine allegorical readings of the biblical text with precise and detailed attention to the nuances of specific words and their meanings. In this manner, Origen draws upon both the very technical tradition of Greco-Roman literary analysis that began with the study of Homer and the equally complex interpretive strategies found in rabbinic literature.[27]

Indeed, one can find similar ways of reading the same biblical text by both Jewish and Christian interpreters in late antiquity. This is readily seen in both the Song of Songs and the book of Ecclesiastes. Both Jewish and Christian readers understood the erotic poetry of the Song of Songs to be an allegorical expression of the love of God collectively for the community (the people of

[25] David Weiss Halivni, *Peshat and Derash: Plain and Applied Meaning in Rabbinic Exegesis* (New York: Oxford University Press, 2018).

[26] Arthur P. Urbano, "Difficulties in Writing the Life of Origen," in Ronald E. Heine and Karen Jo Torjesen, eds., *The Oxford Handbook of Origen* (New York: Oxford University Press, 2022), 118–40.

[27] Gerardo Rodriguez-Galarza, "The Contribution of Bernhard Neuschäfer's *Origenes als Philologe*," in Heine and Torjesen, *Oxford Handbook of Origen*, 160–74.

Israel, or the church, respectively) or of the individual human soul at the end of a process of mystical enlightenment.[28] Ecclesiastes contains many statements that promote the pursuit of pleasure in a world devoid of justice or meaning and was consequently read allegorically. For example, Ecclesiastes 2:24 asserts that "there is nothing better for mortals than to eat and drink and find enjoyment in their toil. This also, I saw, is from the hand of God." In the Midrash—a collection of Jewish re-readings of biblical texts—this verse is read to say that "everything that is said in this scroll about eating and drinking is intended to refer to Torah and good works" (Eccl Rabbah 2:24). Similarly, in his commentary on this verse, Jerome (d. 420) reads it as reference to the Eucharist: "Consequently it is good for us to take up the true food and true drink of the flesh and blood of the Lamb whom we find in the sacred books."[29] Again, it's not a question of a sacred text containing embarrassing elements that must be whitewashed for believers. Instead, it's the other way around: *because* the text is sacred, the reader approaches it with the assumption that its meanings go beyond the most obvious or self-evident reading and contain deeper spiritual or theological truths.

The foundation of Christian biblical interpretation lies in the symbolic reading of the Jewish Scriptures in such a way as to view them as predicting the person and life of Jesus. The earliest Christian texts we have—the letters of Paul—refer more than once to the death of Jesus as happening "in accordance with the scriptures."[30] These Scriptures are, of course, the Jewish texts. All four canonical Gospels cite Old Testament texts and introduce them with a phrase that states that the text has been "fulfilled" by something that Jesus said or did. On the one hand, this approach uses

[28] For discussion of the history of interpretation of the Song of Songs, see Ilana Pardes, *The Song of Songs: A Biography* (Princeton: Princeton University Press, 2019).

[29] Discussion in Thomas M. Bolin, *Ecclesiastes and the Riddle of Authorship* (London: Routledge, 2017), 85–86.

[30] κατὰ τὰς γραφὰς (1 Cor 15:3). See also the opening to Rom 1:1-2, where Paul refers to the "gospel of God" (εὐαγγέλιον θεοῦ) and immediately uses the same verbal root of εὐαγγέλιον to describe how that Gospel has been "promised beforehand" (προεπηγγείλατο) in the Jewish Scriptures, which he understands as prophetic (διὰ τῶν προφητῶν αὐτοῦ ἐν γραφαῖς ἁγίαις).

the same methods we saw in Daniel's rereading of Jeremiah or in the Qumran *pesharim*, namely, the connection of older sacred texts to the time of the interpreter. On the other hand, because it involves the Christian interpretation of Jewish texts, these rereadings often succumb to supersessionist claims and polemical textual appropriation of the Jewish Scriptures. In Galatians 4, for example, Paul rereads the story of Sarah and Hagar in order to create a stunning reversal in which Hagar, the enslaved mother of Ishmael, now becomes the ancestor of the Jews, and Sarah, the mother of Isaac, is now the ancestor of Christians. Paul founds his argument on the assertion that "Hagar is Mount Sinai in Arabia and corresponds to the present Jerusalem, for she is in slavery with her children" (Gal 4:25). Elsewhere, Paul articulates this interpretative approach to allegory by means of an allegorical reading of an Old Testament text. Referring to the biblical account in Exodus 34 of Moses veiling his face after having spoken with God, Paul claims that Jewish readers of "Moses" (i.e., the Pentateuch) are still kept from the text's true meaning by a veil: "But their minds were hardened. Indeed, to this very day, when they hear the reading of the old covenant, that same veil is still there; it is not unveiled since in Christ is it set aside. Indeed, to this very day whenever Moses is read, a veil lies over their minds; but when one turns to the Lord, the veil is removed" (2 Cor 3:14-15).

The epistle to the Hebrews is one extended allegorical reading of the Old Testament which aims to show that Jesus is the fulfillment of all biblical prophecy. The opening lines of the epistle state this approach succinctly: "Long ago God spoke to our ancestors in many and various ways by the prophets, but in these last days he has spoken to us by a Son" (Heb 1:1-2).

Note the corresponding contrast and disjunction between the "long ago" in verse 1 and "*but* in these last days" of verse 2; and the "many and various ways" (v. 1) of divine communication in the prophetic texts (i.e., the Old Testament) have been replaced by the implied clear revelation by means of God's son (v. 2). The claim here is that, while the Jewish prophetic books are true divine communication, which consequently contain deeper meanings that must be teased out, the only correct interpretive key to do this—indeed one revealed by God—is the reading strategy of

Christians. This assertion is made in polemical writings between Jews and Christians. In his debate with the Jewish thinker Trypho, the Christian philosopher Justin (d. ca. 165 CE) ends a string of Old Testament quotations with sarcasm and aggression: "David sung them, Isaiah announced them, Zechariah proclaimed them, and Moses wrote them. Do you know them, Trypho? They are contained in your Scriptures—actually not yours, but ours. For we believe them; but you, reading them do not understand their meaning."[31] Justin's breathtaking claim to Trypho that the Jewish texts are "actually not yours, but ours" is based on his belief that Jewish interpreters read the texts without grasping their true—that is, Christian—meaning.

An influential subset of this approach is the Christian practice of typological reading of the Jewish Scriptures. It is premised on the idea that the Jewish texts contain hidden figures (called "types") that are only revealed after and because of the life of Jesus. As we have already seen, and will see again, this is not a practice devised by Christians. The idea of a "type" (*typos* in Greek) as a model or example or pattern is found as early as in the writings of Plato (d. 348 BCE). Philo of Alexandria, in reference to the Adam and Eve story, notes, "Now these are no mythical fictions, such as poets and sophists delight in, but modes of making ideas visible (*deigmata typōn*) bidding us resort to allegorical interpretation guided in our renderings by what lies beneath the surface."[32] Reading the same biblical text of Genesis 2–3, Paul makes Adam the *typos* of Christ: "Yet death exercised dominion from Adam to Moses, even over those whose sins were not like the transgression of Adam, who is a type of the one who was to come" (Rom 5:14, NRSV). Typological reading abounds in Christian literature. The epistle to the Hebrews views Melchizedek, the enigmatic figure of Genesis 14 and Psalm 110, also as a *typos* of Christ. In the *Epistle*

[31] ἀλλὰ τούτους Δαυῒδ μὲν ἔψαλλεν, Ἡσαίας δὲ εὐηγγελίζετο, Ζαχαρίας δὲ ἐκήρυξε, Μωσῆς δὲ ἀνέγραψεν. Ἐπιγινώσκεις αὐτούς, Τρύφων; ἐν τοῖς ὑμετέροις ἀπόκεινται γράμμασι, μᾶλλον δὲ οὐχ ὑμετέροις ἀλλ ἡμετέροις· ἡμεῖς γὰρ αὐτοῖς πειθόμεθα, ὑμεῖς δὲ ἀναγινώσκοντες οὐ νοεῖτε τὸν ἐν αὐτοῖς νοῦν (Georges Archambault, ed., *Dialogue avec Tryphon* [Paris: Librairie Alphones Picard, 1909]). Translation mine.

[32] Philo, *On the Creation*, 124.

of Barnabas, written sometime in the early second century CE, Isaac bound on the altar for sacrifice in Genesis 22 is read as a type of the death of Jesus, as are multiple aspects of the sacrificial rites of the scapegoat (Leviticus 16) and the red heifer (Numbers 19). Still later, in the sixth century, Gregory the Great, in his influential *Moralia on Job*, describes the righteous sufferer Job as a *typos* of Jesus.

These ancient Christian reading strategies of seeing in the Jewish Scriptures references to Christ in the form of prophecies, allegories, or types continue to this day most notably in the liturgy, which significantly is the place where most practicing Christians encounter the biblical text. Looking at the Catholic Lectionary (which is shared with other denominations under the name Common Lectionary) we can see multiple examples. There is the use of Isaiah 7:14 ("Therefore the Lord himself will give you a sign; the young woman, pregnant and about to bear a son, shall name him Emmanuel") as the first reading in the Fourth Sunday of Advent (Cycle A), which also uses Matthew 1:22-23 in the Gospel ("All this took place to fulfill what the Lord had said through the prophet: 'Behold, the virgin shall be with child and bear a son, and they shall name him Emmanuel,' which means 'God is with us.'"). Similarly, during the Easter Triduum, the Suffering Servant passages from Isaiah are always read on Good Friday alongside one of the Gospel passion accounts; and at the Easter Vigil up to seven readings from the Jewish Scriptures are read, including the binding of Isaac in Genesis 22, long read as a type of Christ as seen above, and two passages from the Suffering Servant texts of Isaiah. As a final example, the first Sunday of Lent has the temptation of the woman by the serpent and the eating of the forbidden fruit in Genesis 3 as the first reading set alongside the temptation of Jesus by Satan in the wilderness from Matthew 4 as the Gospel. Significantly, the second reading for that Sunday is taken from the very same passage from Romans 5 discussed above, where Paul contrasts Adam with Christ and refers to Adam as "the type of the one who was to come."[33]

[33] For these three sets of liturgical readings, I have quoted the NABRE available at the US Conference of Catholic Bishops' website: https://www.usccb.org/offices/new-american-bible/books-bible.

A once widespread method of reading sacred texts that might seem particularly odd to modern readers is the oracular use of Scripture. However, it follows naturally on the idea of the text as being prophetic—that is, as speaking directly to the reader. If the text contains prophetic material, then it can also be used to supply prophecy. One of the more famous examples of this approach is Augustine's well-known account of his conversion, which he describes in his *Confessions*. Lying prone in a garden, Augustine is torn between surrendering his life to Jesus and holding on to his old habits. He then hears a child's voice singing, "*Tolle lege*" ("Pick up and read") repeatedly. In his own words, Augustine understood the child's chant "to be no less than a divine voice commanding me to open a book and read whatever passage I first came upon. . . . And so, stirred by this voice, I returned to the place where I had been sitting with Alypius, for I had set down a book of the Apostle there when I got up and left. I snatched it up, opened it, and read in silence the passage that first caught my eye."[34]

Strictly speaking, Augustine's use of the biblical text (here a small bound volume of Paul's letters) as a means of prophecy is actually a response to a preceding oracle—the child's voice that Augustine believed to be "no less than a divine voice." This method of reading authoritative texts dates back centuries prior to Augustine. Throughout the era of the Roman Republic (ca. sixth century BCE–27 BCE) ancient oracular books attributed to a Greek woman prophet known as the Sybil were kept on the Capitoline Hill in Rome in the temple of Jupiter. In times of particular crisis, selected Roman elite men consulted the books for guidance. In private life, Greek and Roman readers practiced a similar form of random text choice as kind of prophecy, using scrolls of Homer or Vergil. These practices had their own specific terminology, *Homeromanteia* for Homer and *Sortes Vergilianae* for Vergil, and

[34] Augustine, *Confessions*, 8.12.19, trans. Thomas Williams (Indianapolis: Hackett, 2019), 137. Notably, Augustine is supported in this idea by the story in Athanasius's *Life of Antony*, where Antony enters a church just as Matt 19:21 is proclaimed ("If you wish to be perfect, go, sell your possessions, and give the money to the poor, and you will have treasure in heaven; then come, follow me"). Taking the Gospel to be directed to himself by divine intent, Antony sells all he has and embarks on his monastic life.

were accompanied by particular rituals, sometimes including the use of dice. This practice viewed these authoritative poems as having oracular force.[35] In early Judaism, 1 Maccabees recounts how the Jewish army, prior to a battle, engaged in oracular use of the Torah: "And they opened the book of the law to inquire into those matters about which the nations consulted the likenesses of their gods" (1 Macc 3:48).[36] We know from the stories about Francis of Assisi and his first followers that they would often make decisions by opening a book of the Gospels and looking at whatever passage first caught their attention. Writing about his upbringing in an Evangelical Christian household, Timothy Beal describes engaging in this same practice and refers to this as using the biblical text as a Magic 8-Ball.[37]

Another reading strategy based on the idea that every word and phrase of the Bible is equally authoritative and relevant is the practice of prooftexting, in which one quotes or even simply cites a biblical verse to justify a course of action. Perhaps the most famous instance of prooftexting occurs in the story of Jesus being tempted by Satan as recounted in Matthew 4:1-11 and Luke 4:13. There, Satan demands that Jesus do things and justifies each of his commands with a biblical prooftext. Jesus responds to each demand with a prooftext of his own that thwarts Satan. The story doesn't make clear exactly why Jesus' quotations are better than Satan's, apart from the fact that it is the greater authority of Jesus as God's son which gives his use of the Bible more force.

This practice was widespread in antiquity, and both Jewish and Christian preachers and scholars would construct elaborate theological or interpretive arguments founded upon a scaffold of numerous prooftexts arranged in complicated and creative ways.

[35] AnneMarie Luijendijk and William E. Klingshirn, eds., *My Lots Are in Thy Hands: Sortilege and Its Practitioners in Late Antiquity* (Leiden: Brill, 2019); Raquel Martín Hernández, "Using Homer for Divination: Homeromanteia in Context," *CHS Research Bulletin* 2, no. 1 (2013), https://research-bulletin.chs.harvard.edu/2014/03/28/using-homer-for-divination-homeromanteia-in-context/.

[36] καὶ ἐξεπέτασαν τὸ βιβλίον τοῦ νόμου περὶ ὧν ἐξηρεύνων τὰ ἔθνη τὰ ὁμοιώματα τῶν εἰδώλων αὐτῶν.

[37] Timothy Beal, *The Rise and Fall of the Bible: The Unexpected History of an Accidental Book* (New York: Houghton Mifflin, 2012), 2–5.

Simpler prooftexting is done by recourse to a single verse as an authority intended to silence any disagreement or debate. This is what characterizes much of what passes for political and theological discourse in the US at the moment.[38]

Methods and Limits

Oracular use of the biblical text proceeded according to a ritual and was understood as an encounter in which the text spoke directly to the person seeking the oracle. Generally speaking, for Daniel, the nonliteral meaning of a prophetic text was revealed by an angel. For Greek intellectuals, along with Philo, and Origen, allegorical meaning was a skill developed by various means of textual analysis. For Paul, the author of Hebrews, and Justin Martyr, faith in Jesus was the key that unlocked the hidden meanings of Jewish sacred texts. However, as both Jewish and Christian readers continued to engage in this manner of interpretation, rules or principles were developed inductively from the growing body of biblical readings. This shows a development of biblical interpretation as a skill, given that particular inspiration was both rare and beyond human control and that the more general inspiration for Christians of having faith in Jesus did not guarantee meaningful readings. Consequently, there arose the articulation of particular methods or rules for how to engage in meaningful biblical interpretation. Again, these were in part derived from early Greco-Roman scholarship on reading Homer allegorically. In Judaism, lists of interpretive rules (*middoth*) are attributed to the Talmudic rabbis: seven rules for Hillel, thirteen for Ishmael, and thirty-two for Eleazar ben Yose. One of the main underlying principles at work in almost all of these rules is the use of at least one biblical text to help make sense of another, for example by analogy or other similarity, broadly construed. This approach of using Scripture to interpret Scripture is, like others we have discussed, prevalent

[38] This distinction is made also by Diarmaid MacCulloch, who describes modern prooftexting as a "nervous tic . . . which seeks to deal with everyday situations as if the Bible were a collection of instructions" (MacCulloch, *Silence: A Christian History* [New York: Penguin Books, 2013], 237).

both in Jewish and Christian interpretation and also in the earlier Greco-Roman tradition.[39] This strategy will take on added importance during the Reformation when Protestant readers seek to derive interpretive standards for reading the Bible from the Bible itself.

The North African Christian Tyconius (d. 390 CE) developed his own list of principles for biblical interpretation in the fourth century.[40] Tyconius's rules bear some similarity to the principles developed by the rabbis, particularly in the foundational assumption that biblical texts are to be interpreted by other biblical texts, but Tyconius, as is distinctive of much Christian biblical interpretation, adds a linear dimension to his reading of the biblical text. This is an outgrowth of the typological reading of the Old Testament mentioned above, which saw the Jewish Scriptures as predictive. Consequently, Tyconius emphasizes the forward motion of the Bible from the Old Testament into the New Testament and continuing until the return of Jesus. At the same time, Tyconius reads the text allegorically, most notably in his understanding that typological references can refer not only to Jesus but also to the church as the enduring Body of Christ in the world. Throughout his work, there exists a creative tension between the fact that Tyconius is articulating principles to be followed by others—and hence teachable and knowable—and the equally strong claim that the Bible is a book of hidden knowledge not meant to be learned by all. He describes his rules as mystical and compares them to both keys and lamps which help to reveal secret treasures that are also meant to remain hidden to some.[41] Tyconius's *Rules* is the first

[39] "Because I think to best to make sense of Homer through Homer, I usually show by example how he may interpret himself." *'Αξιῶν δὲ ἐγὼ Ὅμηρον ἐξ Ὁμήρου σαφηνίζειν αὐτὸν ἐξηγούμενον ἑαυτὸν ὑπεδείκνυον* (Porphyry, *Homeric Questions*, 1.12-14), in Joel Christensen, "Reading and Teaching Homer: Some Practical Advice," *Painful Signs* (blog), https://joelchristensen.substack.com/p/reading-and-teaching-homer.

[40] Latin text and translation in William S. Babcock, trans., *Tyconius: The Book of Rules* (Atlanta: Society of Biblical Literature, 1989).

[41] "I considered it necessary to write a book of rules and so to fashion keys and lamps, as it were, to the secrets of the law. For there are certain mystic rules [regulae mysticae] which obtain in the inner recesses of the entire law and keep the rich treasures of the truth hidden from some people [veritatis thesauros aliquibus invisibiles faciunt]," in Babcock, *Tyconius*, 3.

extant work on biblical interpretation written by a Christian, and it is referenced and discussed by another North African Christian, Augustine, in his *De Doctrina Christiana*, one of the most influential Christian works on the subject, and which is discussed in detail later in this book.

By Way of Conclusion

Several things should be apparent at the end of this chapter. First is the long-standing and widespread interaction between Jewish and Christian elites and the wider Greco-Roman culture of textual interpretation. We have seen at every turn both Jewish and Christian interpretive strategies nestled comfortably in the larger Greco-Roman context of literary analysis. Second, while Jews and Christians were reading the same texts in similar ways, it is apparent that they did so with the intention of differentiating themselves from each other. These efforts often took on a polemical tone, particularly—but not exclusively—on the part of Christian readers. This seemed necessary to them because the texts they read were not written by Christians. On the one hand, Christians reading these texts as prophecies about Jesus, or as typological precedents to Jesus, or symbolic references to Jesus, are yet more particular iterations of those holding the basic interpretive stance that prophetic texts must somehow have relevance to the reader. On the other hand, we can see from even the earliest Christian texts an awareness of the fact that the reading of Jesus into these texts is in some way a significant break with the interpretive traditions that had already grown out of the texts, and which were present in early Judaism. Paul's use of the term *old covenant* (*palaia diathēkēi*) in 2 Corinthians 3:14 to describe the Jewish texts, alongside his claim that Jewish readers cannot properly read their own texts because they do not believe in Christ, and Justin Martyr's flat-out appropriation of the Jewish texts in conversation with a Jew ("not yours, but ours"), are parade examples of early Christian readers' awareness of this tension. This brings us to our third point: the interpretation of sacred texts in general has ethical dimensions and consequences, and this is particularly so with Christian interpretation of Jewish texts. Recently, two Jewish biblical scholars, Amy-Jill Levine and Marc Zvi Brettler, coauthored a book that highlights the differences between reading the Bible "with and without Jesus," but with an eye for isolating what's at stake in the use of polemics and moving from a bellicose stance to one of possibility, by which they mean a stance in which "we can affirm our own beliefs without negating the beliefs of others."[42] For my own part, writing as a Christian scholar of the Jewish Scriptures, I consider myself to be obligated both to notice and to critique instances of Christian negation of Jewish biblical interpretation in my discussion.

This chapter began with the image of James Albert Ukawsaw Gronniosaw confronted with a silent, closed book. That book opened for Gronniosaw and other enslaved Africans through their reading of the Exodus as both a prophecy and an allegory of their own desire for freedom and of the promise of divine aid in that struggle. As Richard Lischer eloquently notes, enslaved Africans, "bereft of a history," adopted the Bible as their past, and this reading tradition has continued on through the present day.[43] The question of the ethical entailments of our readings, and how we are obliged to respond to them, is discussed in more detail later in this book. For now, the present chapter ends with our second story about the power of the closed book. *The Acts of Andrew* is a Christian text from around the late second century CE that recounts the adventures of the apostle Andrew after the resurrection and ascension of Jesus. Originally written in Greek, the *Acts* survives today in Greek, Coptic, and Armenian fragments and in a Latin summary by the sixth-century bishop Gregory of Tours, from which this story is taken:

> An old man, Nicolaus, came [to Andrew] with clothes rent and said: "I am seventy-four years old and have never departed from filth, prostitution and fornication, things that have dragged me to the brothel. But now it is the third day since I

[42] Amy-Jill Levine and Marc Zvi Brettler, *The Bible With and Without Jesus: How Jews and Christians Read the Same Story Differently* (New York: HarperOne, 2020), 60.

[43] Richard Lischer, *The Preacher King: Martin Luther King, Jr. and the Word That Moved America* (New York: Oxford University Press, 1995), 200.

> heard of your miracles and preaching, which are full of powerful words. And so I thought to myself that I would repent of my ways, come to you, and that you would show me a better way of life. But as I was thinking these things, another thought came that I should give up this idea and not do the good that I was considering. Struggling in my conscience, I took a book of the Gospels and prayed to God that he would make me forget my old ways. After a few days, forgetting the Gospel that I carried with me and inflamed with lustful thoughts, I went to a brothel. And behold, the prostitute, seeing me, said, 'Go away old man! Go away! You are an angel of God. Do not touch me or even come near me, for I see in you a mighty mystery!' "[44]

Set alongside Gronniosaw's encounter with his enslaver's talking book, we have two book owners—Gronniosaw's enslaver and Nicolaus—and two marginalized people—Gronniosaw and the unnamed woman. Each pair has a biblical text between them. In both cases, the book's owner—Gronniosaw's enslaver and Nicolaus—are seemingly insiders confronted with outsiders who do not know the book. And yet both stories present a reversal. It is Gronniosaw's enslaver who reads the Bible but is unable to properly hear the text, given that he has enslaved other human beings. And it is the proverbial dirty old man, Nicolaus, who not only is unable to resist his lustful inclinations but also literally forgets that he carries a book of Gospels about with him. Conversely,

[44] *Acts of Andrew* 28. "Dum haec agerentur, ecce quidam senex Nicolaus nomine, scissis vestibus, venit ad apostolum, dicens: 'Famule Dei, ecce 74 anni sunt vitae meae, in quibus non discessi ab inmunditiis et scorto ac fornicatione, plerumque praeceps deduetus ad lupanar, et exercebam inlieita. Et nunc tertia dies est, in qua audivi miracula quae agis et praedicationes tuas, quae sunt plenae verbis vitalibus, cogitabam enim mecum, ut, relicto hoc opere, venirem ad te, ut mihi ostenderes meliora. Sed dum haec cogitarem, veniebat mihi alius sensus, ut haec relinguerem et non facerem bonum quod cogitabam. Luctante igitur conscientia mea, accepi euangelium! et oravi Dominum, ut haec aliquando me faceret oblivisei. Post dies vero paucos oblitus euangelii, quod super me erat, inflammante cogitatione perversa, abii iterum ad lupanar. Et ecce mulier meretrix videns me, ait: 'Egredere, senex, egredere; angelus enim Dei es tu. Ne contingas me neque adpropinques in hoc loco; video enim in te misterium magnum' " (W. Arndt and B. Krusch, eds., *Gregorii Turonensis Opera*, vol. 1 [Hanover: Impensis Bibliopolii Hahniani, 1884], 842). Translation mine.

the relative outsiders in both accounts, Gronniosaw, the enslaved African, and the nameless prostitute, are the ones who perceive the true power of the book, *without even needing to read it*. In both stories, the power of the biblical text is such that it "speaks" to those who need to hear it and remains closed and silent to those who think that they hear it. The Bible, these stories seem to say, is a book about lifting up the lowly and casting down the mighty, and the book itself goes about its work in doing that apart from, and in spite of, some of its readers.

Chapter 4

Plain Sense

The last chapter explored how readers' assumptions of the Bible's normativity and relevance lead them to read the text in a way that goes beyond its original context and the intentions of its authors. Allegorical reading in particular is founded on the belief that the text can't mean what it says on the surface, but rather that its real meaning lies underneath, or beyond the words on the page. Given this fact, it is reasonable to think that there would be a huge array of different and contradictory biblical interpretations after two thousand years of readerly imagination working on the text. And while there is certainly a plethora of different interpretations in the historical record, as we saw briefly with the rules of Tyconius in the last chapter, strategies were developed to limit the range of acceptable symbolic readings of Scripture. Different religious communities also developed their own traditions of symbolic interpretations that were perpetuated in sermons, hymns, and catechesis. This chapter will explore what is probably the most influential of these strategies, the grounding of interpretation on the text's so-called plain meaning.

Literal Meanings

The foundation of symbolic readings in Christian (and Jewish) biblical interpretation has always been the words on the page. Whatever a reading offered, no matter how fanciful, must somehow be shown to connect to the words of the text. This foundational adherence to the words came to be known as the text's literal meaning (from the Latin *littera*, "letter"). Now, this is an observation so obvious as to be practically useless, but it's important to bear in mind that interpreters of the Bible used the idea of a text's literal meaning as a way to ground their readings and adjudicate between readings. It is no coincidence that Origen, the most creative of allegorical readers in the early church, was also the first Christian to engage in critical, detailed study of the biblical texts in varied translations. A technological feat in its day, Origen's Hexapla was a massive series of volumes that laid out the text of the Old Testament in multiple versions arranged in six columns, complete with an annotation system that highlighted the differences between them.[1] And while the history of Christian biblical interpretation often highlights those thinkers who argued for a closer connection with the literal meaning, the overwhelming majority of Christian biblical interpretation reflects the claim by Aquinas that, since the literal sense is intended by the author, and the author of the Scriptures is the eternal and infinite God, then the literal sense of the Scriptures can encompass vast expanses of meaning.[2] Nevertheless, by the Middle Ages there arose a collection of authoritative allegorical interpretations which were copied and later printed alongside of and around the biblical text. By the thirteenth century, an authoritative collection, called the *Glossa Ordinaria*, contained a set selection of interpretations ("glosses") of biblical texts, mainly from earlier Latin writers such as Jerome, Ambrose, and Augustine. A structured fourfold method of nonliteral reading was developed, basing itself on Origen and Augustine, often called the *quadriga*, which saw the literal as the surface meaning, with progressive depth found in three nonliteral types of interpretation: allegorical, moral, and anagogical (i.e., spiritual ascent).

[1] Anthony Grafton and Megan Williams, *Christianity and the Transformation of the Book: Origen, Eusebius, and the Library of Caesarea* (Cambridge, MA: Harvard/Belknap, 2006), 86–132.

[2] "Moreover, since the literal sense is the sense intended by the author, and since the author of Sacred Scripture is God, who comprehends all things at once by His intellect, it follows that, as Augustine says in *Confessions* 12, it is not inappropriate for a single Scriptural passage to have more than one sense even with respect to the literal sense" (ST I-I, q.1, a.10, trans., Alfred J. Freddoso, https://www3.nd.edu/~afreddos/summa-translation/TOC.htm).

Underlying this understanding of the biblical text as a vast reservoir of divine meanings is the idea that this content should not be available to all but rather was reserved for the spiritually mature. Given that, for centuries, literacy was limited to the ruling and clerical classes, this spiritual maturity tracked with educational levels and social status. For example, in 1199 Pope Innocent III wrote the Bishop of Metz in response to reports that laypeople were gathering privately to read biblical texts in translation. The pope seems more concerned about the secrecy of these meetings and the fact that they are not led by a cleric than the mere fact that people are engaging with the Bible. Nevertheless, Innocent III makes clear that "so great is the depth of divine Scriptuure that not only the simple and unlearned but even the prudent and learned are not capable enough to capture its understanding," and reiterates that "clearly, no simple or unlearned person should presume to grasp the sublime nature of the sacred Scripture, nor to preach it to others."[3] A more dramatic illustration of this idea comes from the life of an early twelfth-century saint. Preserved in the two medieval biographies of Norbert of Xanten (ca. 1075–1134) is the story of the saint's exorcism of a young girl who had been possessed for a year. While Norbert was reading from the Gospel over the girl, the demon,

> flaunting his knowledge, recited, through the mouth of the girl, the Canticle of Canticles from beginning to end. Then, repeating word for word, he translated the same Canticle of Canticles into French. Once again he proclaimed the whole thing word for word in German through the mouth of the girl who, while she was well, knew nothing but the Psalter.[4]

[3] "Tanta est enim divinae Scripturae profunditas, ut non solum simplices et illiterati, sed etiam prudentes et docti non plene sufficiant ad ipsius intelligentiam indagandam . . . ne videlicet simplex aliquis vel et indoctus praesumat ad sublimitatem Scripturae sacrae pertingere vel eam aliis praedicare" (Innocent III, *Cum ex injuncto*, Latin text *Regestorum Lib. II. Epistola CXLI*, PL 214, cols. 695–98, quotation from col. 696; translation mine).

[4] Chap. 10 of *Vita A*, trans. Theodore Antry, O. Praem., https://premontre.org/wp-content/uploads/2021/02/vita.pdf.

Note how the story revolves around the presumption, which we saw in the previous chapter, about the inherent power of the biblical text. Norbert reads the from the Gospels over the possessed girl in order to oust the demon. The demon's response is twofold: first, it recites the Song of Songs, presumably in Latin (which is the language of Norbert's Gospel text). This is perhaps the demon's way to show that the biblical text has no power over him and is also an allusion to the New Testament texts where Satan quotes the Bible in his temptation of Jesus (Matt 4:1-11; Luke 4:1-13).[5] Significantly, the demon next recites the entirety of the Song of Songs in the two vernacular languages of the girl and the assembled crowd. In Christian biblical interpretation going as far back as Origen, the Song of Songs was understood to be a book to contain profound esoteric, mystical truths, which made it unsuitable for any but the most spiritually mature.[6] Note how the text makes clear that the only biblical text the girl knew before her possession was the Psalms. By reciting a biblical book reserved for religious elites—and by doing so in the vernacular languages of the people—the demon embodies the chaos envisioned by our pious author of a world where the holiness of spiritual truths is regularly violated by their widespread access to all and sundry.

What was demonic for the twelfth-century author of this hagiography became a centerpiece of the Reformation three centuries later. This was due in part to the heightened interest in reading primary sources from antiquity that was typical of the Renaissance. Rather than read the *Glossa* containing the interpretations of earlier, authoritative Christian teachers, intellectuals in Europe wanted to read the biblical text on its own. Moreover, they wanted to read the text in the original languages, which they could now do because of greater access to the study of Greek and Hebrew. The development of typeset printing in the 1450s led to a powerful combination

[5] Shakespeare's well-known quote from *The Merchant of Venice*: "The devil can cite Scripture for his purpose!" Antonio to Bassanio re: Shylock (I.iii.107) also plays on long-established Christian antisemitism with the claim that Jewish readers do not know how to read the biblical text correctly, a baseless claim that goes back at least to Justin Martyr in the second century, as discussed in chap. 3.

[6] Discussion in Thomas M. Bolin, *Ecclesiastes and the Riddle of Authorship* (London: Routledge, 2017), 28–32.

of new knowledge and increased access that would change how the Bible was viewed to this day. Up to this point, Western theologians were all clerics who read Jerome's Latin Vulgate. Theology as a scholarly pursuit viewed the biblical material as a source text upon which to build theological claims. Only a few Christians prior to the Renaissance were known to read biblical Hebrew—Jerome, a thousand years earlier, being the most notable. Now priests who taught theology could read the Bible in Hebrew, Aramaic, and Greek. One of those priests was Martin Luther, professor at the University of Wittenberg. While the Reformation is said to "begin" with Luther's posting of the Ninety-Five Theses in 1517, the real theological heart of Luther's conflict with Rome is clearer in the writings produced in the following year after his meeting with the papal legate, Cardinal Cajetan, in Augsburg. On the one hand, the dispute was over how salvation is effected in a human soul, but underlying this was the question of which sources were authoritative in making theological claims and forming dogma, and more specifically the question of the limits (if any) of papal authority. For Cardinal Cajetan, it was important to assert the power of the pope to dispense indulgences, which he did using the theological method laid down by scholastics in the Middle Ages, which included appeal to papal decrees, canon law, and John 20:23 ("If you forgive the sins of any, they are forgiven them; if you retain the sins of any, they are retained"). Luther, on the other hand, relied primarily on scriptural passages, because they were for him the highest authority under which all other authorities should be subordinated, even the pope's. Consequently, he responded to Cajetan's appeal to papal decrees by asserting that such decrees are to be obeyed only if they agree with the Bible.[7] In his written summary of the three-day encounter, Luther states that Cajetan "never produced a syllable from the Holy Scriptures against me."[8]

There is not space here to do justice to Luther's voluminous written output and theological thought (which developed and changed over time), but his impact is such that he deserves a bit

[7] See Suzanne Hequet, "The 1518 Proceedings at Augsburg," *Lutheran Quarterly* 32 (2018): 60–70.

[8] Hequet, "The 1518 Proceedings at Augsburg," 66.

more of our attention. Luther railed against the centuries-long tradition of reading the Bible allegorically, and indeed the entire view of the fourfold meaning of Scripture. For Luther, the heart of the Christian faith was God's direct address to the individual believer. This took place most clearly in the words of the Bible, which was where the Holy Spirit was most present and active.[9] One was closest to the Spirit when paying careful attention to the literal meaning of the Bible's words. In this way, Luther expressed a "robust confidence in the clarity of the Scriptures when dealt with honestly and with faith."[10] In response to an author who accused him of focusing on the letter of the Bible and not its spirit, Luther wrote a vigorous defense of the literal meaning as the place where one encountered God's message of salvation, calling it "the whole substance, nature, and foundation of Holy Scripture," and asserting that "if one abandoned it, the whole Scripture would be nothing." In contrast, the spiritual meaning "counts in no dispute and does not stand the test."[11] Luther, most famously at the Diet of Worms in 1521, where he refused to recant his theological positions, argued that the Bible alone was the final arbiter in terms of doctrine for Christians.[12] Everything else—papal decrees, conciliar teachings, church tradition—was subordinate to the testimony of the Bible, which spoke clearly to the individual Christian about God's grace and salvation. This connection is important: *because* the Bible is the source of our knowledge of salvation, *it can be understood by anyone*. For Luther, it is unthinkable that God would

[9] Robert Kolb, "Current Perspectives on Luther's Biblical Interpretation," *Lutheran Quarterly* 36, no. 3 (2022): 251–52.

[10] Mark D. Thompson, "Biblical Interpretation in the Works of Martin Luther," in Alan Hauser and Duane Watson, eds., *A History of Biblical Interpretation*, vol. 2 (Grand Rapids, MI: Eerdmans, 2009), 303.

[11] Martin Luther, "Answer to the Hyperchristian, Hyperspiritual and Hyperlearned Book by Goat Emser in Leipzig Including Some Thoughts Regarding His Companion, the Fool Murner," trans. Eric Gritsch and Ruth Gritsch, in *Luther's Works* 39, ed. Eric Gritsch (Minneapolis: Fortress Press, 1970), 177. See also the discussion in Joel R. Beeke, "The Perspicuity of Scripture," *Puritan Reformed Journal* 7, no. 2 (July 2015): 45–64.

[12] "Luther spoke of the need for the church and for Christians to rely on scripture alone within a specific context: regarding the authority of the church to make final decisions about doctrine" (Jillian E. Cox, "Martin Luther on the Living Word: Rethinking the Principle of *Sola Scriptura*," *Pacifica* 29 [2016]: 7–8).

make the essential salvific message obscure or require the individual Christian to rely on specialists to interpret it for them. Naturally, Luther used his training in Hebrew and Greek to translate the Bible into German, which could then be printed and distributed widely to Christians.

It's safe to say that the ability to read the Bible in the original languages, due to the cultural impact of the Renaissance and the technological development of the invention of movable-type printing, shaped the way that the Reformation unfolded and the role the Bible played in it. There had been reform efforts in the church before which were also tied to the Bible. The compelling power of Francis of Assisi stemmed from his authentic living out of evangelical simplicity. The English translation of the Bible from Jerome's Latin attributed to John Wycliffe in the fourteenth century was part of a reform effort.[13] But while the Bible played a role in earlier reform efforts, the new circumstances of Luther's day made the Bible itself a point of contention. In other words, prior to Luther, efforts at church reform would appeal to the Bible as an authoritative source of how to live an authentic Christian life. For Luther and his opponents, one of the issues under debate was exactly how the Bible acted as an authority and, by extension, who was properly suited to offer correct interpretations of the Bible. One unavoidable consequence of the proliferation of printed Bibles in vernacular languages is that increased access to the biblical text led almost necessarily to multiple, competing interpretations. This is due, as we have already seen, to the nature of how people make sense of texts. Luther saw this in his own lifetime, as his ideas were taken up by others and carried to places he never intended. Not even interpreters of Luther could stay on the same page!

Luther's assertion of the Bible's supreme doctrinal authority and its clarity are two of his ideas that later Reformers intensified. His belief that the Bible occupied a sole, privileged place in terms

[13] Wycliffe died in 1384. At the Council of Constance in 1415, he was declared a heretic, and his remains were ordered to be removed from consecrated ground. His corpse was exhumed from its grave in Lutterworth, England, burned, and the ashes thrown into the nearby River Swift. The Council of Constance also condemned and executed the Czech reformer Jan Hus.

of authority became a slogan of later Reformers—*sola scriptura*—and more authority was granted to the Bible over larger parts of Christian life. Alongside this, the Bible was believed to be more and more clear to the ordinary believer, something called the perspicuity of Scripture. For example, the 1646 Westminster Confession of Faith, a foundational document of Reformed churches that developed from John Calvin's reforms, states that, while

> all things in Scripture are not alike plain in themselves, nor alike clear unto all . . . yet those things which are necessary to be known, believed, and observed for salvation, are so clearly propounded, and opened in some place of Scripture or other, that not only the learned, but the unlearned, in a due use of the ordinary means, may attain unto a sufficient understanding of them.[14]

To reiterate: this democratization of biblical access and interpretation quickly led to competing interpretations. In 1523, the Reformer Ulrich Zwingli, a minister in Zurich, urged his fellow Christians to engage in the biblical texts for themselves. However, he was soon confronted with opponents whose reading of the biblical text differed with his on the key issue of baptism.[15] Zwingli's response, significantly, was to establish a school in Zurich to train ministers in Greek and Hebrew. In other words, Zwingli's reaction to conflicting biblical interpretations was recourse to scholarly expertise, which implies that the biblical text is not clear to all believing Christians. Zwingli reconciled these views by stating that the Holy Spirit was essential to correct biblical interpretation and that the

[14] Available at the Presbyterian Church of America website: https://www.pcaac.org/wp-content/uploads/2022/04/WCFScripureProofs2022.pdf. John Calvin, writing to Cardinal Jacopo Sadoleto in 1539, asserts that all beliefs are to be tested by the Bible and that highest concern of the church is "humbly and religiously to venerate the Word of God and submit to its authority" (John Calvin and Jacopo Sadoleto, *A Reformation Debate*, trans. Henry Beveridge, ed. John Olin [Grand Rapids, MI: Baker Books, 1966], 75).

[15] "By 1525, the perspicuity of Scripture had become problematic, as some of the people of Zurich had read the Bible for themselves, as recommended by Zwingli, and had reached conclusions that clashed with Zwingli's own" (Benjamin Sargent, "Biblical Hermeneutics and the Zurich Reformation," *Evangelical Quarterly* 86 [2014]: 330).

Spirit could be given to any Christian. Alongside that, however, pastors were to have the ability to engage the biblical text as scholars.[16] This was codified in the Second Helvetic Confession of 1564, which stated that authentic biblical interpretation depended in part upon correct understanding of the biblical languages. Proper biblical interpretation relied both on spiritual gift and learned skill.

What separated the Reformers' biblical interpretation from the way Catholic theologians had practiced it was not simply that Luther, Calvin, Zwingli, and others were finally reading the Bible for its plain meaning and in its original languages. As the previous chapters have discussed, every act of reading, but particularly of reading the Bible, requires readers to engage in strategies that will allow the text to speak to them. The Reformers, notably, retained the interpretation of the Old Testament that saw it as predicting Jesus, a way of reading that had its own scriptural authority because this was how the New Testament read those texts. Inevitably, the spread of access to Bibles in printed translations caused religious divisions to multiply too. In the century after Luther's death in 1546, the Reformation had spread and branched out into multiple traditions, all of which had theological disagreements but all of whose positions were grounded in how they read the biblical text. Reformers were no longer engaged in the biblical interpretation of medieval Catholic theologians who read the Vulgate, folded biblical texts into ancient Greek philosophical thought, and used the scholastic form of argumentation. Nevertheless, despite the claim of the Bible's sole or highest authority over Christian life, Reformation theologians were still interpreting the biblical text like their medieval forebears, using organizing principles external to the Bible, whether that be reading the Old Testament as predicting or being fulfilled by Jesus or subordinating New Testament texts that emphasized actions to the Pauline emphasis on faith over works, or sharing Luther's continued embrace of infant

[16] "Zwingli placed the learning of biblical languages at the heart of ministerial and general education in Zurich. In doing so, he placed a greater emphasis on the languages than Martin Luther, for whom they were also of vital importance" (Sargent, "Biblical Hermeneutics," 332).

baptism without any biblical warrant. As always, the biblical text continued to be a site of creative theologizing, albeit now with recourse to Greek and Hebrew words rather than the glosses of the early church fathers.

For instance, in his 1531 lectures on the Song of Songs, Luther entirely eschews the allegorical reading that had been the staple of the Christian tradition since Origen and argues instead that this is a writing of Solomon undertaken in his capacity as king and that it is about the political challenges he faced during his reign. Solomon did this by writing "figuratively" about his kingship in the Song of Songs. Luther grounds the *origins* of the text in the historical figure of Solomon, something that allegorical reading did not go out of its way to do, but he is forced by the nature of the text to read it figuratively, a move that he justifies by attributing this meaning to the historical Solomon. In the end, however, Luther, Origen, and all the other Christian readers of the Song of Songs engage in a process of reading that begins from the premise that the words cannot mean what they appear to on the surface.[17]

The Bible and the Church Part Ways

The upshot of the expanded access to the Bible, its increased importance in the lives of Christians, and the ongoing disagreements over its supposedly clear meaning was over a century of bloody religious war across Europe. The historian Jacques Barzun wryly and correctly points to "the moral paradox of 'wars of religion' in the name of a Christ who preached the brotherhood of man. On that injunction there seemed to be a meeting of minds; it meant: 'Be my brother or I will kill you.'"[18]

In this environment many intellectuals were looking for meaning and ethical advice outside of religion, which to them only seemed to engender division and violence. Yet despite the criticism of organized religions and their political entailments, the Bible itself still occupied a place of importance, which required people

[17] See the discussion in Endel Kallas, "Martin Luther as Expositor of the Song of Songs," *Lutheran Quarterly* 2 (1988): 323–41.

[18] Jacques Barzun, *From Dawn to Decadence: 500 Years of Western Cultural Life* (San Francisco: HarperCollins, 2000), 23.

to engage with it. In other words, it became possible for someone to set themselves apart from religion but still engage with the Bible as a book with cultural and historical authority.

Scientific discovery was a visible place where the Bible's authority was receding and in need of rearticulation. Two examples show the different approaches taken in this regard. In 1615, already under pressure from some in the Catholic Church for his demonstration of the heliocentric solar system, Galileo wrote a defense of himself to Christina, Grand Duchess of Tuscany. The letter is Galileo's response to claims that he has attacked the veracity of the Bible with his observations, given that the Bible's cosmology puts a stationary earth at the center with the sun moving through the sky. Consequently, the letter is about not only science but also about biblical interpretation and its role in the proper relationship between religion and science. The letter itself is a master class in rhetorical artistry, as Galileo moves from pious humility to sharp criticism of his antagonists in the church. What concerns us here is his view of the Bible. Drawing on long-standing Catholic theological tradition, Galileo distinguishes the special revelation found in the Bible with the general knowledge of God that is demonstrated by nature.[19] Crucially for Galileo, these are not simply two different ways of learning the same things about God, but instead two very different types of revelation. Whereas nature responds to careful observation and speaks clearly to those with the requisite training in the languages of mathematics and physics, the Bible "is often very abstruse, and may say things which are quite different from what its bare words signify."[20] This is a far cry from Luther and the later Reformers, for whom the clarity of the biblical text in its literal meaning was the foundation of their interpretive theory. Also, given that the Catholic Church at this time was on its guard against anything that looked like Reformation theology,

[19] This is partially in debt to Augustine, who described creation as a book written by God. See also the discussion in Bjarke Mørkøre Stigel Hansen, "Biblical Hermeneutics in Galileo's 'Letter to the Grand Duchess Christina': On the Issue of Negative Theology," *Studia Theologica: Nordic Journal of Theology* 74 (2020): 75–78.

[20] Galileo Galilei, "Letter to the Grand Duchess Christina," in Stillman Drake, ed., *Discoveries and Opinions of Galileo* (New York: Anchor-Doubleday, 1957), 181. Text also available at https://inters.org/galilei-madame-christina-Lorraine.

it is hardly coincidental that Galileo emphasizes the problems with the text's literal meaning.[21] Here Galileo engages in a complicated interpretive dance as he moves between the two "books" of Scripture and nature. At the same time that he states that the Bible's meaning is difficult to grasp, Galileo also repeatedly argues that the Bible uses simple language about the natural world so as not to confuse the uneducated.[22] This is a feature and not a bug of the text, because Galileo also affirms that the Bible cannot contain falsehood and, moreover, that the biblical authors knew that the earth moved around the sun.[23] Relying on Augustine, Galileo asserts that no two truths can contradict each other and in the process takes the formerly unified understanding of special and natural revelation and separates them into two independent realms, what the evolutionary biologist Stephen Jay Gould termed "non-overlapping magisterial."[24] Moreover, as the Bible's mysteries need to be interpreted by the authorities of the church, so too do nature's complexities require expert analysis. In this way, Galileo puts himself and other natural scientists on par with the church; both are trained authorities in interpreting their respective sources of revelation. But Galileo goes further, comparing scientists to the biblical authors themselves:

> Regarding the state of rest or motion of the sun and earth, experience plainly proves that *in order to accommodate the common people it was necessary to assert of these things precisely what the words of the Bible convey*. Even in our own age, people far less primitive continue to maintain the same opinion for reasons

[21] Galileo continues, "Hence in expounding the Bible if one were always to confine oneself to the unadorned grammatical meaning, one might fall into error" (Galilei, "Letter to the Grand Duchess," 181).

[22] "Hence I think that I may reasonably conclude that whenever the Bible has occasion to speak of any physical conclusion (especially those which are very abstruse and hard to understand), the rule has been observed of avoiding confusion in the minds of the common people which would render them contumacious toward the higher mysteries" (Galilei, "Letter to the Grand Duchess," 182).

[23] "Far from pretending to teach us the constitution and motions of the heavens and the stars, with their shapes, magnitudes, and distances, the authors of the Bible intentionally forbore to speak of these things, though all were quite well known to them" (Galilei, "Letter to the Grand Duchess," 184).

[24] Stephen Jay Gould, *Rocks of Ages: Science and Religion in the Fullness of Life* (New York: Ballantine, 1999).

> which will be found extremely trivial if well weighed and examined, and upon the basis of experiences that are wholly false or altogether beside the point. Nor is it worthwhile to try to change their opinion, they being unable to understand the arguments on the opposite side, for these depend upon observations too precise and demonstrations too subtle, grounded on abstractions which require too strong an imagination to be comprehended by them. Hence even if the stability of heaven and the motion of the earth should be more than certain in the minds of the wise, *it would still be necessary to assert the contrary for the preservation of belief among the all-too-numerous vulgar.*[25]

Put into a corner when his discoveries contradicted biblical cosmology, Galileo was forced to affirm both the Bible's authority and the validity of scientific investigation. As a Catholic living in a Catholic country, Galileo distanced himself from Reformation thought by reaffirming the Bible's complicated meaning hidden under the literal sense and the corresponding need for the church to oversee interpretation. But he also attributed a similar depth to nature, which likewise needed its own authorities to discern its hidden workings. Both the Bible and the natural world were opaque to nonspecialists, who failed to grasp both realms' inner reality because they misunderstood their respective surface appearances.

A century after Galileo and in a Protestant country, Isaac Newton was another giant of the early scientific period whose *Principia Mathematica* revolutionized physics, astronomy, and mathematics. His three laws of universal motion are still used today, and his name is used to describe the thoroughly mechanistic cosmology that typified much of the philosophical and scientific thought that followed him. But Newton also wrote extensively on the Bible and theology. Consonant with the Reformation tradition, he read the biblical text in its original languages and consulted the Targums, which are early Jewish translations of the Hebrew Bible into Aramaic.[26] Newton's extensive religious writings were controversial

[25] Galilei, "Letter to the Grand Duchess," 199–200 (italics added).

[26] "When Newton died in 1727, he left in his library a collection of thirty-two copies of the Bible, both in the original and in vernacular translations, namely in Hebrew, Syriac, Greek, Latin, English, and French, as well as a copy of the Walton Polyglot Bible" (Michael Joalland, "Isaac Newton Reads the King James

(among other things he denied the doctrine of the Trinity). Consequently, they were not published in his lifetime and the bulk of them were unknown until the 1930s. Newton was particularly fascinated by biblical prophecy, particularly in the apocalyptic books of Daniel and Revelation.[27] Among his unpublished papers is an untitled treatise on revelation in which Newton offers interpretive rules for allowing the reader "to know when an interpretation is genuine and of two interpretations which is the best."[28] Newton was a brilliant reader of the Bible. He read the biblical languages and ancient translations, correlated the biblical text with extrabiblical historical and cultural data, and was sensitive to the contexts of individual biblical books and the entire canon. He understood that both Daniel and Revelation were written in times of persecution and hence that their imagery had to refer to political realities in their day.[29] It is ironic, then, that he erroneously denied that the great beast of the book of Daniel represented the Seleucid king Antiochus IV, a great persecutor of Jews.[30]

If Galileo falls back on traditional Catholic understanding of the Scriptures as full of hidden meaning, Newton lies squarely in the Reformation's view of the perspicuity of the Bible.[31] To those

---

Version: The Marginal Notes and Reading Marks of a Natural Philosopher," *Proceedings of the Bibliographical Society of America* 113 [2019]: 299).

[27] See the posthumously published *Observations upon the Prophecies of Daniel and the Apocalypse of St. John* (London: J. Darby & T. Browne, 1733), available at https://www.gutenberg.org/files/16878/16878-h/16878-h.htm.

[28] This and all following quotations, both in the text and in the notes, are from Isaac Newton, "Untitled Treatise on Revelation," https://www.newtonproject.ox.ac.uk/view/texts/normalized/THEM00135. I have modernized the spelling.

[29] "The original of the figurative language of the prophets was the comparison of a kingdom to the world and the parts of the one to the like parts of the other."

[30] "Thus in Daniel's vision of the four beasts, it would be grossly absurd to interpret, as some politicians of late have done, the fourth beast of Antiochus Epiphanes and his successors; since that is described to be the most terrible, dreadful, strong, and warlike beast of all the four, and the prophet dwells far longer upon the description of that than of all the others put together: whereas the kingdom of Antiochus Epiphanes and his successors was both less and weaker and less warlike than any of the three before him."

[31] Moreover, Newton lamented the state of the church in his day and looked back to early Christian history as a golden age: "Where are they that live like the primitive Christians, that love God with all their hearts and with all their souls and with all their might, and their neighbor as their selves?"

who would protest the difficulty of the book of Revelation, Newton retorts, "if there was no need of it, or if it cannot be understood, then why did God give it? Does he trifle?" This clarity of the Scriptures is predicated upon the mercy of God to reveal salvation to humanity. Thus, for Newton, all unfulfilled prophecies can be correctly interpreted, provided that the reader stay close to the biblical text's literal meaning. One of his interpretive rules requires that readers "choose those interpretations which are most according to the literal meaning of the Scriptures unless where the tenor and circumstances of the place plainly require an allegory." Like Galileo, who had to address both the clarity and opacity of the biblical text, Newton can both affirm the intelligibility of biblical prophecy while at the same time claiming that the text is also a proving ground where the good and evil are sorted according to their ability to understand it:

> For God is just as well as merciful and punishes wickedness by hardening the wicked and visiting the sins of the fathers upon the children. But the design of [biblical prophecy] is to try men and convert the best, so that the church may be purer and less mixed with hypocrites and lukewarm persons.

If Galileo the Catholic saw both nature and the Bible to be filled with depths of meaning underneath an accessible exterior, Newton viewed nature to be as perspicuous as the Bible:

> Truth is ever to be found in simplicity, and not in the multiplicity and confusion of things. As the world, which to the naked eye exhibits the greatest variety of objects, appears very simple in its internal constitution when surveyed by a philosophic understanding, and so much the simpler by how much the better it is understood, so it is in these visions.[32]

Here we can see how the two distinct ways of looking at the Bible, the older way of seeing it as a book with hidden meanings and the Reformers' assumption of the text's clarity, played out in the

[32] Although he qualifies this by asserting how "contrary it is to God's purpose that the truth of his religion should be as obvious and perspicuous to all men as a mathematical demonstration."

biblical interpretations of two scientists, each representing one of these ways. What's more, their understanding of the biblical text was similar to how they approached their interpretation of the natural world. Galileo turned the book of nature into a book like the Bible that held hidden meaning. Newton turned the God of the Bible into a plain-speaking scientist.

The Bible Outside the Church

At the time he posted his Ninety-Five Theses in 1517, Martin Luther was a biblical scholar, Catholic priest, Augustinian monk, and professor at the University of Wittenberg. The ensuing cultural shifts in Europe permanently separated the identity of religious authority and biblical scholar. The widespread access to the biblical text and biblical languages meant that before long laypeople such as Newton could engage deeply with the Bible and, eventually, that laypeople would constitute the makeup of biblical scholars at universities. The Bible began a new stage in its history outside of the institutional churches and their professional personnel. Michael Legaspi describes this change as a shift wherein the Bible as *Scripture*—a sacred text as a source for theology—changed into a view of the Bible as a source of Western tradition (what Legaspi calls "the cultural Bible") and also to the study of the Bible as a collection of ancient writings subject to linguistic, literary, and historical analysis much like the Homeric poems (Legaspi's "academic Bible"). The impetus for this was, in part, a desire to find common ground around the Bible in a place not dominated by the doctrinal disputes unleashed by the Reformation.[33] Ultimately, the project to establish a cultural Bible failed, and academic biblical studies retreated into the university and became the purview of a small group of specialists—a situation that continues to this day:

[33] Michael C. Legaspi, *The Death of Scripture and the Rise of Biblical Studies* (New York: Oxford University Press, 2010). "To men and women of the Enlightenment, though, it was precisely the particularity and incommensurability of these religious identities that had led to war, fraud, and superstition in modern life. As impediments to the kind of moral, irenic, and happy society that Enlightenment figures hoped to create, they had to be disallowed" (164).

> The Reformation engendered a crisis of authority in which authority itself—its location, its nature, its sources—was contested. As a result of this crisis, the ecclesial underpinnings of the scriptural Bible became too weak, too fragmented to sustain its place at the center of Western Christendom. It was moved to the boundaries, where, throughout the sixteenth and seventeenth centuries, it fueled confessional and theological programs. . . . Many of the tools and much of the material that would be later used to create the academic Bible were developed in the two centuries following the Reformation.[34]

European intellectuals who had hostility toward organized religion for its ethical shortcomings turned that sentiment to the Bible, specifically the Old Testament. The belief in the ongoing development of culture led Christian thinkers such as Immanuel Kant to view Judaism (and the Old Testament) as expressing a primitive religious viewpoint limited to a particular national or ethnic group and focused on the observance of external rules rather than inner change.[35] This view is, of course, nonsense and reveals more about persistence of antisemitism in thinkers like Kant than anything about the biblical text or Judaism. Elites in the nascent United States were taking a similar editorial approach. Thomas Paine, the American revolutionary, wrote in 1793 a scathing criticism of the Bible called *The Age of Reason* where he described the Bible as "a history of the grossest vices, and a collection of the most paltry and contemptible tales."[36] Toward the end of his life, Thomas Jefferson constructed a private Bible for himself by slicing passages from the four Gospels in multiple languages and pasting them into a book which he entitled *The Life and Morals of Jesus of Nazareth* and from which all miracles and references to the supernatural were removed. Like Newton before him, Jefferson kept this volume private; it was only long after his death that it was published under the title *Jefferson's Bible*.[37]

[34] Legaspi, *Death of Scripture*, viii.

[35] For an overview, see Wojciech Kozyra, "Kant on the Jews and Their Religion," *Diametros* 17 (2020): 32–55.

[36] Thomas Paine, *The Age of Reason*, 200th Anniversary Edition (n.p.: Wet Water Publications, 1992), 16.

[37] Commentary, history, images, and text available at the Smithsonian Institution website: https://americanhistory.si.edu/JeffersonBible/#1.

The Reformation opened a Pandora's box of competing biblical interpretations. It is difficult to underestimate its impact on biblical interpretation in Western Christianity to this day. Directly, it made Bible reading itself a place of contention and division and, as interpretations diverged, more new biblical translations proliferated to offer textual support for them. Indirectly, the ability of both clergy and later lay academics to access the biblical texts in Hebrew, Aramaic, and Greek helped to erode the centuries-long belief in the Bible's uniqueness as the text began to be subjected to the kinds of grammatical and historical analysis used on ancient Greek and Latin writings. If early Jewish and Christian readers of the Bible borrowed the allegorical approach of Greco-Roman intellectuals at the turn of the Christian era, post-Enlightenment European academics borrowed the analytical approaches of classical studies to dissect the Bible into sources and competing viewpoints.

The roots of academic biblical study lie in the study of original languages and biblical manuscripts undertaken by Erasmus in the early 1500s with his newly edited printed edition of the New Testament, which became one of the texts used to make the King James translation a century later. Such careful attention to the text (another expression of uncovering the literal meaning) wasn't limited to the Bible. Widespread access to the poems of Homer in the original led scholars to explore questions of the poems' composition, specifically whether the *Iliad* and the *Odyssey* contained earlier writings. Soon these kinds of questions were applied to the Pentateuch, traditionally believed to have been written by Moses. To that end, Richard Simon, an Oratorian priest in Paris who was a scholar of Semitic languages, published a lengthy and detailed study in 1678 that claimed that Moses could not have written the Pentateuch due to linguistic and compositional inconsistencies in the text. Simon's book appeared only eight years after Baruch Spinoza's *Tractatus Theologico-Politicus* which claimed that the Pentateuch was written by the priest Ezra after the Babylonian exile. Spinoza, a Dutch Jewish philosopher, had already been expelled from the synagogue by this time, and Simon's fate was similar—he was expelled from the Oratorian order on the publication of his book.

But the cat was out of the bag. In 1753 Jean Astruc, a pastor's son, physician, and Catholic convert, published a book in which he showed how the biblical text was comprised of doublets—two versions of the same story—and that these doublets often used different names for God. He surmised from this that Moses had used different written sources to compose the Pentateuch. Despite Astruc's desire to preserve Moses as the author of the Pentateuch, his work became the foundation for critical analysis of the first five books of the Bible ever since. Over 250 years later, scholars still divide the two creation stories in Genesis 1–3, or the flood story in Genesis 6–9, or the commissioning of Moses by God in Exodus 3 and 6, following the principles first articulated by Astruc. By the late 1700s critical biblical studies were being done by non-clergy in German universities, and by the end of the 1800s, this type of study focusing on historical and linguistic issues was being done by scholars in England and the United States. Notably, in terms of the Old Testament, the biblical text was seen for the most part as a record of belief and practice that had been left behind. This was in part a reaction to religious dogmatism, in part a recurrence of the ancient Christian belief that the Old Testament was "perfected" by the New, and in part a pernicious European anti-semitism.[38] Once biblical scholarship shifted to history and moved away from theological polemics, this fundamentally changed the way the Bible was thought about. "Literal" meaning was limited to what the words meant in their ancient cultural context. The focus of biblical scholarship was exclusively on the past. Meaning came from long ago and was intended only for others. Consequently, biblical scholarship engaged in a quest to uncover older sources and to use extrabiblical writings and archeological data to "illuminate" the Bible. This continues to this day. In much of its work, academic biblical scholarship has been mainly talking to itself; even when it occurs in the context of training clergy, it

[38] Writing about German biblical scholarship in the 1700s, James Turner observes, "The record of a slow, relapsing struggle to get from polytheism to monotheism, the Old Testament had no spiritual lessons to teach modern people" (James Turner, *Philology: The Forgotten Origins of the Modern Humanities* [Princeton: Princeton University Press, 2014], 116).

still is far removed from what Christians go to the Bible expecting and looking for.

The retreat of academic biblical studies from contemporary theological meanings of the Bible left the cultural space occupied by the biblical text open to interpretations by people for whom the Bible was a book of divine teachings that should be read with an eye to its plain meaning but who did not have much formal guidance as to what constituted that meaning. This brings us back to our starting point in chapter 1 and the role that the Bible has played in disputes over moral and social issues in the US. While elites like Jefferson edited out the parts of the Bible that didn't agree with their views of science, ethics, or cosmology, and Christians trained in biblical languages labored behind the walls of seminaries and universities, most Americans in the 1800s were reading their King James Bibles believing that their interpretations accorded with the text's plain sense. As discussed in chapter 1, Southerners who supported slavery found in the Bible's literal meaning multiple places of support for the position, seeing the Bible as a text that communicates specific things that God wants people to do or to avoid. Abolitionists, on the other hand, faced with the Bible's overt embrace of slavery in both the Old and New Testaments, were led to read the text in a nonliteral way, arguing that certain passages pointed to values or ideals that argued against slavery. Biblical scholars, as James Turner details, "mostly spoke to each other" and were careful—if they valued their jobs—to avoid making public any negative historical or theological judgments on the text.[39]

The North-South divide in biblical interpretation continued after the Civil War. Both the war and Reconstruction left the South economically devastated for decades. White Southerners' hostility toward the North manifested in many ways, one being a form of populism that contrasted heretical educated elites with faithful, Bible-reading Christians. A parade example of this dichotomy is the 1925 Scopes "Monkey Trial." Intended as a media spectacle from the outset, the state of Tennessee—and the historical truth of the Bible—were represented by William Jennings Bryan, three-time

[39] Turner, *Philology*, 210–26; quotation on 210.

presidential candidate and populist whose famous "Cross of Gold" speech during the 1886 presidential campaign argued passionately for the interests of working people across the country and against wealthy East Coast business owners. On the other side, teacher John Scopes was represented by Clarence Darrow, an agnostic who had made his name in part by defending two young murderers from wealthy families in Chicago.[40] Covering the trial for the *Baltimore Sun* was H. L. Mencken, who consistently mocked and belittled the local inhabitants and their belief in biblical creation rather than evolution (Mencken is the first person in print to have used the term *Bible Belt* to describe the Southern US).[41]

The Bible in the Catholic Church

The story I've been telling in this chapter has thus far been one that takes place in Protestant milieux, beginning necessarily in Europe and ending in the US. The Catholic Church's understanding of the Bible follows a different path from that opened by the Reformation before the two trajectories partially come together in the middle of the last century. At Session IV of the Council of Trent (April 8, 1546) several doctrinal statements about the Bible were

[40] Darrow's agnosticism was an issue during the trial, as the transcripts show; see Jeffrey P. Moran, *The Scopes Trial: A Brief History with Documents* (Boston: Bedford St. Martins, 2002), 99–100.

[41] In referring to police coming to Dayton, Tennessee, for the trial, Mencken writes, "But all other atheists and anarchists now have public notice they must shut up forthwith and stay shut so long as they pollute this bright, shining, buckle of the Bible belt with their presence" (H. L. Mencken, "Law and Freedom, Mencken Discovers, Yield Place to Holy Writ in Rhea County," *Baltimore Evening Sun*, July 15, 1925). Elsewhere, after describing several individuals in the most negative way possible, Mencken ends a column stating, "Such is human existence among the fundamentalists, where children are brought up on Genesis and sin is unknown. If I have made the tale too long, then blame the spirit of garrulity that is in the local air. Even newspaper reporters, down here, get some echo of the call. Divine inspiration is as common as the hookworm. I have done my best to show you what the great heritage of mankind comes to in regions where the Bible is the beginning and end of wisdom, and the mountebank Bryan, parading the streets in his seersucker coat, is pointed out to sucklings as the greatest man since Abraham" (H. L. Mencken, "Yearning Mountaineers' Souls Need Reconversion Nightly, Mencken Finds," *Baltimore Evening Sun*, July 13, 1925), https://archive.org/details/CoverageOfTheScopesTrialByH.l.Mencken.

passed. Among these, the bishops required that the "old Vulgate edition" (*vetus et vulgata editione*) be used in all preaching, teaching, and exposition on the grounds that the translation's authority was founded on the fact of its long use in the church.[42] Trent's decree forbade any interpretation of the Bible that went contrary to the teaching of the church or to the unanimous interpretation of "the Fathers," a phrase that most often referred to the main early Latin-writing theologians, Augustine, Jerome, Ambrose and Gregory the Great. Finally, the council forbade the printing of any Bibles without ecclesiastical license, noting in particular that such printed editions often contained notes that offered heterodox interpretations. These strictures rested upon the foundational claim that the institutional church alone was the judge of Scripture's true meaning (*sancta mater Ecclesia, cuius est iudicare de vero sensu et interpretatione Scripturarum Sanctarum*). Trent's message was clear: it repudiated everything that Luther, Calvin, and their followers were claiming about the Bible.

In terms of the origins of critical biblical scholarship as an academic enterprise, it's safe to say that the Catholic Church had very little to do with it for quite some time. As we saw above, the two Catholics who did engage in newer critical analysis of the Bible did so at their own risk: Richard Simon was expelled from his religious order, and Jean Astruc published his book anonymously. That being said, the church still made use of some scholarly methods, most notably the study of ancient manuscripts to correct errors in the biblical text. Trent's decrees on the Bible ordered the publication of a corrected text of the Vulgate (*quam emendatissime imprimatur*). That same month (April 1546) a group of bishops at Trent wrote to the pope to ask that, alongside the Vulgate, the Hebrew and Greek biblical texts be also corrected in this manner. In the 1590s, Popes Sixtus V (himself a humanist scholar) and

[42] "Statuit et declarat, ut haec ipsa vetus et vulgata editio, quae longo tot saeculorum usu in ipsa Ecclesia probata est, in publicis lectionibus, disputationibus, praedicationibus et expositionibus pro authentica habeatur, et ut nemo illam reiicere quovis praetextu audeat vel praesumat" (Decree Concerning the Canonical Scriptures), English translations in H. J. Schroeder, *The Canons and Decrees of the Council of Trent* (St. Louis: Herder, 1941), 17–19, and at https://www.bible-researcher.com/trent1.html.

Clement VIII commissioned and promulgated corrected editions of the Vulgate.[43] Moreover, Catholic vernacular Bibles were also published, notably the Douay-Rheims, an English translation of the Vulgate for English Catholics. Published in the early 1600s, the Douay-Rheims was revised in the 1770s by Richard Challoner and went on to become the most popular biblical translation for English-speaking Catholics until the Second Vatican Council.

It is often thought by both Catholics and non-Catholics that the church outright forbade laypeople to read the Bible on their own before the Vatican II. Strictly speaking, this is not true. As the Douay-Rheims demonstrates, Catholic vernacular Bibles were published with ecclesiastical approval, and various popes granted indulgences to lay Catholics who reverently read the Bible for a set period of time. Even Pope Innocent III, in the letter mentioned at the beginning of this chapter, was more concerned about laypeople reading the Bible in groups without ecclesiastical supervision than the mere fact that they are reading the text. Indeed, he notes in his letter that the desire to understand the Bible is itself a good thing but qualifies this with the concern that laypeople are engaging in this activity outside of the liturgical and catechetical structures of the church.[44] Wim François details how the picture of Catholic Bible reading before and through the Reformation is more complicated and interesting than is usually thought, noting that "the late medieval Catholic Church did not forbid the reading of the Bible in the vernacular, and that there was simply no central

[43] James M. Vosté, "The Vulgate at the Council of Trent," *Catholic Biblical Quarterly* 9 (1947): 9–25.

[44] "Licet autem desiderium intelligendi divinas Scripturas, et secundum eas, studium adhortandi reprehendendum non sit, sed potius commendandum, in eo tamen apparent merito arguendi, quod tales occulta conventicula sua celebrant, officium sibi praedicationis usurpant, sacerdotum simplicitatem eludunt et eorum consortium aspernantur qui talibus non inhaerent" ("The desire to understand the divine Scriptures is licit, and as they say, to encourage their study is not to be blamed but rather to be praised. In this, however, these people appear to deserve the charge, because they conduct their meetings in secret, take for themselves the office of preaching, ridicule the simplicity of priests, and shun those who are not part of their group" [Innocent III, *Cum ex injuncto*, Latin text *Regestorum Lib. II. Epistola CXLI*, PL 214, cols. 695–98, quotation from cols. 695–96]; translation mine.)

Roman policy pertaining to Bible reading in the vernacular—let alone an outright ban—that could have been in force everywhere in Western Europe, and that biblical books circulated in most of late medieval Western Europe's linguistic regions."[45] It's more accurate to say that the Catholic Church was very concerned about laypeople reading the Bible without clerical guidance for fear that they would arrive at interpretations contrary to church teaching. The experience of the Reformation churches demonstrated that access to the Bible led to competing interpretations. Luther, Calvin, Zwingli, and others strove to balance widespread Bible reading by congregants with doctrinal and interpretive guardrails to prevent heterodox interpretations. These efforts had limited success. For lay Catholics, exposure to the Bible occurred in closely regulated contexts, such as liturgical celebrations or formalized private devotions. Consequently, biblical texts were situated in an interpretive neighborhood that supplied clues and cues to lead the reader to correct interpretation safely within the boundaries of Catholic doctrine and reading tradition.

Regarding critical biblical studies, the Catholic Church kept the enterprise at arm's length for a long time, regarding the search for sources behind the biblical text with suspicion and outright condemnation. In response to the doctrinal debates that roiled Protestant denominations over the results of critical biblical studies throughout the nineteenth century, in 1893 Pope Leo XIII wrote an encyclical on biblical studies reaffirming the primacy of the Vulgate and the authority of the Latin fathers for biblical interpretation. He also established, in 1902, the Pontifical Biblical Commission (PBC) to maintain oversight over the teaching and research of Catholic academics, all of whom at that time were clerics and consequently could be directly disciplined by the church. In a series of *responsa* in the early twentieth century, the PBC firmly rejected modern critical biblical study and reaffirmed traditional beliefs about the historical nature of Genesis 1–3, the Mosaic authorship of the Pentateuch, and a host of other issues concerning the history and authorship of biblical books. It also played a role

[45] Wim François, "Vernacular Bible Reading in Late Medieval and Early Modern Europe: The 'Catholic' Position Revisited," *Catholic Historical Review* 104 (2018): 25.

in the silencing of the Dominican biblical scholar Marie-Joseph Lagrange (1855–1938). The PBC's role as a regulatory body continued up to Vatican II, when in 1964 it issued an important document on the Gospels that played a significant role in the council's Dogmatic Decree on Divine Revelation (*Dei Verbum*).[46] In the reorganization of the Roman Curia in 1971, the PBC was repurposed as an advisory body and in that capacity issued a series of important and detailed documents on a variety of topics bearing on the interpretation of the Bible. Importantly, in its new role, the PBC fully embraced the critical study of the Bible that had developed gradually over the preceding two centuries. As the PBC itself notes in its foundational 1993 document, *On the Interpretation of the Bible in the Church*:

> The historical-critical method is the indispensable method for the scientific study of the meaning of ancient texts. Holy Scripture, inasmuch as it is the "word of God in human language," has been composed by human authors in all its various parts and in all the sources that lie behind them. Because of this, its proper understanding not only admits the use of this method but actually requires it.[47]

This is not the place to give a detailed discussion of the PBC and the development of the church's understanding of biblical studies. Many good histories of this exist.[48] What I want to stress here, alongside this gradual development in regard to the church's attitude toward biblical studies, is the significant step forward made by Vatican II on the reading of the Bible by laypeople. "Easy access to Sacred Scripture should be provided for all the Christian faithful . . . since the word of God should be accessible at all times, the Church by her authority and with maternal concern

[46] Thomas M. Bolin, "The Biblical Commission's Instruction, *On the Historical Truth of the Gospels (Sancta Mater Ecclesia)* and Present Magisterial Attitudes Toward Biblical Exegesis," *Gregorianum* 93 (2012): 765–85.

[47] Dean P. Béchard, trans., *The Scripture Documents: An Anthology of Official Catholic Teachings* (Collegeville, MN: Liturgical Press, 2002), 249.

[48] See Ronald D. Witherup, *Biblical Fundamentalism: What Every Catholic Should Know* (Collegeville, MN: Liturgical Press, 2001), 31–48, and Bolin, "Biblical Commission's Instruction."

sees to it that suitable and correct translations are made into different languages, especially from the original texts of the sacred books."[49]

In the wake of the council, and for around twenty years or so afterward, the engagement of US Catholics with the Bible experienced a flourishing as a new biblical translation from the Hebrew and Greek, the New American Bible, replaced the Douay-Rheims, with its much older English rendering of the Vulgate. Simultaneously, a generation of Catholic biblical scholars, still clerics and religious at this point, were trained in critical methods and began to produce writings aimed to provide nonspecialist Catholics with access to the latest in biblical scholarship. The work of scholars such as Raymond Brown, Dianne Bergant, Jerome Murphy-O'Connor, John Dominic Crossan, John Craghan, and Alice Laffey, along with resources such as *The Jerome Biblical Commentary* and the *Collegeville Bible Commentary*, played an important role in empowering lay Catholics to read the Bible with historical and literary sensitivity.

This state of affairs among Catholic laypeople in the US has not been sustainable, however, for a variety of reasons. One I want to highlight here is that, since the late 1980s, the theological viewpoints of many active US Catholics have become more aligned with those of Evangelical Protestants. As discussed in chapter 1, the work of Steven Millies shows how political and social issues, abortion being the premier one, led a large number of American Catholics—both clergy and laity—to partner politically, and to a certain extent theologically, with Evangelical Protestants (themselves the descendants of the religious opponents of Clarence Darrow in the Scopes Monkey Trial), beginning in the 1980s and continuing to this day.[50] Here is where our discussion of the Bible in the Catholic Church meets up with the narrative about the Reformation and the rise of critical biblical studies earlier in this

[49] Paul VI, *Dei Verbum* (Dogmatic Constitution on Divine Revelation) 22, The Holy See (November 18, 1965), https://www.vatican.va/archive/hist_councils/ii_vatican_council/documents/vat-ii_const_19651118_dei-verbum_en.html.

[50] Steven Millies, *Good Intentions: A History of Catholic Voters' Road from Roe to Trump* (Collegeville, MN: Liturgical Press, 2018), 29–61.

chapter and with the discussion in chapter 1 about where we are and how we got here.

One or Many

The Reformation was a conflict over multiple issues, one of them being the source of authority for Christian life. For Luther and the other Reformers, the Bible was the primary and final authority for the individual Christian. The biblical text, containing both divine disclosure (what God is like) and divine communication (what God wants us to do), was indispensable. A logical presupposition was that the Bible was clear in what God wanted us to know and to do. How could it be otherwise, given that it was necessary for salvation? This understanding of the Bible as both clear and necessary meant that the role of the Christian church was to provide individual Christians with access to the Bible and to encourage and support their reading. The Christian church's mission was to preach the Gospel, found in its fullness in the Scriptures; the church could be said to exist for the sake of the Bible. Conversely, prior to the Reformation, and for centuries afterward, the Catholic Church understood itself as the means of salvation, through the sacraments, and the Bible as a resource for doctrine and dogma. As such, it was the purview of trained clerics with the expertise to correctly interpret a text that was seen as containing hidden depths. Lay Catholics encountered the biblical text in clearly defined contexts: prayers taken from the Bible, such as the Our Father, psalms selected and arranged in a Book of Hours, or Sunday Gospel readings. These contexts functioned as guardrails to prevent improper or even independent interpretation of the text. The church's maintenance of Latin as the language of liturgy and, to a great extent, private prayer and devotion, further ensured that the faithful saw the biblical text as first and foremost the church's book, preserved and read in the boundaries set by the church. There is an underlying tension in these different approaches to the biblical text, a dilemma between the two goods of accessibility to the text and uniformity of interpretation. If the Bible is God's Word to a fallen humanity, then it stands to reason that people should have access to it. This was the position of the

Reformers. However, the greater the accessibility to the text, the greater the number of interpretations generated, which results in the fracturing of the reading community. Consequently, to preserve the unity of the group, the range of interpretations should be limited. This was the approach of the Catholic Church from Trent to Vatican II.

This isn't to say that Luther and the other Reformers didn't see the potential problems that expanded accessibility to the biblical text could lead to. As we saw above, when faced with divergent interpretations in Zurich, Ulrich Zwingli doubled down on the newfound interest in biblical languages and judged interpretations based on how well they were grounded in the Hebrew and Greek text of the Bible. Luther took a different and more traditional route. Mark D. Thompson charts how Luther's biblical interpretation developed throughout his life, moving away from the medieval tradition's fourfold sense of Scripture but never abandoning the ancient principle that read much of the Old Testament as referring to Jesus. The significant shift that Thompson describes is the distinction Luther made between law and gospel in his biblical interpretation. Building on the older distinction between the letter and the spirit of the text, first articulated by Paul in 2 Corinthians 3 and used to distinguish literal from allegorical readings, Luther reconfigured this distinction and used the two terms to designate different kinds of content in the Bible.[51] Simply put, for Luther, the law and gospel distinction was found throughout the Bible, summed up by the observation that "whatever contains promises is a book of the Gospel; where commandments are found, we have a book of law."[52] Because for Luther, gospel held greater authority

[51] Mark D. Thompson, "Biblical Interpretation in the Works of Martin Luther," in Alan J. Hauser and Duane Frederick Watson, eds., *A History of Biblical Interpretation*, vol. 2 (Grand Rapids, MI: Eerdmans, 2009), 299–318: "Letter and spirit were not so much two levels of meaning as two elements in a dynamic, which can be traced throughout the OT and the NT. Both are at work in the single literal sense of the text" (Thompson, "Biblical Interpretation," 309). The Pauline text is 2 Cor 3:5-6: "Our competence is from God, who has made us competent to be ministers of a new covenant, not of letter but of spirit; for the letter kills, but the Spirit gives life."

[52] Quoted in Thompson ("Biblical Interpretation," 310) from Luther's 1540 published sermon on Matt 11:2-10 (LW 11.72–97).

than law, which could only underscore the inability of humanity to live up to the law's requirements, this distinction provided a method of adjudicating between competing interpretations and negotiating contradictions in the Bible without recourse to allegorical reading or abandoning the principle of the Bible's clarity.

For its part, the Catholic Church took a little longer to acknowledge the worth of widespread access to the Bible by laypeople. Vatican II's Dogmatic Constitution on Divine Revelation (*Dei Verbum*) was one of the first documents brought forward for debate in 1962 but one of the last texts approved at the council's final session in 1965. The struggle over its editorial history at the council is a fascinating story in itself.[53] Of relevance to our discussion are three statements of *Dei Verbum* regarding biblical authority and interpretation. First, and most importantly, the council affirmed the primacy of the divine Word in the life of the church, stating clearly that the magisterium "is not above the word of God, but serves it" (*DV* 10) and that the church venerates the biblical text in the same way as it does the Blessed Sacrament (*DV* 21). For those familiar with the history outlined in this chapter, the message is unmistakable: the Bible is more than the sourcebook for dogma and is not secondary to the sacraments in the lives of Christians. Second, in addition to mandating continuous and easy access to the biblical text for all the faithful, as mentioned above, *Dei Verbum* goes further in acknowledging that the encounter with the text by the lay faithful yields authentic insight into the meaning of the Scriptures: "For there is a growth in the understanding of the realities and the words which have been handed down. This happens through the contemplation and study made by believers, who treasure these things in their hearts through a penetrating understanding of the spiritual realities which they experience" (*DV* 8). There is no denying that these are significant developments in official Catholic teaching on biblical interpretation, but alongside these statements *Dei Verbum* also affirms the authoritative role of the institutional church in authenticating and guaranteeing right interpretation. Quite literally in the same sentences

[53] For a discussion of this document's history at the council, see Ronald D. Witherup, *Scripture: Dei Verbum* (Mahwah, NJ: Paulist, 2006).

where the above quoted phrases occur, the council reasserts that, while the teaching office serves the Word of God, "the task of authentically interpreting the word of God, whether written or handed on, has been entrusted exclusively to the living teaching office of the Church" (*DV* 10) and that, while the interpretations of the lay faithful lead to greater understanding of the biblical revelation, it also reaffirms that it is in "the preaching of those who have received . . . Episcopal succession" where one can be certain of the sure gift of truth" (*DV* 9).

Conclusion

The impetus for this book, as described in the introduction and chapter 1, is to describe the origins and state of biblical interpretation among US Christians in general and Catholics in particular. It assumes that the current state of biblical interpretation in this context is flawed, in part mired in the paths laid down in the debates over slavery and racial equality and in part, as I have detailed in this chapter, over the insular and limited nature of the way academic biblical study has been practiced for the past two centuries. Despite the widespread teaching of academic biblical studies in Protestant universities and seminaries across the country for close to 150 years and in Catholic institutions for at least fifty years, most Americans are still unfamiliar with this approach to the Bible. There exists "a great divide" between what biblical scholars do with the text and what nonacademic Bible readers want when they go to the text.[54] And while this disconnect manifests itself in different ways, the fundamental reason for it is that the majority of Bible readers come to the text with different assumptions, expectations, and questions than those of biblical scholars.

For Christians, the Bible is ultimately a single book with a single, divine author. This in part is due to the fact that we encounter the

[54] I borrow this phrase from Barbara E. Walvoord, who, in a large survey of faculty and students in introductory religion courses, noted the disconnect between students, who came to the class wanting to explore ultimate questions of meaning, and faculty, who wanted students to acquire skills in critical thinking and analysis (Walvoord, *Teaching and Learning in College Introductory Religion Courses* [Oxford: Blackwell, 2008]).

Bible as a single book, but even before that became technologically possible with the invention of printing in the fifteenth century, people still understood the Scriptures as a coherent set of writings with a unity of theme and purpose. As we saw in this chapter, critical biblical studies began with the identification of different sources behind the biblical texts, founded upon the identification of differences—in language, theology, theme, or details. This method has been the dominant one for two centuries in the field, and to this day biblical scholarship engages in or assumes the presence of earlier sources, or editorial insertions, in practically every biblical book. Scholarship's view of the Bible as an anthology of different texts with different authors, often with competing viewpoints, is at odds with the traditional view of most Bible readers of the Bible as a single text. Timothy Beal's book addresses this disconnect, and he urges his readers to acknowledge the Bible as a "polyvocal" text that "canonizes contradiction" and places dialogue at the heart of the religious life and theological dialogue.[55]

This is easier said than done, as the dominant understanding of the Bible (what Beal calls the Bible's iconic image) is the traditional one. This is apparent in the Pew Research Center research data cited in the introduction about the surprisingly large number of Americans who believe that it is both feasible and desirable for the Bible to be used in the creation of civil laws. But also, and despite five hundred years of focus on the "plain sense" of Scripture, the assumption of the text's sacredness—and hence its ongoing relevance—also means that symbolic readings or attempts to find the deeper (i.e., directly relevant) meaning of the biblical text have persisted. We still read allegorically, although academics find it problematic.[56] Interestingly, readers are for the most part allergic

[55] Timothy Beal, *The Rise and Fall of the Bible: The Unexpected History of an Accidental Book* (New York: Houghton Mifflin, 2012). "The Bible canonizes contradiction. It holds together a tense diversity of perspectives and voices, difference and argument—even and especially, as we have seen, when it comes to the profoundest questions of faith, questions that inevitably outlive all their answers. The Bible interprets itself, argues with itself, and perpetually frustrates any desire to reduce it to univocality" (173).

[56] For example, Timothy Troutner notes that modern scholars dismiss Origen's biblical interpretation as unhistorical, but then tries to demonstrate Origen's ongoing relevance by applying a principle of progressive revelation to make

to allegory in texts other than the Bible. Authors certainly are. Famously, in the preface to the second printing of *The Lord of the Rings*, J. R. R. Tolkien strongly pushed back against readers who saw the trilogy as an elaborate allegory of the Second World War.[57] But when it comes to the Bible, readers expect and resonate with symbolic or nonliteral readings. In his book-length study of Martin Luther King Jr.'s preaching, Richard Lischer demonstrates how King drew more from the African-American interpretive tradition than he did from his graduate courses in modern biblical analysis.[58] This stands to reason. When seen as a single text with a single, divine author, the Bible's meaning is assumed to be timeless, essential, and existentially relevant to the reader. This is not necessarily the case when one sees the Bible as a collection of ancient texts with different authors from different times and with different viewpoints. At its best, the historical-critical method works as a control on certain interpretations, but as we have seen, most Bible readers do not have ready access to this scholarship. And if they do, there is still the need for a second step, a move from the conclusions of what a text's meaning was when it was written to the text's meaning now. In their 1993 document discussed above, the Pontifical Biblical Commission calls this process "actualization," which refers to the rereading of texts "in the light of new circum-

---

Origen's approach more palatable to modern scholarship (Troutner, "Sowing Seeds of Progressive Revelation: Origen on the Knowledge of the Prophets," *Scottish Journal of Theology* 75 [2022]: 123–36).

[57] "As for any inner meaning or 'message,' it has in the intention of the author none. It is neither allegorical nor topical. . . . But I cordially dislike allegory in all its manifestations, and always have done so since I grew old and wary enough to detect its presence. I much prefer history, true or feigned, with its varied applicability to the thought and experience of readers. I think that many confuse 'applicability' with 'allegory'; but the one resides in the freedom of the reader, and the other in the purposed domination of the author" (J. R. R. Tolkien, *The Fellowship of the Ring* [Boston: Houghton Mifflin, 1954], xiv). Less subtly, here is Ernest Hemingway's response to attempts to find symbolism in *The Old Man and the Sea*: "There isn't any symbolism. The sea is the sea. The old man is an old man. The boy is a boy and the fish is a fish. The sharks are all sharks no better and no worse. All the symbolism that people say is shit" (Hemingway, letter to Bernard Berenson, September 13, 1952, in Carlos Baker, ed., *Ernest Hemingway: Selected Letters 1917–1961* [New York: Scribner, 2003], 780–81).

[58] Richard Lischer, *The Preacher King: Martin Luther King, Jr. and the Word That Moved America* (New York: Oxford University Press, 1995), 198–205.

stances and applied to the contemporary situation of the people of God."[59] This is, in effect, a return to the ways of reading the biblical text discussed in chapter 3, such as Daniel's reinterpretation of Jeremiah's prophecy or the Qumran *pesharim*. As a solution, this is less than satisfactory, because such reading ignores the significance of the historical biblical authors and their intended meanings. The fact that most Bible readers are unfamiliar with biblical scholarship doesn't render it irrelevant.

The Reformers' focus on the plain sense was founded on the conviction that the Bible was necessary for salvation and that, as such, was intended by God to be comprehensible. The Bible's necessity and clarity rendered the long centuries of allegorical reading and resulting theological and doctrinal assertions obsolete and asserted that they were fundamental misinterpretations of the Bible. The subsequent rise of academic biblical study was meant to use the Bible as something other than an authoritative book for Christians, but the theological consequences of that kind of analysis couldn't be ignored, despite the mutually reinforcing barriers erected by churches and academics. The happy collaboration between the Catholic Church and biblical scholarship initiated sixty years ago has proven, I think, to be an exception to the inevitable journey that has brought us to the current state of affairs. A large number of Americans of all religious groups or none see the Bible as an authority, communicating rules to live by or disclosing what God is like. They see it as a necessary resource for constructing a better society and refer to it when debating pressing social issues. This has always been the case in the US. Is there a way we can stop the seemingly constant cycle in which people on opposite sides of issues rely on the Bible to support their respective positions? We have seen that both the Reformers and the Catholic Church relied on interpretive guardrails with the hope of squaring the circle between advocating widespread access to the biblical text and preserving doctrinal unity. Are there any other possible guardrails that would work in the US social landscape, where Bible readers of many Christian denominations or none look to the text for guidance?

[59] Béchard, *Scripture Documents*, 303.

Chapter 5

Reading from the Outside In

It's worth stopping at this point to recap the discussion thus far. All interpretation is a creative act, but not a solitary act. It occurs in the interaction between texts (or readers) and readers (or hearers), all of whom are influenced by their own cultural and historical contexts, which shape the assumptions they bring to the interpretive act. From its beginnings, the Bible has been a site of interpretation insofar as the collection of texts in the biblical canon are assembled based on interpretive choices and many of them engage in interpretation with others in the collection. In the words of Timothy Beal, "the Bible is interpretation all the way down."[1] The history of Christian biblical interpretation can be understood as the process on a spectrum, with the biblical text on one end and limitless interpretations on the other. Because the biblical text is understood as inspired and normative, reading communities navigate between the two poles of staying rooted to the sacred text while also acknowledging its ongoing relevance and authority. A watershed moment in the history of this process is the Reformation's call to be grounded in the literal meaning of the text, an attempt to move down the spectrum closer to one of the poles. An unintended consequence of this focus on the biblical text's literal meaning has been the rise and flourishing of the field of academic biblical studies, which has used and developed literary, historical, linguistic, and other scholarly methods over the past three centuries. Because

[1] Timothy Beal, *The Rise and Fall of the Bible: The Unexpected History of an Accidental Book* (New York: Houghton Mifflin, 2012), 101.

of the doctrinal conflicts inherent in the work of academic biblical studies, the field has increasingly separated itself from the interpretive life of the various Christian communities. Today, most Americans, whether practicing Christians or not, view the Bible as an authoritative text that offers specific guidelines to pressing moral questions and social issues. Their interpretive strategies are practically divorced from the methods and results of academic biblical study but owe more to the interpretive strategies that hardened in the conflict over slavery in the nineteenth century. The Bible's authority and interpretive power is thus subsumed under the ideologies still at war in our polarized culture, albeit over different issues than that of the antebellum US. The way out lies in the search for an external interpretive principle from which the diverse and often confusing biblical material can be fruitfully used in informing our collective thinking about moral and social issues. Both the Catholic and Reformation churches sought to find this principle in doctrinal concepts that would allow for the ongoing relevance of the biblical text for believers without being locked into the strictly historical dimension revealed by academic biblical studies.

This chapter will further explore those doctrinal concepts which, along with other external standards, function as interpretive guardrails that limit the ways the text can be interpreted with theological, ethical, or other values that stand outside of the text and, at least implicitly, exert authority over the biblical material. These boundaries are the good fences that make for good readers mentioned below, or that at least try to do so. We have already touched upon some of the older methods in chapters 3–4, such as the early Christian strategy of reading Jesus typologically into Old Testament narratives or Martin Luther's adaptation of the law-gospel distinction to separate biblical texts into two categories of different theological force. In this chapter we will look closely at the old idea of the rule of faith as a guardrail to interpretation before moving to a discussion of more recent scholarly and academic attempts at using the Bible to shape and support contemporary ethical positions. This latter discussion will bring us back to the beginning of the book and the problems inherent in how contemporary American Christians use the Bible to debate morally fraught social issues.

Good Fences Make Good Readers

One of the first things students in undergraduate biblical studies classes learn is that communities precede their authoritative texts because they are the groups that produce those texts. So too has official Catholic teaching stressed that the New Testament is the product of the early church and is therefore an expression of a faith that already existed and not just the source of the faith. This is most definitively and fully expressed in Vatican II's Dogmatic Constitution on Divine Revelation (*Dei Verbum*). In the preceding chapter I discussed how *Dei Verbum* marked a watershed moment in the Catholic Church regarding the authority of the Bible and the need for widespread access to the biblical text by all the lay faithful. Introduced in the fall of 1962 at the first session of the council, the original draft reaffirmed the Council of Trent's claim that there are two sources of revelation: Scripture and tradition. This position was Trent's rejection of the Reformers' claim that the Bible alone (*sola scriptura*) was the source of revelation and the ultimate authority in the life of the Christian community. The 1962 draft was rejected by the bishops at the council and work commenced on a new document. The two theologians who emerged as some of the main architects of this new draft were the Dominican theologian Yves Congar and the young German priest Joseph Ratzinger, who later became Pope Benedict XVI.[2] Congar had published an important book in 1960 that argued that tradition was the very identity of the church that was passed on from generation to the next and not simply a body of teachings identifiable as something separate from the Bible.[3] Ratzinger, whose theological influence would grow after the council, had already written a book dealing with the theology of history. Congar and Ratzinger, along with other

[2] In addition to Congar and Ratzinger, other theologians who either wrote detailed critiques of the first draft or contributed language to the new document include Edward Schillebeeckx, Beda Rigaux, Karl Rahner, and Jean Daniélou. See the detailed discussion in Jared Wicks, SJ, "Vatican II on Revelation—From Behind the Scenes," *Theological Studies* 71 (2010): 637–50.

[3] Yves Congar, *La Tradition et Les Traditions: Essai Historique* (Paris: Fayard, 1960), issued in translation as *Tradition and Traditions: An Historical and a Theological Essay*, trans. Michael Naseby and Thomas Rainborough (London: Burnes and Oates, 1966).

theologians, set about reorienting the Catholic understanding of revelation, and their efforts both created an ecumenical bridge with the Reformation churches and provided Catholic theology with a more nuanced, historically accurate, and long-term expression of the relationship between the church and the Bible.

This is not the place to discuss the entire contents of *Dei Verbum*. What concerns us is the document's second chapter, "Handing on Divine Revelation," which makes three important points:

First, revelation is not found primarily in the Bible, but in the person of Jesus, whom John's Gospel calls the Word of God. Both the life and teachings of Jesus constitute the fullness of revelation and he imparted this to the apostles—the nascent Christian community. The apostles and their successors, whom the Catholic Church understands to be bishops, are therefore entrusted with the transmission of the life and teachings of Jesus.

Second, it is from the preaching of the apostles that Scripture arises. Scripture is a part of the larger tradition originating with Jesus and handed on by the church. "Sacred tradition and Sacred Scripture form one sacred deposit of the word of God" (*DV* 10) whose "divine wellspring" is the life and teaching of Jesus.[4] Moreover, "through the same tradition the Church's full canon of the sacred books is known, and the sacred writings themselves are more profoundly understood and unceasingly made active in her" (*DV* 8). This affirms the idea that the Christian community precedes the writing and collection of the biblical text but goes further. *Dei Verbum* understands tradition—rooted in the person of Jesus—as the source not only of Scripture, but also of the interpretation

[4] Paul VI, *Dei Verbum* (Dogmatic Constitution on Divine Revelation), The Holy See (November 18, 1965), https://www.vatican.va/archive/hist_councils/ii_vatican_council/documents/vat-ii_const_19651118_dei-verbum_en.html. More fully: "Hence there exists a close connection and communication between sacred tradition and Sacred Scripture. For both of them, flowing from the same divine wellspring, in a certain way merge into a unity and tend toward the same end. For Sacred Scripture is the word of God inasmuch as it is consigned to writing under the inspiration of the divine Spirit, while sacred tradition takes the word of God entrusted by Christ the Lord and the Holy Spirit to the Apostles, and hands it on to their successors in its full purity, so that led by the light of the Spirit of truth, they may in proclaiming it preserve this word of God faithfully, explain it, and make it more widely known" (*DV* 9).

of Scripture. The process of revelation, then, is not simply content, but the means of interpreting that content, with the very first act of interpretation being the collection and arrangement of that content into the biblical canon.

Third, and perhaps most importantly, *Dei Verbum*'s view of the interpretive role of tradition allows for adaptation. The relevant section is worth quoting in full:

> This tradition which comes from the Apostles develops in the Church with the help of the Holy Spirit. For there is a growth in the understanding of the realities and the words which have been handed down. This happens through the contemplation and study made by believers, who treasure these things in their hearts through a penetrating understanding of the spiritual realities which they experience, and through the preaching of those who have received through Episcopal succession the sure gift of truth. For as the centuries succeed one another, the Church constantly moves forward toward the fullness of divine truth until the words of God reach their complete fulfillment in her. (*DV* 8)

Basing itself on the inexhaustibility of the biblical text, a belief that supported centuries of allegorical and symbolic interpretation, *Dei Verbum* allows for interpretations to develop both through the preaching of the institutional church but also, importantly, through the ongoing engagement of the texts by all the faithful. Interpretation is not only part of the process of revelation but is itself a process that grows and changes over time.[5]

By uniting the long-separated concepts of Scripture and tradition, *Dei Verbum* sought to move away from Trent's bifurcated understanding of those concepts and to build a bridge to the Reformation emphasis on the priority of Scripture but without sacrificing magisterial authority. Consequently, *Dei Verbum* states plainly that the church's "teaching office is not above the word of God, but serves it, teaching only what has been handed on, listening to it devoutly,

[5] I'm aware that use of the word "change" may be problematic, and that the council avoided this term so as not to imply that essential teachings could ever change. I take up this question of change below.

guarding it scrupulously and explaining it faithfully . . . it draws from this *one deposit of faith* everything which it presents for belief as divinely revealed." At the same time, however, *Dei Verbum* also reaffirms Trent's assertion that the institutional church alone is the judge of Scripture's true meaning: "the task of authentically interpreting the word of God, whether written or handed on, has been entrusted *exclusively* to the living teaching office of the Church" (*DV* 10, emphasis added).[6]

What this brief discussion of a portion of *Dei Verbum* seeks to show is how contemporary Catholic teaching seeks to affirm the primacy of the Bible and to allow for ongoing biblical interpretation, but within stated limits. This is a strategy with a long pedigree and was referred to most often over the centuries as the rule of faith. This term, which is used by both early Greek and Latin theologians as far back as the second century, refers to doctrinal affirmations that will appear later in the various creeds and that function as a standard for the proper interpretation of the Bible. For example, here is Irenaeus of Lyons, writing in the late second century:

> This then is the order of the rule of our faith . . . God, the Father, not made, not material, invisible; one God, the creator of all things . . . The Word of God, Son of God, Christ Jesus our Lord, who was manifested to the prophets according to the form of their prophesying and according to the method of the dispensation of the Father: through whom all things were made; who also at the end of the times, to complete and gather up all things, was made man among men, visible and tangible, in order to abolish death and show forth life and produce a community of union between God and man . . . The Holy Spirit, through whom the prophets prophesied, and the fathers learned the things of God, and the righteous were led forth into the way of righteousness; and who in the end of the times

[6] In its affirmation that "Holy Mother Church is the judge of the true sense and interpretation of the Sacred Scriptures" (Decree Concerning the Edition and the Use of the Sacred Books), Trent's message was clear: it repudiated everything that Luther, Calvin, and their followers were claiming about the Bible. On the other hand, *Dei Verbum* seeks to affirm the Reformation principles of the primacy of Scripture and its efficacy in the lives of the lay faithful while preserving the magisterium's role as the ultimate judge in biblical interpretation.

> was poured out in a new way a upon mankind in all the earth, renewing man unto God.[7]

This rule of faith is used to correctly interpret the Scriptures.[8] Elsewhere, Irenaeus describes the Christian "who keeps unchangeable the Rule of the Truth received through baptism" and, by virtue of this, can both "recognize the names and sayings and parables from the Scriptures" used by (for Irenaeus) heterodox Christians, while also rejecting their "blasphemous" interpretations of the biblical text.[9]

This is expanded by Augustine in his work on biblical interpretation, *De Doctrina Christiana*. For Augustine, the rule of faith constitutes those essential truths of Christianity that have come to us first from the unambiguous portions of the Bible and second from the authority of the church (*De Doct Christ*, 3.2.2).[10] It is important to notice here that Augustine understands the Bible to be consistent in its theological message but varied in its level of interpretive difficulty. There are easier and more difficult parts of the Bible to read, but regardless of their relative complexity, they each individually and all together teach the same faith.[11] Augustine is here applying the, already in his time, ancient practice of using Scripture to interpret Scripture, which itself derived most likely from

[7] Irenaeus, *The Demonstration of the Apostolic Preaching*, trans. Armitage Robinson (New York: Macmillan, 1920), 21.

[8] "Scripture, then, is an excellent source for the Rule of Faith. It is divine and must be believed. But the Scriptures are not always clear, nor did all of Scripture exist from the beginning. Hence it is not an absolute Rule of Faith. Scripture is ultimately subject to the criterion of tradition, of the doctrine of the Church, of the Rule of Truth itself" (Dominic Unger, introduction to *St. Irenaeus of Lyons: Against the Heresies Book 1* [New York: Newman Press, 1992], 10).

[9] Irenaeus, *Adv. Haer* 1.9.4. Translation in Unger, *St. Irenaeus of Lyons*, 48.

[10] Augustine is not referring to papal or curial authority, which was not universally recognized in the church of his day. Rather, church authority encompasses what is believed by a majority of the churches in his day, with precedence given to those churches of an earlier foundation (see *De Doctrina Christiana*, 2.8.12). Vincent of Lerins, born some fifteen years after Augustine, developed an influential motto for defining tradition as that which has been believed "everywhere, always, and by everyone" ("quod ubique, quod semper, quod ab omnibus").

[11] Augustine makes this point throughout *De Doctrina Christiana*, e.g., 2.6.7-8; 2.9.14.

Greek interpretation of Homer, discussed in chapter 3. Augustine affirms that we are obligated to discover the authors' intentions behind the words but that authorial intent is not the final arbiter of the texts' meaning. In some cases we are bound to go beyond an author's intended meaning, as for example when Augustine advises readers always to read metaphorically certain theologically rich terms, such as *sabbath* or *sacrifice*, since to read them as referring only to the seventh day of the week or an act of ancient religious worship is to miss their point entirely (*De Doct Christ*, 3.5.9). Naturally, the long-standing Christian practice of reading Jesus symbolically into the texts of the Old Testament, which Augustine also advocated, is another example of going beyond an author's intended meaning.

This ancient concept of the rule of faith is encompassed in *Dei Verbum*'s description of tradition, which embraces the Scriptures and guides their proper interpretation so that "sacred tradition, Sacred Scripture and the teaching authority of the Church, in accord with God's most wise design, are so linked and joined together that one cannot stand without the others" (*DV* 10). This standard for proper biblical interpretation comes from *outside* the Bible and functions as a necessary limit on interpretation ("one cannot stand without the other") because the Bible is an ancient and foreign collection of documents that originated across several centuries. Significantly, this strategy creates an external standard by which biblical texts are interpreted, in which case the standard can be said to have more authority than the text.

Protestant doctrine, which does not give tradition significant authoritative weight, derives the rule of faith from the Bible itself. For example, the Smalcald Articles, a statement of doctrine written by Martin Luther in 1537, states that "the Word of God shall establish articles of faith, and no one else, not even an angel."[12] Similar statements are found in the Second Helvetic Confession (1562) and the Westminster Confession (1646), both Calvinist documents, and in the Anglican Thirty-Nine Articles (1571).[13] This

[12] https://bookofconcord.org/smalcald-articles/ii/#sa-ii-ii-0015.

[13] Charles Dodge, *Systematic Theology*, vol. 1 (Grand Rapids, MI: Eerdmans, 1940; originally New York: Charles Scribner's, 1871), 151–53.

creates a problem, however, in that the proper interpretation of the Bible is the problem that the Bible as the rule of faith is supposed to solve. Protestant thinkers were aware of this and addressed it in a couple of ways. Here we can see a reliance on Augustine's strategy of interpreting difficult parts of the Bible on the basis of more clear passages. As we saw in the last chapter, Luther used the dichotomy between law and gospel, with the latter having more authority, to adjudicate between biblical texts and their meanings. Luther seems to be building on the idea from Augustine. This reliance on the clear parts of the Bible implicitly moves to a privileging of those texts in terms of what the biblical message is. In other words, *clear* quickly becomes a term that also encompasses *authoritative*. This results in what is often referred to as a canon within a canon—the idea that, while all the biblical texts are holy and authoritative, some are more so than others on the basis of their content, determined by external criteria brought to the text by the reader. For Luther, the "gospel" component of the entire Bible comprised those texts that contained what he called "promises" and, importantly, that he held to be more theologically significant than the texts he classified as "law." But this classification depended upon how Luther sorted these texts and required him to base his criteria on the particular way he interpreted certain biblical texts as essential—in this case the writings of Paul—regarding the contrast between law and gospel. In other words, although the dichotomy claims a biblical pedigree, the criteria by which Luther distinguished between law and gospel were determined by his own external criteria on how to sort them.[14] Luther and later Reformers also expanded Augustine's idea of reliance upon the clear parts of Scriptures and, seemingly, combined it with the belief we find in Irenaeus of the baptized Christian's ability to correctly interpret the Bible, to make the claim that, to the faithful Christian, all of the Bible taught clearly *what was necessary for salvation*. In other words, what Christian readers most needed from the Bible was accessible. The obvious problem with this, of course, is

[14] Luther also included the Creed—a nonbiblical text—as part of the rule of faith (Todd R. Hains, *Martin Luther and the Rule of Faith: Reading God's Word for God's People* [Downers Grove, IL: IVP Academic, 2022]).

that baptized Christians do not all agree on how biblical texts should be interpreted or even on which ones are clear. Clear to whom? And clear about what? Here we see the tension that was highlighted by the Reformation's call for universal access to the Bible by the faithful: the more readers there are, the more interpretations and, hence, the greater potential for reduced doctrinal uniformity among believers. Navigating this tension is part of the reason for the rule of faith, in that it is intended to instill in readers a standard that limits interpretations to an acceptable range of options and brings about intra-ecclesial uniformity. In the words of Charles Cosgrove, "In theory the rule of faith is the clear teaching of scripture; in fact, it is an orthodox conception of the essential teachings of scripture."[15] This standard is based on something external to the Bible, despite its claims to be biblical. In response to this problem and to the lack of theological potential in much historical-critical work on the Bible, there has arisen an approach called the theological interpretation of Scripture (TIS), which is a return by Protestant theologians to the early understanding of the rule of faith as an external standard by which to interpret the Bible.[16]

The external nature of the rule of faith for interpreting the Bible is a feature and not a bug of biblical interpretation; it is necessary for interpretation to happen. For Christians it has been essential from day one, given that Christian reading of the Jewish Scriptures required interpretations that supported the belief in Jesus as the Son of God and were informed by that very same belief. The interpretive principles and strategies discussed above in chapter 3 are examples of this, although they were not always referred to as "the rule of faith." Nor are they always referred to by that term today, although this reading strategy is evident throughout Christian history. Recall Frederick Douglass's distinction between the

[15] Charles Cosgrove, *Appealing to Scripture in Moral Debate: Five Hermeneutical Rules* (Grand Rapids, MI: Eerdmans, 2002), 160.

[16] "Practitioners of TIS respect external theological parameters as guides for interpretation. If one writes in and for the church, it is legitimate to be bound by ecclesiastical confessions, argue TIS authors" (Robert Plummer, "Contra Origen: Martin Luther on Allegorizing the Biblical Text," in Robert L. Plummer and Channing L. Crisler, eds., *Always Reforming: Reflections on Martin Luther and Biblical Studies* [Bellingham, WA: Lexham Press, 2021], 16).

false Christianity of North American slaveowners and "the Christianity of Christ." Both could point to biblical texts for support, but one was clearly immoral.[17] In the same way, Martin Luther King Jr. "ultimately let the *church* guide his interpretation of Scripture. When the Bible is read as the church's book, the interpreter always works within the boundaries of the church's convictions about God."[18]

In Catholic moral theology since Vatican II, we see not only the reaffirmation of tradition and the magisterium as external standards of biblical interpretation, but also a focus on particular biblical texts as clear or particularly important in this endeavor. In his 1993 encyclical on Catholic moral teaching, *Veritatis Splendor*, Pope John Paul II affirms the foundational nature of the Ten Commandments in Exodus 20 and the Beatitudes of Matthew 5–7.[19] Fifteen years later the Pontifical Biblical Commission would make these same two texts the pillars of their detailed document on the Bible and morality.[20] The document views the Bible as a book of revealed morality with a single overarching message that is fulfilled in the New Testament revelation. While modern historical and literary insights of biblical scholarship are used, they are subsumed under this larger theological purpose.[21] This in part explains the length

[17] Frederick Douglass, *Narrative of the Life of Frederick Douglass, An American Slave* (Boston: Anti-Slavery Office, 1845), 118.

[18] Richard Lischer, *The Preacher King: Martin Luther King, Jr. and the Word That Moved America* (New York: Oxford University Press, 1995), 210.

[19] John Paul II, *Veritatis Splendor* (Encyclical Letter Regarding Certain Fundamental Questions of the Church's Moral Teaching) 12, August 6, 1993, https://www.vatican.va/content/john-paul-ii/en/encyclicals/documents/hf_jp-ii_enc_06081993_veritatis-splendor.html. It is noteworthy that every section of the encyclical is prefaced by a brief biblical quotation in a manner used for centuries by Christian authors, i.e., as a starting point for theological reflection with little attention to the text's context in the Bible.

[20] Pontifical Biblical Commission, "The Bible and Morality: Biblical Roots of Christian Conduct," May 11, 2008, https://www.vatican.va/roman_curia/congregations/cfaith/pcb_documents/rc_con_cfaith_doc_20080511_bibbia-e-morale_en.html.

[21] Which the commission notes: "It is certainly a delicate project, the reason being that the biblical canon is a complex collection of inspired texts, a collection of books by different authors dating back to very diverse epochs; they express a multitude of theological views, at times in a context of legislation or of prescriptive dicta; at other times they are narratives illustrating the revelation of the

and complexity of this text. The application portion of the document begins with the enumeration of two "fundamental criteria" based on the two paradigmatic biblical texts: "The two basic texts set at the head of our document, the Decalogue and the beatitudes, will serve to illustrate the two general criteria for precisely the reason that they possess a foundational character on the literary as well as on the theological level" (94). The Ten Commandments are the foundational text for the first fundamental criteria of "conformity with the biblical concept of human nature," while the Beatitudes underlie the second fundamental criteria of "conformity with the example of Jesus."[22]

To Know the Good and to Do It

To discuss how the Bible is used in contemporary debates about right behavior is to engage in an ethical exercise. In addition to appeal to the rule of faith in its many manifestations, another way that interpretations have been limited is by the use of external ethical concepts to both evaluate biblical texts and to seek how to apply them to present situations. The term *biblical ethics* refers to two separate but related interpretive process. The first involves articulating the ethical visions found in the Bible. This is a descriptive task which refrains from making any judgements about the quality or ongoing relevance of those ethical principles. The second process results in the development of a working ethical vision that is based all or in part on ethical principles derived from the Bible. This is a normative task which involves making claims about the continued relevance and moral force of some (but not all) ethical principles in the Bible.[23] Space prohibits a comprehen-

---

history of salvation; they also present concrete examples of moral conduct, whether positive or negative. Moreover, in the course of time they betray a diversified evolution and refinement of moral sensitivity and motivation" (Pontifical Biblical Commission, "Bible and Morality," 92).

[22] Pontifical Biblical Commission, "Bible and Morality," 95–102.

[23] I borrow this distinction from the way that biblical theology is bifurcated into descriptive and constructive approaches, first articulated in 1787 by Johann Philipp Gabler (John H. Hayes and Frederick Prussner, *Old Testament Theology: Its History and Development* [Atlanta: John Knox, 1985]).

sive review of the academic work done on biblical ethics, but I want to highlight some examples of the different ways this is undertaken by contemporary biblical scholars and theologians. This overview will demonstrate that, similar to the use of an external dogmatic standard to guide biblical interpretation, attempts to generate a biblically informed ethic rely on philosophical and moral principles derived from outside the Bible, which are used to limit and shape the reading of biblical texts.

Let's begin with examples of descriptive and normative approaches by two significant figures in modern biblical studies. First is John Barton's 2014 volume, *Ethics in Ancient Israel*. In the introduction, Barton makes clear the book's descriptive aim: "We are *not* concerned with any present applications" of ancient Israelite ethical thought.[24] To drive the point home, on the very last page of the volume, Barton writes: "Some readers will have been waiting, more or less patiently, for me to answer the question, How should we apply the 'ethics of the Old Testament' today? They have been disappointed so far and are going to continue to be disappointed."[25] That's not to say that Barton's agenda is purely descriptive. He is, on the one hand, critiquing a long-held theological view that saw biblical ethics as grounded only in the sovereign authority of God—that is, that something ought to be done simply and only because God demands it. At the same time, Barton wants to argue against the views of many scholars of antiquity who assert that ancient Israelite ethics is completely different from what we see in early Greek philosophical thought.[26] Consistent with how biblical scholarship works, which we discussed in previous chapters, Barton notes the tremendous diversity in the viewpoints found in the Bible and uses scholarly genre designations, such as wisdom literature or Deuteronomic thought,

[24] John Barton, *Ethics in Ancient Israel* (New York: Oxford University Press, 2014), 11. Italics in original. See also, "I am concerned with the Hebrew Bible or Old Testament not as the scriptures of Judaism or Christianity, but as evidence for the thinking of ancient Israelites and Jews" (Barton, *Ethics in Ancient Israel*, 4).

[25] Barton, *Ethics in Ancient Israel*, 276.

[26] "There was something in ancient Israel that corresponds, even if only inchoately, to the reflection on morality that would eventually become moral philosophy" (Barton, *Ethics in Ancient Israel*, 13).

to group texts. Significantly, Barton's description of the Bible's ethical content draws upon using outside concepts—virtue ethics, narrative ethics, divine-command theory, natural law. What Barton demonstrates is that the variety of biblical texts contain a range of ethical thinking. For instance, Barton notes multiple examples in the early Jewish literature to use the Bible to create "ethical digests," which reduce and summarize biblical ethics to a manageable size. He then goes on to identify these digests in the Bible itself, for example in Psalm 15, Job 31, Isaiah 3:10-11.[27] On the other hand, complex narratives such as the David story in 1–2 Samuel offer a sophisticated view of characters that show "unvarnished and complex characters for the reader/hearer to contemplate. They invite the audience to see the moral difficulties, and especially the interplay of moral choice with luck of divinely engineered fate that makes human life the complicated thing that it is."[28] There are two things to note about Barton's discussion. First is that, while Barton is engaged in a descriptive task in terms of the ethics in the Hebrew Bible, he is also making an argument on the worth of those texts in terms of their relationship with early Greek philosophy. His description supports the claim that the ethics of the ancient Israelites are not completely different from the rational philosophical thought of the ancient Greeks. This argument implies a value claim for the Bible as, at least in part, witness to philosophical or rational—as opposed to purely theological—ethical reflection, and that this is something that's good to think about the Bible. Second is that Barton relies extensively on historical-critical scholarship to date the biblical texts and to sort them into genres developed by biblical scholars, which he then subjects to analysis by ethical concepts drawn from outside the Bible.

Next is John J. Collins's 2019 book, *What Are Biblical Values?*[29] In contrast to Barton, although equally as clear about his intent from the outset, Collins affirms: "My purpose in this book is to examine

[27] Barton, *Ethics in Ancient Israel*, 227–44.

[28] Barton, *Ethics in Ancient Israel*, 171.

[29] John J. Collins, *What Are Biblical Values? What the Bible Says on Key Ethical Issues* (New Haven: Yale University Press, 2019). The book grew out of a course on biblical ethics that Collins taught at Yale Divinity School.

what the Bible actually says, what values the Bible actually affirms, on several key issues. . . . I am not attempting a descriptive account. . . . My interest is in the relevance of the ancient texts to modern situations."[30] Collins applies a number of external limiting factors to how the Bible's ethical content should be interpreted. He combines both the limits of the traditional role of faith with the insights of critical biblical scholarship's focus on grammatical and contextual issues. In this both-and approach, doctrine and scholarship combine to guide biblical interpretation. However, the overriding criterion for Collins seems to be ethical principles derived from sources other than the Bible that, when in conflict with the biblical text, take precedence. He states in his introduction that "the Bible needs to be placed in dialogue with everything we know about ethical living from other sources." In a discussion of whether the Bible can be said to support modern ethics surrounding the rights of women, he says that "if we find a particular biblical position reprehensible, the ethically responsible course is to say so, not to give the benefit of the doubt to whatever position we find congenial."[31] In other words, while Collins is not engaging in a descriptive account, neither is he treating the Bible as a unqualified normative text. Rather, he constructs an ethical worldview *with* the Bible and not *from* the Bible, using external criteria of justice and right behavior and highlighting biblical texts that support those standards.[32] Collins observes that the wide variety of viewpoints in the Bible requires that there be "some hierarchy, some criteria, by which the values can be assessed."[33]

I want to stress that the fact that Barton and Collins draw upon external ideas to make descriptive and normative claims about the Bible is not a criticism of their work. Rather, it demonstrates my claim that there is no other way to use the Bible in making moral arguments. The work of these two biblical scholars is

[30] Collins, *What Are Biblical Values?*, 2.

[31] Collins, *What Are Biblical Values?*, 15, 86.

[32] For example, Collins describes Matthew 25, where Jesus separates the sheep from the goats based on whether they aided the poor, hungry, sick, and imprisoned as "the bottom line on biblical values" (Collins, *What Are Biblical Values?*, 208).

[33] Collins, *What Are Biblical Values?*, 211.

representative of what other exegetes do.[34] Not surprisingly, it's also what we see in the work of Christian ethicists who draw on the Bible in their work. In an article surveying the state of biblical ethics as it is practiced by ethicists and biblical scholars, Lúcás Chan, a Catholic ethicist, notes the problems inherent in generating a biblical ethics based on the literary and ethical diversity of material in the Bible. In a survey of two major books on biblical ethics produced by biblical scholars, Chan points out that the authors insufficiently interact with the work of ethicists and do not ground their ethical assertions in external frameworks, for example, virtue ethics.[35] When he turns to the work of ethicists engaging the Bible in their work, Chan notes their "rather selective use of Scripture" and "less than satisfactory exegesis," along with too great a concern with "interpreting the text's meaning for the contemporary world than with first examining its original meaning to see whether the text can be rightly employed."[36] For Chan the root problem preventing a compelling articulation of biblical ethics is found in the disciplinary silos created by the highly technical academic training required of both biblical scholars and ethicists. He sketches out a program of continued integration and collaboration in the hope of bridging this gap and leading to a "thinking outside the box" that will engage multiple areas of theological study, such as ecological studies and sacramental theology alongside biblical studies and ethics—most specifically virtue ethics, with its focus narratives that allow values to be derived by watching how biblical characters act in certain situations, as opposed to the exclusive or dominant approach of looking at biblical rules and thinking about how to apply them today.[37]

[34] See the discussion in the introduction by Carly Crouch, ed., in *The Cambridge Companion to the Hebrew Bible and Ethics* (Cambridge, UK: Cambridge University Press, 2021), 1–5. She describes the volume as an attempt to bring together normative and descriptive approaches.

[35] Yiu Sing Lúcás Chan, "Biblical Ethics 3D," *Theological Studies* 76, no. 1 (2015): 115, discussing Richard B. Hays, *The Moral Vision of the New Testament* (San Francisco: HarperCollins, 1996), and Frank J. Matera, *New Testament Ethics: The Legacies of Jesus and Paul* (Louisville: Westminster John Knox, 1996).

[36] Chan, "Biblical Ethics 3D," 116.

[37] Yiu Sing Lúcás Chan, *The Ten Commandments and the Beatitudes: Biblical Studies and Ethics for Real Life* (Lanham, MD: Rowman & Littlefield, 2012).

Regarding the process of application of biblical rules, Charles Cosgrove sheds light on some important aspects of how scholars attempt to do this in moral debate. First is the essential distinction between a rule and its moral justification. While biblical rules are often justified by the simple fact of being in the Bible, Cosgrove notes too that all moral rules also have justifications grounded in particular values. For example, the biblical assertion that "whoever blesses a neighbor with a loud voice, rising early in the morning, will be counted as cursing" (Prov 27:14) is grounded in the justification that one should not rouse another person from sleep too early in the day. In turn, this justification is based upon the larger value that one ought to be good to their neighbors, to "bless" and not "curse" them. What is essential to understand is that the further one moves up this chain of rule to justification to value, the more authoritative the concepts become. Justifications carry more moral weight than the rules that express them. This is because, as Cosgrove notes, no rule can account for every conceivable situation, and consequently the justification is used to generate new rules for new situations that can in some way be said to be "faithful" to the Bible.[38] Importantly in this regard, there are some rules that in some situations ought to be broken in order to uphold the justification and underlying value the rule is meant to express. To return to the text from Proverbs, there are situations where one would be obligated to wake their neighbor early in the morning in order to do them good, for instance if their house were on fire. Specific sets of rules cannot foresee every situation, and that is why modern legal codes are constantly revised. The Bible, however, as a text with divine authority, cannot be explicitly emended. Instead, hermeneutical rules are used to adapt the Bible

[38] "The warrant for treating the justification for a biblical rule as weightier (for us) than the rule itself is that transferring biblical rules from their ancient cultural contexts into modern contexts tends to disrupt the relation between the rules and their justifications so severely that confidence in the rules is undermined (or ought to be)" (Cosgrove, *Appealing to Scripture*, 19). Cosgrove adds, however, that "[t]he question of weighting comes into play not as a general argument for taking scripture only at its highest levels of generality, but rather in those cases where a given level of generality calls for something different from the level(s) below it in view of changed circumstances in our time and place" (Cosgrove, *Appealing to Scripture*, 47).

to situations it did not foresee.[39] However, "sometimes the justifications for biblical moral rules . . . contain assumptions that we find morally problematic and that conflict with moral principles found elsewhere in the Bible."[40] Here Cosgrove notes the tension between the historical reality of the Bible being a collection of once separate writings with the theological belief that it is a single book with a single unifying message.

Cosgrove next emphasizes the necessity that moral argument function analogically and be case-based. To identify a biblical rule's underlying justification and then seek to formulate an applicable modern rule involves the creation of an analogy between the ancient situation and the modern one—a comparison of the two that seeks similarities by appeal to some third thing, not mentioned in the text. A common example is how Christians read the biblical prohibition against worship of other gods. In the context of ancient Israelite culture, the rule is literal: there are many gods available to honor, pray to, and sacrifice to. You may only honor, pray to, and sacrifice to the God of Israel. For contemporary Bible readers, this text does not apply at the rule level, because for the most part we do not live in a culture where there are multiple different gods to worship. Yet the repeated insistence of this prohibition in the Bible tells us that it is important to God and, consequently, should be important to us. The rule is thus reinterpreted in such a way that understands "idols" or "other gods" to be modern temptations such as wealth, success, fame, beauty, or the like. This is a widespread interpretive move, so much so that it's made unconsciously, but it's worth breaking down to see how the

[39] "Biblical concepts are not disembodied concepts to be applied from above; they are explicit or implicit rules (however general) that assume some set of their applications" (Cosgrove, *Appealing to Scripture*, 67). This makes biblical ethics "case-based," which allows for analysis of narratives and view of individuals in narratives as exemplars of character (Cosgrove, *Appealing to Scripture*, 68–69). Note that for some Christians, the Bible as a divinely inspired text has foreseen everything. This kind of interpretation, then, is not attributed to the skill of the interpreter but to the foresight of God and the biblical authors.

[40] Cosgrove, *Appealing to Scripture*, 24. This reality conflicts with the belief in "scripture as properly interpreted only where it is construed according to certain substantive principles, conceived as intrinsic to scripture itself, taken as a whole" (Cosgrove, *Appealing to Scripture*, 157).

analogy works, using the prohibition from Ten Commandments (Exod 20:3):

> Biblical rule: "You shall have no other gods before me."
>
> Justification: As the only source of life and blessing, God deserves the highest honor.
>
> Modern rule: You should not omit Sunday worship or daily prayer and replace that time with going to the gym.

You should already be able to see potential interpretive gray areas with this. For example, what if one misses Sunday worship in order to pick up extra shifts at work to feed their family? Is not care for the well-being of children important to God? Or does one honor God only with their time? What if I make a monetary donation to my church in place of my attending Sunday worship? To answer these questions, we would most likely generate more rules, or qualify the one above. These new rules might very well be based on other biblical texts and their justifications. It's not as if there's a better way to do this. "Appeal to any mode in which the Bible speaks morally properly involves case-based analogical reasoning. . . . All moral reasoning is inherently analogical, and all analogical reasoning is inherently case-based."[41] The problem appears when, as mentioned above, the justifications for biblical rules are themselves problematic. An example of this is the repeated injunction against intermarriage throughout the Hebrew Bible, which is founded on the justification that the religious beliefs of outsiders are a corrupting influence on the religion of the ancient Israelites.

Back to the Beginning

In chapter 1 we saw that proslavery readers relied on the historical fact that both the Old and New Testaments come from cultures that practiced enslavement and that biblical texts presuppose the practice. Added to this was the belief that the Table of Nations in Genesis 10 accurately described the origins of various

[41] Cosgrove, *Appealing to Scripture*, 85–86.

ethnic groups and that Noah's curse of Ham's son was also historical and perpetually valid. Each of these interpretations relied on a reading of the biblical text at its most literal level, which readers believed to be the "plain sense" of Scripture, a reading based on the Reformation belief in the clarity of the Bible as divine communication. On the other hand, abolitionists for the most part appealed not to specific texts that they believed could be applied directly to their context, but rather to parts of the Bible that they believed bore witness to what God was like and what God valued, namely freedom and equality. They viewed the Bible in terms of divine disclosure. This way of interpretation is a good example of how the Bible is applied analogously to modern situations. Statements in the biblical text are used to derive a principle operating at a higher level of abstraction about what values those statements express. These values are then used to formulate a "biblical" norm for the contemporary situation. With the abortion issue we see the same dynamic at work. On the one hand, antiabortion readers point to biblical texts that articulate larger concepts that indicate the importance of human life for God in general and unborn life in particular. In other words, the Bible discloses that part of God's character is to desire life for human beings both before and after their birth (see the texts discussed in chapter 1).[42] Those on the opposite side of this issue often point to the fact that the Bible says nothing at all specifically about abortion.[43] Signifi-

[42] "The argument against abortion in most instances is substantial, if indirect. In other words, even though direct statements are not present in the Bible, we will see that there are teachings that would lead to a strong presumption against the practice of abortion" (Tremper Longman, *The Bible and the Ballot: Using Scripture in Political Decisions* [Grand Rapids, MI: Eerdmans, 2020], 135). See also Bert Jan Lietaert Peerbolte, who notes that "approaching the question of abortion from the perspective of the sacred character of life can certainly be underpinned with biblical references" (Peerbolte, "Ending a Life That Has Not Begun: Abortion in the Bible," in *The Bible in Political Debate: What Does It Really Say?*, ed. Frances Flannery and Rodney A. Werline [London: Bloomsbury, 2016], 51).

[43] "In sum, the Bible is not very explicit about abortion. The sanctity of life is clearly asserted" (Peerbolte, "Ending a Life," 54). Similarly, Longman notes that "the Bible does not support the equation that abortion is the moral equivalent of the unjustified killing of a human person after birth" (*Bible and the Ballot*, 150). My quotation of the same two authors pointing out the ways the Bible is read on both sides of this debate is to underscore that I am not making any assump-

cantly in this regard, Kira Schlesinger's chapter on this question in her book, *Pro-Choice and Christian*, is entitled, "What the Bible Does (and Doesn't) Say."[44] This silence can be interpreted in many ways. At its most expansive, it could mean that abortion is allowed because it is not specifically prohibited. This kind of interpretation was hotly debated during the Reformation: Is something allowed if the Bible doesn't specifically prohibit it, or are the only things allowed those things which the Bible specifically supports? The latter position came to be known as the regulative principle, and it was used in debates over the role of music in Christian worship. For some proponents of the regulative principle, the only music permissible in worship was taken from the Psalms because they were the only biblically based hymnody. In the United States this interpretation went even further regarding the use of musical instruments in worship. The Disciples of Christ and Church of Christ divided in the early twentieth century because, while the Disciples believed that the use of musical instruments in church was acceptable, the group that formed the Church of Christ believed that musical instruments were forbidden because the New Testament did not specifically allow for them.

Arguments based on what the Bible specifically does and doesn't say understand the text as communication, telling us what God does or doesn't want. Broadly speaking, then, we see an interesting parallel between abolitionist and antiabortion biblical interpretation on the one hand and between supporters of slavery and proabortion readers on the other. These parallels between the contemporary positions on abortion with those of the debate over slavery say nothing at all about the moral value of either side in the contemporary debate. And while some antiabortion proponents compare themselves to the antebellum abolitionists, this equation has not gone uncriticized. In a detailed analysis, Bryan N. Massingale notes that modern attempts by the US Catholic hierarchy to equate

---

tions on their own position but rather want to highlight how both authors are engaging in careful and responsible interpretation.

[44] Kira Schlesinger, *Pro-Choice and Christian: Reconciling Faith, Politics, and Justice* (Louisville: Westminster John Knox, 2017), 55. Compare the discussion in Collins, *What Are Biblical Values?*, 50–58.

antiabortion positions with abolitionist movements two centuries ago overlook the historical reality that the Catholic Church in the antebellum US was engaged in the trafficking of enslaved Africans and their descendants (discussed above in chapter 1). Massingale also points out that the parallel is forced insofar as the issue at stake with the enslaved wasn't their acknowledgement as persons, but rather their rights as citizens, whereas one of the divisive issues in the debates around abortion is the point when fetuses can be understood as unborn children, and, hence, as persons.[45] Not all readers who support abortion in certain circumstances read the Bible simply as communication rather than disclosure. As I discussed in chapter 1, Schlesinger uses an expansive understanding of the concept of life to embrace more than biological life but something that includes social, economic, political, and gender issues and which ultimately strives for liberation. This reading is not based on specific texts, but rather on a particular way of interpreting larger narrative arcs or themes in the Bible. Alongside this, Schlesinger brings the ancient interpretive strategy of reading the entire Bible through the story of Jesus.[46]

The Catholic Church's Use of the Bible in Teaching about Life

Finally, let's take another brief look at the section on abortion in the *Catechism of the Catholic Church* also discussed above in chapter 1. As pointed out earlier, this section occurs in a larger discussion about the value of human life. Not surprisingly, the majority of the biblical texts cited in this larger section come from the Ten Commandments and the Sermon on the Mount, the two

[45] Bryan N. Massingale, "A Parallel That Limps: The Rhetoric of Slavery in the Pro-Life Discourse of U.S. Bishops," in Nicholas P. Cafardi, ed., *Voting and Holiness: Catholic Perspectives on Political Participation* (Mahwah, NJ: Paulist, 2012), 158–77.

[46] "We all read Scripture through a certain lens, what scholars call a hermeneutic. . . . As Christians, we are taught to read the Bible, even the Old Testament, through the lens of the life, death, and resurrection of Jesus Christ. God's pro-life action through Christ trumps other stories of when God has been the dealer of death, such as in the tenth plague" (Schlesinger, *Pro-Choice and Christian*, 64).

biblical passages designated as foundational for Catholic moral thought by both Pope John Paul II and the Pontifical Biblical Commission. As part of the "Witness of Sacred History," *CCC* cites and explains three biblical rules[47]:

> 2260 The covenant between God and mankind is interwoven with reminders of God's gift of human life and man's murderous violence:
>
> > For your lifeblood I will surely require a reckoning. . . . Whoever sheds the blood of man, by man shall his blood be shed; for God made man in his own image. (Gen 9:5-6)
> >
> > The Old Testament always considered blood a sacred sign of life (Lev 17:14). This teaching remains necessary for all time.
>
> 2261 Scripture specifies the prohibition contained in the fifth commandment: "Do not slay the innocent and the righteous" (Exod 23:7). The deliberate murder of an innocent person is gravely contrary to the dignity of the human being, to the golden rule, and to the holiness of the Creator. The law forbidding it is universally valid: it obliges each and everyone, always and everywhere.

Understood as commands which communicate something God wants, these rules, in order, say that the penalty for murder is death (Gen 9:5-6) and that the fifth commandment ("You shall not kill.") is narrowed to refer to the killing of the good (Exod 23:7). Note that this latter text is given absolute authority: "it obliges each and everyone, always and everywhere." Except when it doesn't, because the next section details instances where one is justified in taking another's life in self-defense. Here the nonbiblical Catholic moral concept of double-effect as articulated by Thomas Aquinas is cited: "The act of self-defense can have a double effect: the preservation of one's own life; and the killing of the aggressor . . . the one is intended, the other is not" (*CCC* 2263). This exception, however, does not limit the universal obligation in paragraph 2261,

[47] As in chapter 1, the biblical quotations here are those used in the *CCC*.

because the situation implies that the person being defended against is in fact trying to kill an innocent person. This makes the act of killing in self-defense partially an expression of Genesis 9's rule mandating capital punishment expressed in paragraph 2260—partial because the biblical rule is to be enforced after someone has shed another person's blood and not before they can do so, as in the case of self-defense. In other words, the paragraph supporting self-defense expands the biblical command of Genesis 9 to something like, "Whoever sheds the blood of a man *or is about to shed it*, by *man may* his blood be shed." This expansion of the rule is, however, really a limitation, but that doesn't become apparent until the next paragraph, where the CCC acknowledges the practice of capital punishment throughout history but goes on to argue for its immorality in part due to "an increasing awareness that the dignity of the person is not lost even after the commission of very serious crimes," which leads to the affirmation that capital punishment "is an attack on the inviolability and dignity of the person" (CCC 2267). One may certainly point to biblical passages that can be used to illustrate human dignity. In fact the very citation of Genesis 9 here in the CCC can be used: "for God made man in his own image." The concept, however, cannot be said to be fully biblical and certainly is not operative regarding capital punishment, which is mandated in several places in the Bible. In other words, this section of the CCC on human life and when it is permissible to take it begins with biblical norms—communications about what we are supposed to do—but goes on to qualify and even to supersede them on the basis of values that stand in part outside the text.

The outright forbidding of capital punishment in the CCC is a recent development, occurring only in the pontificate of Pope Francis, in August 2018. Here we see at work the principles of *Dei Verbum* discussed above: the idea of the development of understanding in how biblical texts are read and the supervisory role of the magisterium in evaluating those changes. Significantly, a group of Catholic theologians, philosophers, and priests wrote a document protesting this change by stating that "to teach that capital punishment is always and intrinsically evil would contradict Scripture. That the death penalty can be a legitimate means of securing retributive justice is affirmed in Genesis 9:6 and many other biblical texts, and the Church holds that Scripture cannot teach moral error."[48]

Sometimes a changed interpretation of a biblical text is placed into the text itself. In a story that did not gain much attention in the anglophone Catholic world, Pope Francis changed a phrase in the Italian version of the Our Father from "lead us not into temptation" ("non indurci in tentazione") to "do not abandon us to temptation" ("non abbandonarci alla tentazione") in part because the traditional reading ran the risk of portraying God as the source of temptation rather than our salvation from it.[49] This is not a matter of translating the Greek verb of Matthew 6:13 more clearly. The verb (*eisenengkēs*) clearly means "to lead to, to bring to," or the like. Rather, this is a change in the wording of a text on the grounds of a theological claim derived in part, but not exclusively, from other biblical texts.

[48] Various, "An Appeal to the Cardinals of the Catholic Church," *First Things*, August 15, 2018, https://www.firstthings.com/web-exclusives/2018/08/an-appeal-to-the-cardinals-of-the-catholic-church.

[49] "Per questa ragione, mantenere nella situazione attuale la traduzione 'non c'indurre in tentazione' non darebbe all'uomo d'oggi una corretta immagine di Dio, perché confonderebbe Dio con il seduttore. Il demonio nel paradiso terrestre tentò Adamo ed Eva perché voleva indurre la sua caduta, voleva il male dell'uomo, desiderava far soccombere i nostri progenitori. E tutto ciò niente ha a che vedere con le intenzioni di Dio. Per questo ben venga il cambiamento" ("For this reason, keeping the translation 'lead us not into temptation,' would not give a modern person the correct image of God because it would confuse God with a seducer. In the earthly paradise the devil tempted Adam and Eve because he wanted to lead them into their fall, he wanted evil for humankind, he wanted to make our ancestors succumb. None of this has anything to do with God's intentions. For this reason the change is welcome" ["Perché Papa Francesco ha deciso di cambiare il Padre nostro," *Agenzia Giornalistica Italia*, August 14, 2018, https://www.agi.it/blog-italia/idee/post/2018-08-14/padre_nostro_papa_francesco-4267420/]. My translation.) The change is not simply to the use of the Our Father in the liturgy. The official biblical translation of the Italian episcopal conference has also emended the text of Matt 6:13 (https://www.bibbiaedu.it/CEI2008/nt/Mt/6/) with a note that reads, "God cannot lead a person to evil but can submit them to a test. The meaning of this petition could be: do not submit us to a test too great for our weak defenses, or also: do not leave us alone to face Satan and his temptations." My translation.

Conclusion, On Needing a Place to Stand

The purpose of this chapter has been to make clear that any biblical interpretation that seeks to apply some aspect of the text to modern moral life requires an external standpoint—be it Christian theological belief or the priority of certain moral values—from which to read the text. We can only read the Bible from a standpoint outside of the Bible's contexts and with the intention to have the text speak to situations that are external to it.[50] The standard view that the Bible is a single book with a unified message is a standpoint that is not found in the Bible itself nor supported by literary and historical study. Moreover, as discussed in chapter 2, we are ourselves embedded in our own historical and cultural contexts and cannot completely extricate ourselves from them in order to fully grasp the meaning intended by the biblical authors. The goal is not to escape our contingency, but to be conscious of it, to interrogate its biases, and to be open to other standpoints. Biblical interpretation is not like an algebra equation. We do not solve for "x" by arriving at a single reading. As Kathleen Gallagher Elkins notes, "Not all interpretive conflicts are necessarily problems to be resolved in favor of a single 'better' interpretation. Instead, the ethical results of various interpretive choices can be the basis for adjudicating among interpretations."[51] We make the decisions on these ethical results at least in part from values that are formulated outside of the biblical text and, hopefully, with both an awareness of our own limited viewpoint and an openness to the viewpoints of others. When we read from a certain standpoint (as we all must do) we cannot see everything. Being open to the readings of others whose own limited standpoints are different from ours helps us to fill in those gaps.[52] Given the polariza-

[50] See also the incisive observation of Michael C. Legaspi: "In order to interpret the Bible, one must have a point of reference outside the passage he or she is interpreting. Biblical texts can only be interpreted in relation to *something* else: a concept, a question, a belief, a historical reality" (Legaspi, *The Death of Scripture and the Rise of Biblical Studies* [New York: Oxford University Press, 2010], 164).

[51] Kathleen Gallagher Elkins, *Mary, Mother of Martyrs: How Motherhood Became Self-Sacrifice in Early Christianity* (Cambridge, MA: Feminist Studies in Religion Books, 2018), 33.

[52] This is discussed in more detail in Thomas M. Bolin, *Ecclesiastes and the Riddle of Authorship* (London: Routledge, 2017), 3–4.

tion present in the US in general and the Catholic Church in particular, this openness to the readings of others becomes even more important. In the final chapter I will make a case for this openness to others being the place from which we should read.

Chapter 6

Reading in the Kingdom of Love

The last chapter made clear that all biblical interpretation that views the Bible as a guide for contemporary life broadly construed demands that the reader engage the text from an external, predetermined ethical or theological stance from which the varied and often difficult biblical material can be interpreted and applied. These external vantage points function as necessary limits that focus on what the reader believes makes the text important. Traditionally, these limits were generated by Christian religious communities and referred to as the rule of faith. Modern biblical scholars and theologians have added other external standards to the rule of faith derived from various ethical approaches. These predetermined stances are often chosen unconsciously due in part to the reader's own circumstances of historical embeddedness, which embraces religious tradition, ethnicity, gender, class, and a host of other factors. In response to the polarization present in US society in general and the American Catholic Church in particular, I want to propose in this chapter that the interpretive stance from which we ought to be reading the Bible in this difficult moment is Augustine's rule of love.

Once More, Augustine

Throughout this book I have referred to Augustine's major work on biblical interpretation, *De Doctrina Christiana*, which is best translated as *On Christian Teaching*.[1] And here I want to focus on

[1] As Edmund Hill points out in his translation of *De Doctrina Christiana*, it is more accurate to understand the Latin *doctrina* not simply as content, but rather

it in greater detail. By way of background, Augustine's own intellectual journey to Christianity involved a struggle with biblical interpretation. He writes in the *Confessions* that on first reading, he found its style uncouth compared to the classical Latin writers he was studying as part of his training in rhetoric. His sojourn with the Manichees lasted so long in part because he could not find a way to interpret the anthropomorphic descriptions of God in the Bible nonliterally. It was, Augustine says, only when he came to Milan and heard the preaching of its bishop, Ambrose, that would "lift the mystical veil" of the biblical texts "and uncover their spiritual sense" (*Confessions*, 6.4.5).[2] Later in the *Confessions*, after a long and detailed attempt to understand Genesis 1:1-2, Augustine asserts that biblical texts can be interpreted in a variety of ways so long as none of them is contrary to the truth.[3] Famously, Augustine asserts about these opening verses of the Bible, "So when one person says, 'He [the biblical author] meant what I say,' and another says, 'No, he meant what I say,' I think it would be more pious for me to say, 'Why not both, if both are true?' " (*Confessions*, 12.31.42).[4] Augustine's interpretive flexibility is something that characterizes much contemporary hermeneutics and in part leads Peter Brown to call *De Doctrina Christiana* both Augustine's most creative and most modern work.[5] All indications are that

---

as a process, i.e., not teaching as a body of material but rather as an active process (Edmund Hill, OP, trans., *Saint Augustine: Teaching Christianity (De Doctrina Christiana)* [Hyde Park, NY: New City Press, 1996], 95).

[2] Thomas Williams, trans., *Augustine: Confessions* (Indianapolis: Hackett, 2019), 82–83.

[3] "What harm does it do me if these words can be understood to bear other meanings, all of which are true? What harm does it do me if what I think the writer of those words meant is different from what someone else thinks he meant? Certainly all of us who read try to investigate and understand what the author we are reading meant to say; and when we believe that the author was truthful, we do not dare suppose that he said anything we know or think is false. So as long as each of us is trying to discover in the Holy Scriptures what their author meant, how is it objectionable if someone interprets them as meaning something that you, the Light of all truthful minds, show to be true, even though that is not what the author meant—when what the author meant was also true, just not that particular truth?" (*Confessions*, 12.18.27, in Williams, *Augustine: Confessions*, 236–37).

[4] Williams, *Augustine: Confessions*, 247.

[5] Peter Brown, *Augustine of Hippo* (Berkeley: University of California Press, 1969), 259–69.

Augustine began writing *De Doctrina Christiana* sometime around 396, soon after his ordination as Bishop of Hippo Regius in North Africa. After completing the first three-quarters of the work—which deal with how one ought to interpret the Bible—Augustine then set it aside, where it remained unfinished for thirty years. In the last years of his life, somewhere around 426–427, he added the final quarter of the work, which deals with sharing the fruits of one's biblical interpretation with others. Augustine's most influential idea from *De Doctrina Christiania* is what he calls the rule of love ("regula dilectionis"), which he discusses alongside the rule of faith, a concept we covered in some detail in chapter 5. This chapter will describe and apply Augustine's rule of love to our contemporary situation of reading the Bible in a polarized society and church.[6]

For Augustine, strictly speaking, the rule of love is that part of the rule of faith that is derived from the unambiguous parts of the Bible and set alongside the essential truths of the Christian faith handed down through tradition. In his search for the clearest part of the Bible that articulates the essence of faith, Augustine uses Jesus as his model reader and looks to the story of the Great Commandment (Matt 22:34-40; Mark 12:28-34; Luke 10:25-37). In this story, Jesus is approached by a scholar of the law, an expert in the biblical text, specifically the Pentateuch, who asks Jesus to name the greatest of all the commandments. The scholar's question understands the text to be communication, telling the reader something God wants them to do. For context, later Jewish tradition, first recorded in the Talmud, states that there are a total of 613 commandments in the Torah, although lists of these do not appear to have been drawn up until the Middle Ages. In response to the

[6] I want to mention Jonathan L. Walton's recent book (*A Lens of Love: Reading the Bible in Its World for Our World* [Louisville: Westminster John Knox, 2018]). While the title is similar to Augustine's use of love as an interpretive rule, Walton draws on historical-critical research to argue that the default position of God in the Bible, despite texts that might argue otherwise, is one of solidarity with the poor and oppressed. Consequently, Walton's lens of love is a viewpoint derived from the Bible. In this way, Walton's interpretive approach is an example of selecting a particular ethical stance in the Bible that is determined to be important, in part, by external standards as discussed in chap. 5. In no way does this detract from the importance of Walton's book or of his argument.

scholar's question Jesus responds with two commandments: a person should love God with all their heart, soul, mind, and strength (Deut 6:4) and love their neighbor as themselves (Lev 19:18). Because Jesus identified these two texts out of the entire biblical corpus as the greatest, Augustine will assert that the entire moral teaching of the Bible is love of God and love of neighbor, "the rule of love that God has set for us" (*De Doct Christ*, 1.22.21).[7]

I want to reiterate that Augustine doesn't set this reading strategy alongside others. Rather, it is the fundamental assumption that one must bring to their reading of the Bible and the essential criterion by which one judges every interpretation of every biblical text: "So if it seems to you that you have understood the divine scriptures, or any part of them, in such a way that by this understanding you do not build up this twin love of God and neighbor, then you have not yet understood them" (*De Doct Christ*, 1.36.40).[8] As someone who read the biblical texts allegorically, as discussed in chapter 3, Augustine uses the rule of love as the interpretive lens to determine which biblical passages are to be read literally or metaphorically.

> And here, quite simply, is the one and only method: anything in the divine writings that cannot be referred either to good, honest morals or to the truth of the faith, you must know is said figuratively. Good honest morals belong to loving God and one's neighbor, the truth of the faith to knowing God and one's neighbor. As for hope, that lies in everybody's own conscience, to the extent that you perceive yourself to be making progress in the love of God and neighbor, and in the knowledge of them." (*De doct christ*, 3.10.14)[9]

[7] Hill, *Teaching Christianity*, 115. All translations of *De Doctrina* are taken from Hill. Paula Fredriksen refers to the twofold commandment of love as Augustine's "interpretive North Star" (*Augustine and the Jews: A Christian Defense of Jews and Judaism* [New Haven: Yale University Press, 2008], 192).

[8] Hill, *Teaching Christianity*, 124. Elsewhere, Augustine asserts that "the serious student" ("se exercet . . . studiosus") of the biblical books will find "nothing in them other [than]" ("nihil in eis aliud") the teaching that we are to love God and our neighbor (*De Doct Christ*, 2.7.10).

[9] Hill, *Teaching Christianity*, 176.

Augustine realizes that this is no easy task. Like many other Christian readers in antiquity, he understood the Bible's sacred status to imply also that it was a book of deep wisdom that would be difficult to interpret.[10] But the mercy of God also provided for clear parts of the text to help those who were not yet ready for the more arcane parts of the Bible. In his own stunning use of metaphor, Augustine exhorts his readers "to take pains to turn over and over in your mind what you read, until your interpretation of it is led right through to the kingdom of love" (*De Doct Christ*, 3.15.23).[11]

So, the content of faith is love—love of God and love of neighbor. But, of course, *love* is a small word that covers a multitude of sins—many of which involve a complete lack of clarity on just exactly what love is. Augustine goes to great pains to clarify exactly what he means by love in *De Doctrina Christiana*, so much so that the entire first book is devoted to an exploration of just this question. Augustine's discussion is rather abstract and based on an understanding of reality that he owes to his reading of Greek philosophy. Everything hinges on a crucial distinction between things that are to be used and those that are to be enjoyed. "Things that are to be enjoyed make us happy; things which are to be used help us on the way to happiness" (*De Doct Christ*, 1.3.3).[12] The only things worthy of enjoyment for their own sake are those which are unchangeable and eternal—and only one thing matches that description—God himself. But where does this leave human beings? Are we to be used or enjoyed? For Augustine, human beings are not to be enjoyed for their own sake, but rather "used"—enjoyed for the sake of something else. This is because, unlike God, we are finite and mutable; consequently, other people (and ourselves) are to be loved contingently, for the sake of God (*De Doct Christ*, 1.22.20). This kind of language, unsurprisingly, might make people uneasy, and Augustine was aware of this too, for he

[10] In the *Confessions* (3.5.9) when Augustine recounts his first attempt to read the Bible, he describes it as "lofty within, and veiled in mysteries" (Williams, *Confessions*, 33).

[11] Hill, *Teaching Christianity*, 179.

[12] Hill, *Teaching Christianity*, 107.

says in the middle of this discussion that "other people must not take offense" at you if you love them not for their own sake but for God's (*De Doct Christ*, 1.22.21). This is because the upshot of Augustine's metaphysical discussion is that to love others for the sake of God is to ground the finite, human love that is subject to death in the eternal love of God. At the same time, our love of others is how we show our love of God.

This unity of love of God and neighbor is a significant point. There are other ways to arrive at it than through Platonic philosophy, which I describe below. First, I want to look at the Gospel accounts of the Great Commandment utilizing some of the tools of historical-critical biblical scholarship that will contribute to this discussion. The table on the following page shows the story in its three different iterations.

The first thing to notice is how much longer Mark's account is than Matthew's. This is important because most biblical scholars think—with significant support—that Matthew and Luke used Mark as source material for their respective Gospels. This means that differences between Mark and the other two Gospels can often reveal some of the theological aims of the authors of Matthew and Luke based on how they changed the material they found in Mark.[13] The material from Mark missing in Matthew and Luke is the second exchange between the scribe and Jesus, where the scribe wholeheartedly agrees with and elaborates on Jesus' answer to the question of the Great Commandment and then, significantly, Jesus tells the scribe that he is "not far from the kingdom of God." This positive view of the scribe is actually foregrounded in the opening of Mark's story, where we are told that the scribe seeks to question Jesus because he sees how knowledgeable Jesus is ("seeing that he answered them well, he asked him"). In Mark's version, in other words, the scribe's question to Jesus is posed out of respect for Jesus' demonstrated knowledge, and the scribe's

[13] For an important new way of thinking about the composition of the Gospels based on recent historical insights into bookmaking and the role of enslaved scribes and copyists, see the discussion in Candida R. Moss, *God's Ghostwriters: Enslaved Christians and the Making of the Bible* (New York: Little, Brown, 2024), 140–97.

Mark 12:28-34	Matt 22:34-40	Luke 10:25-37
28 One of the scribes came near and heard them disputing with one another, and seeing that he answered them well, he asked him, "Which commandment is the first of all?" 29 Jesus answered, "The first is, 'Hear, O Israel: the Lord our God, the Lord is one; 30 you shall love the Lord your God with all your heart, and with all your soul, and with all your mind, and with all your strength.' 31 The second is this, 'You shall love your neighbor as yourself.' There is no other commandment greater than these." 32 Then the scribe said to him, "You are right, Teacher; you have truly said that 'he is one, and besides him there is no other'; 33 and 'to love him with all the heart, and with all the understanding, and with all the strength,' and 'to love one's neighbor as oneself,'—this is much more important than all whole burnt offerings and sacrifices." 34 When Jesus saw that he answered wisely, he said to him, "You are not far from the kingdom of God." After that no one dared to ask him any question.	34 When the Pharisees heard that he had silenced the Sadducees, they gathered together, 35 and one of them, an expert in the law, asked him a question to test him. 36 "Teacher, which commandment in the law is the greatest?" 37 He said to him, " 'You shall love the Lord your God with all your heart, and with all your soul, and with all your mind.' 38 This is the greatest and first commandment. 39 And a second is like it: 'You shall love your neighbor as yourself.' 40 On these two commandments hang all the law and the prophets."	25 An expert in the law stood up to test Jesus. "Teacher," he said, "what must I do to inherit eternal life?" 26 He said to him, "What is written in the law? What do you read there?" 27 He answered, "You shall love the Lord your God with all your heart, and with all your soul, and with all your strength, and with all your mind; and your neighbor as yourself." 28 And he said to him, "You have given the right answer; do this, and you will live." 29 But wanting to vindicate himself, he asked Jesus, "And who is my neighbor?" 30 Jesus replied, "A man was going down from Jerusalem to Jericho, and fell into the hands of robbers, who stripped him, beat him, and took off, leaving him half dead. 31 Now by chance a priest was going down that road, and when he saw him he passed by on the other side. 32 So likewise a Levite, when he came to the place and saw him, passed by on the other side. 33 But a Samaritan while traveling came upon him, and when he saw him he was moved with pity. 34 He went to him and bandaged his wounds, treating them with oil and wine. Then he put him on his own animal, brought him to an inn, and took care of him. 35 The next day he took out two denarii, gave them to the innkeeper, and said, 'Take care of him, and when I come back I will repay you whatever more you spend.' 36 Which of these three, do you think, was a neighbor to the man who fell into the hands of the robbers?" 37 He said, "The one who showed him mercy." Jesus said to him, "Go and do likewise."

endorsement of Jesus' answer elicits from Jesus an endorsement of the scribe's knowledge.

The differences from Mark's positive appraisal of the scribe are apparent in Matthew's retelling. Rather than a question motivated out of acknowledgement of Jesus' command of the text of the Torah, the scholar of the law in Matthew is testing Jesus. In Matthew, this verb is only used to negatively describe the motives of certain people who interact with Jesus, beginning with the devil in Matthew 4, who is also called "the tempter," a Greek noun taken from the same root as the verb "to test." By placing the devil as the first tester of Jesus and using the term exclusively elsewhere in his Gospel to describe the scribes, Pharisees, and Sadducees, Matthew equates the opposition Jesus faces from his Jewish co-religionists with diabolical activity. It comes as no surprise, then, that Matthew's rendition of the Great Commandment does not contain the scribe's positive response to Jesus' answer nor Jesus' praise of the scribe, as we find in Mark. Matthew ends the account with Jesus' response, which thwarts the legal scholar's attempt to test Jesus.[14]

Luke's account is the most distinctive. First, the teacher of the law does not ask Jesus for the Great Commandment, but rather what a person must do to inherit eternal life. Note, however, that as in Matthew, here the legal scholar is testing Jesus. Because he is interacting with a scholar of the law, Jesus answers the question with one of his own: How do you read the Torah? What do you think the text teaches about what to do for salvation? It is the scholar, and not Jesus, who then goes on to cite the texts from Deuteronomy 6 and Leviticus 19. Jesus, in perhaps a muted version of the approval of the scribe in Mark's Gospel, tells the legal scholar that his answer is correct. Luke's version reverses the speakers, insofar as it is Jesus asking the scholar for the most important part of the Torah, what "must be done to inherit eternal life." Luke also portrays the legal scholar negatively, because the entire encounter is an attempt to test Jesus.

[14] This kind of story was called a *chreia* in the Greco-Roman world. See the discussion in chap. 3.

Here is where Luke's account goes its own way because the legal scholar follows up with a second question about the interpretation of Leviticus 19:18, a question that is still debated today: Who is the neighbor we are commanded to love? Jesus responds with the parable of the Good Samaritan and then asks the scholar a final question, which leads to the answer to the scholar's second question: the neighbor is the one who shows mercy. Luke's expansion of the story as we find it in Mark is worth exploring more closely, and I want to highlight some of its important features. First, in a manner similar to Matthew and different from Mark, the account in Luke views the legal scholar negatively. He seeks to test Jesus (v. 25) and to vindicate himself (v. 29). Comparing the structure of Luke's account with that of Mark helps to illustrate this. Here is the entire exchange as Mark constructs it:

Scribe asks a question (Mark 12:28)
Jesus answers (Mark 12:29-31)
Scribe affirms Jesus's answer (Mark 12:32-33)
Jesus affirms scribe's viewpoint (Mark 12:34)

Mark's exchange and structure is brief and tightly arranged. In contrast, here is Luke's structure:

Lawyer asks a question (Luke 10:25)
Jesus asks a question (Luke 10:26)
Lawyer answers (Luke 10:27)
Jesus affirms lawyer's answer (Luke 10:28)
Lawyer asks another question (Luke 10:29)
Jesus answers (Luke 10:30-35)
Jesus asks another question (Luke 10:36)
Lawyer answers (Luke 10:37)

The number and arrangement of interactions in Luke are significantly larger and more complex than what we find in Mark. The reason for this appears to be Luke's desire to include the parable of the Good Samaritan here. Its length is clearly disproportionate to the questions and responses we see in Mark, Matthew, and the first part of Luke's account where he is following Mark. Luke's two significant changes to Mark are that he has reversed the question-and-answer pattern so that it is the lawyer who quotes the biblical text instead of Jesus and that Luke has the lawyer ask a follow-up question based on the biblical text, which allows Luke to include the Good Samaritan story here. Notice how the parable does not exactly "fit" the context. The lawyer wants to know who the neighbor is that needs love. Jesus tells a story about someone showing mercy to a stranger in need, yet the point of the parable is that the neighbor is the one who shows that mercy, not the one who receives it. In other words, the lawyer wants to know who the neighbor is to be loved and the parable tells him that the neighbor is the one who shows mercy to someone in need.[15] It's important to note that the parable of the Good Samaritan occurs only in Luke and that our examination of its context seems to show that Luke has greatly adapted a story he found in Mark to create an opportunity to use the parable—possibly another text that Luke has taken from elsewhere—as an illustration of Leviticus 19:18.

The Good Samaritan

Luke's elaboration of the Great Commandment story underscores Augustine's point that this is at its heart an example of Jesus engaging in biblical interpretation about what is necessary and most important for faith. It is so important to Luke that he uses a parable of Jesus to emphasize his interpretation of one of the biblical rules under discussion. What does the parable tell us about what it means to love one's neighbor? This is not the place to engage in a full investigation of the history and later interpretation of the Good Samaritan story.[16] What I want to do instead is arrive

[15] Mark A. Proctor argues that the Greek concept of neighbor (*plēsion*) implies reciprocity and that therefore the Samaritan and the wounded man are neighbors to each other (Proctor, "'Who Is My Neighbor?' Recontextualizing Luke's Good Samaritan [Luke 10:25-37]," *JBL* 138, no. 1 [2019]: 203–19).

[16] Here is but a sampling of recent books and articles: Emerson B. Powery, *The Good Samaritan: Luke 10 for the Life of the Church* (Grand Rapids, MI: Baker Academic, 2022); Jeanine Brown and Kazuhiko Yamazaki-Ransom, "The Parable of the Good Samaritan and the Narrative Portrayal of Samaritans in Luke-Acts,"

at a reading that is consistent with Augustine's rule of love. Much modern interpretation of the parable attempts to arrive at a meaning based on what is known about ancient ethnic relations between Jews and Samaritans in the time of Jesus, or about the significance of the first two passersby being a priest and a Levite. These approaches are valid intellectual exercises, but they often have overlooked ethical implications that need to be noticed and addressed. Regarding the issue of the Samaritan's ethnicity vis-à-vis the other characters in the parable and Jesus' audience, the long-standing dominant interpretation of the parable in biblical scholarship has been to read it against a backdrop a perceived deep mutual hatred between Jews and Samaritans. This in turn gives Jesus' parable force because a member of a despised group for Jesus' Jewish audience is the hero of the story. However, in a detailed study of the evidence, Matthew Chalmers concludes that, "There is little reason to assume that Luke 10:25-37 is primarily explained by reference to Jewish-Samaritan hostility, even if it belongs to a world in which some tension between Jewish and Samaritan Israelites persisted."[17] While ancient literary sources demonstrate a tension between Jews and Samaritans, they also make clear that this is an *intrareligious* tension. Samaritans are not hated outsiders but members of the same larger ethnic group, "Israel." Consequently, the Samaritan in the parable is not a bitter, hated enemy of the injured man nor of Jesus' Jewish audience, nor does the appearance of the Samaritan in the parable necessarily shock,

Journal of Theological Interpretation 15 (September 21, 2021): 233–46; Matthew Chalmers, "Rethinking Luke 10: The Parable of the Good Samaritan Israelite," *JBL* 139, no. 3 (January 1, 2020): 543–66; Anthony G. Keddie, " 'Who Is My Neighbor?' Ethnic Boundaries and the Samaritan Other in Luke 10:25-37," *Biblical Interpretation* 28, no. 2 (March 2020): 246–71; Michael P. Knowles, "What Was the Victim Wearing? Literary, Economic, and Social Contexts for the Parable of the Good Samaritan," *Biblical Interpretation* 12, no. 2 (April 2004): 145–74; Joshua Eugene Leim, "To Inherit Eternal Life: Jesus, the Lawyer, and Luke's Soteriological Grammar," *Bulletin for Biblical Research* 31, no. 2 (July 7, 2021): 167–90; Rimer Roukema, "The Good Samaritan in Ancient Christianity," *Vigiliae Christianae* 58, no. 1 (February 2004): 56–74; Kyriakos Stavrianos, "The Parable of the Good Samaritan in Patristic Thought," *Greek Orthodox Theological Review* 57, nos. 1–4 (2012): 29–48; Ruben Zimmermann, "The Good Samaritan (Luke 10:30–35) and the Parables in Luke," in *Puzzling the Parables of Jesus: Methods and Interpretations* (Minneapolis: Augsburg Fortress, 2015).

[17] Chalmers, "Rethinking Luke 10," 544.

surprise, or otherwise indict Jesus' Jewish listeners for their perceived hatred of Samaritans. This last point is important because it underscores the need to be aware of the implications of our readings. Many people read this parable with the mistaken assumption that Jews and Samaritans hated each other, and then apply the parable today for the laudable goal of challenging Christians to move beyond long-standing hatreds and dare to see an enemy as a person in need of mercy. The problem with this reading—apart from the fact that it's historically inaccurate—is its unintended consequence of depicting ancient Jews as bearing a general and bitter hatred for another ethnic group and therefore as in need of Jesus' radical teaching of kindness and mercy. Such wholesale negative depiction of Jews in the New Testament occurs with many other texts and contributes to supersessionist or outright antisemitic readings of the biblical texts.

A second interpretive strand that is also prone to these unacceptable types of readings centers on the idea of ritual purity as an explanation for the behavior of the priest and the Levite. According to this interpretation, the priest and the Levite were concerned to maintain ritual purity because of their liturgical roles in temple worship. The man left "half dead" on the roadside is believed by them to be dead and, because contact with a corpse in Jewish law (e.g., Num 19:11; 31:19) brings temporary ritual impurity, the priest and the Levite steer clear of the injured man. As with the issue of the relationship between Jews and Samaritans, it is possible that the priest and Levite are motivated in part by ritual concerns. This would make the parable in part align with critiques in the Hebrew Bible where God faults the Israelites for placing ritual or liturgical service over the demands to care for the poor and the weak (e.g., Isa 1:10-17; Amos 5:21-25). However, as Amy-Jill Levine points out, if this prioritization of ritual purity is generalized as a characteristic of all Jews in the time of Jesus, then it is a return to supersessionist Christian stereotypes of Judaism as a legalistic religion that is replaced by Jesus' teaching of mercy.[18] This modern reading is a variant of an allegorical inter-

[18] Amy-Jill Levine, *Short Stories by Jesus: The Enigmatic Parables of a Controversial Rabbi* (San Francisco: HarperCollins, 2014), 90–95.

pretation that goes back at least as far as Origen, which saw the injured man as the human soul, Jesus as the Samaritan, and the priest and the Levite as the old covenant which had no power to save.[19] This interpretation is picked up by other Greek Christian writers such as John Chrysostom and also by Latin Christian authors, including Augustine, who, in another writing, says that the priest and the Levite represent the "priesthood and ministry of the Old Testament which are of no use for salvation."[20]

The interpretive problem with these two readings isn't so much in the basic insights they offer, but rather in the exaggeration of them. Samaritans are not hated outsiders in Israel but, as Chalmers notes, a "limit case to delineate belonging."[21] And while this particular priest and this particular Levite might avoid the injured man out of fear of ritual impurity, this does not mean that Judaism as an entire religion can be described as overly concerned with ritualistic legalism. Both of the supersessionist readings discussed above overlook the setting of the parable: a debate between two Jewish men—Jesus and the lawyer—about the most important part of the law. Consequently, the Samaritan represents a positive example of living out the law, while the priest and the Levite are in this instance perhaps examples of an erroneous prioritization of other parts of the law concerning ritual purity over what Jesus and the lawyer have agreed is the most important part of the law—love of God and neighbor. This explains a feature of the parable that can be easily overlooked: in describing the behavior of the priest and the Levite, Jesus notes that they "passed by on the other side" (vv. 31-32) while the Samaritan stops to help. In

[19] Roukema, "Good Samaritan in Ancient Christianity," 62; and Stavrianos, "Parable of the Good Samaritan," 33.

[20] "Sacerdotium et ministerium Veteris Testamenti significant, quod non poterat prodesse ad salutem" (*Questions on the Gospels*, 2.19, in J. Migne, PL 35:130, my translation). For analysis of this reading of the parable alongside that in *De Doctrina Christiana*, see Mike Higton, "Boldness and Reserve: A Lesson from St. Augustine," *Anglican Theological Review* 85, no. 3 (2003): 447–56. Fredriksen notes that, while Augustine argues that the Jews cannot read the Bible for its "higher" meaning, he nevertheless acknowledges that the Jews, unlike all other peoples, worshiped God in accordance with the laws God had given them (*Augustine and the Jews*, 193–94).

[21] Chalmers, "Rethinking Luke 10," 545.

other words, and consistent with the interpretation I'm offering here, the three travelers who encounter the injured man are already on the same side of the road as he is. Reading the parable as a hated Samaritan reaching out to the injured man overlooks this key fact. The parable is not about the Samaritan crossing an ethnic boundary to help someone in need; it's about the priest and the Levite creating a boundary in order to avoid offering help. The parable is not about crossing a line to get in, but about creating one to get out, or rather creating one to put another person outside. A key component of the parable is the warning against taking a neighbor, one whom we are to love, and placing them outside of that ethical obligation.

Circles and Boundaries

At this point, we can return to the lawyer's question for which the parable is the answer. The lawyer acknowledges the validity of the biblical injunction to love one's neighbor. His question—Who is my neighbor?—is founded on the assumption that not everyone will fit into this category. In other words, the lawyer's question of how to interpret the rule is founded upon the assumption that a boundary should be drawn to place some people outside of the category of neighbor. In its portrayal of the priest and the Levite in contrast with that of the Samaritan, the parable shows that understanding the commandment from the stance of where to draw a boundary is to misunderstand it. A brief poem by the American poet Edwin Markham (1852–1940) eloquently expresses the point:

> He drew a circle that shut me out—
> Heretic, rebel, a thing to flout.
> But Love and I had the wit to win:
> We drew a circle that took him in![22]

Like Jesus and the lawyer, contemporary Christians reading this text are required to ask exactly which individuals constitute the

[22] Edwin Markham, "Outwitted," *The Literary Digest* 49 (July–December 1914): 801.

neighbor, or rather to determine how big a circle to draw in order to encompass all those the commandment says are to be loved. In much the same way that US history can be seen as an extended interpretive interaction with Jefferson's statement in the Declaration of Independence that "all men are created equal," with many of the struggles throughout American history focusing on specifically who are the "men" to whom this equality is granted, so too can much of Christian history be seen as a story of whom to include in the circle of those who are to be loved. Likewise, those moments in both American history and Christian history where institutions fell short of their potential are, unsurprisingly, when the interpretations of these authoritative texts were used to draw small circles encompassing only a privileged few entitled to dignity and love.[23]

But not all Christian circles have been small. In *De Doctrina Christiana*, after articulating the rule of love, Augustine answers the lawyer's question himself: "it is clear that every single human being is to be counted as a neighbor" (*De Doct Christ*, 1.30.32).[24] This is reaffirmed in the Second Vatican Council's Pastoral Constitution on the Church in the Modern World (*Gaudium et Spes*), which mandates that "everyone must consider his every neighbor without exception as another self."[25] The language of Vatican II allows no wiggle room: everyone is obligated by the rule, and it applies to all without exception. This is a circle whose circumference embraces the entire human race; it cannot get any larger. In one of his homilies on John's Gospel, commenting on John 5:8 ("Jesus said to him, 'Stand up, take your mat and walk' ") Augustine clarifies exactly what this love looks like and what it entails:

[23] Diarmaid MacCulloch traces the oscillations of this circle in Christian history through use of the concept of silence (MacCulloch, *Silence: A Christian History* [New York: Penguin Books, 2013]).

[24] Hill, *Teaching Christianity*, 120. And elsewhere: "All people are to be loved equally; but since you cannot be of service to everyone, you have to take greater care of those who are joined to you by a turn, so to say, of fortune's wheel, whether by occasion of place or time, or any other such circumstance" (*De Doctrina Christiana*, 1.28.29, in Hill, *Teaching Christianity*, 118).

[25] Paul VI, *Gaudium et Spes* (Pastoral Constitution on the Church in the Modern World) 27, The Holy See (December 7, 1965), https://www.vatican.va/archive/hist_councils/ii_vatican_council/documents/vat-ii_const_19651207_gaudium-et-spes_en.html.

> Always be thinking, the whole time, that one must love God and neighbor. . . . Always think about them, reflect on them, observe them, practice them, fulfill them. In terms of precept, love of God comes first; but in terms of practice the love of neighbor comes first. . . . But, because you do not yet see God, you will deserve to see him by loving your neighbor. . . . So then, love your neighbor, and contemplate in yourself the source of your loving your neighbor; there, as best you can, you will see God. Begin, therefore by loving your neighbor. Break your bread to the hungry, bring the one who is needy, without a roof over his head, into your house. If you see him naked, clothe him, and do not look down upon your own (*Tract in Ioh*, 17.7–9).[26]

Augustine is deftly moving between a number of biblical texts here. While ostensibly discussing John 5:8, he draws upon the story of the Great Commandment and goes on to use Matthew 25 (Jesus separating the sheep from the goats) to describe what love of neighbor looks like: care of the hungry and the needy. The result of this, in addition to the salvation promised by Jesus in Matthew 25 for those who do such things, allows Augustine to cite 1 John 4:16 ("those who abide in love abide in God, and God abides in them") and make the bold claim that those who love their neighbors will be able to "see" God abiding in themselves.

Bringing the rule of love to contemporary biblical interpretation, we can look at some examples from recent and ongoing social debates. This book began with the story of Attorney General Jeff Sessions citing Romans 13:1 to justify the separation of migrant children from their families and their subsequent incarceration. In response to the attorney general's use of the biblical verse, the Catholic bishops of Orange County, California, wrote a strongly worded rebuke which pointed out the shortcomings of proof-texting, specifically in its disregard for the history of this verse's use to support both Nazi German rule and chattel slavery in the United States. Importantly, the bishops begin their response to Sessions with the call to "the people of God and our nation's lead-

[26] Edmund Hill, OP, trans., *Saint Augustine: Homilies on the Gospel of John 1–40* (Hyde Park, NY: New City Press, 2009), 312–13.

ers *to love our neighbors*, to tell the truth, and to journey together with respect for human dignity and the common good" (emphasis added).[27] The neighbors being defended by the bishops are those very migrants whom many in our country see as dangerous and unwanted. Against a drawing of a boundary (and what are borders if not such boundaries?) the bishops affirm that the circle demanded by the Gospel is wider than one which views needy men, women, and children seeking protection as threats. More broadly speaking but equally apt, in its 1993 document on biblical interpretation, the Pontifical Biblical Commission asserts firmly that, "clearly to be rejected also is every attempt at actualization set in a direction contrary to evangelical justice and charity, such as, for example, the use of the Bible to justify racial segregation, anti-Semitism or sexism whether on the part of men or of women."[28]

Augustine means for the rule of love to unite people in their behavior in every way, which includes their reading of the Bible. In the words of Brian Stock, for Augustine, "love operates vertically, descending from the text to the reader, and horizontally, as readers relate to audiences. Christianity emerges as a textual community built around shared principles of interpretation."[29] These shared principles are characterized by viewing fellow readers as neighbors deserving of love. We see Augustine put this expansive vision of biblical interpretation into practice when he discusses multiple interpretations of Genesis 1:1, culminating in the affirmation that multiple interpretations are true and united by the ultimate truth which is God.[30]

What might this look like? In the introduction, I drew upon Pope Francis's encyclical *Fratelli Tutti* and the importance it places

[27] Kevin Vann, Timothy Freye, and Thanh Thai Nguyen, "On Taking Human Persons (and Holy Scripture) Out of Context," *Orange County Catholic*, June 20, 2018, https://occatholic.com/diocese-of-orange-bishops-on-taking-human-persons-and-holy-scripture-out-of-context-2/.

[28] Dean P. Béchard, trans., *The Scripture Documents: An Anthology of Official Catholic Teachings* (Collegeville, MN: Liturgical Press, 2002), 305.

[29] Brian Stock, *Augustine the Reader: Meditation, Self-Knowledge, and the Ethics of Interpretation* (Cambridge, MA: Belknap, 1998), 196.

[30] "In this diversity of true interpretations, let Truth itself bring forth harmony" (*Confessions*, 12.30.41, in Williams, *Augustine: Confessions*, 246).

on dialogue.[31] Unsurprisingly, in a teaching document arguing for social friendship, the main biblical text used by Pope Francis is the parable of the Good Samaritan, with an entire chapter of the encyclical devoted to it. I want to point out that the pope refrains from one of the supersessionist exaggerations discussed above. His reading of the parable does claim that Samaritans were "impure, detestable, dangerous," to Jews in Jesus' day (82), but he does not explain the actions of the priest and the Levite by appeal to a false caricature of Judaism as overly concerned with ritual purity. Pope Francis reads the encyclical through the lenses of social, political, and economic realities. The problem with the behavior of the priest and the Levite is that they lack concern for the common good and feel that their time is a scarce resource not to be "wasted" on concern for strangers. "The story of the Good Samaritan is constantly being repeated. We can see this clearly as social and political inertia is turning many parts of our world into a desolate byway, even as domestic and international disputes and the robbing of opportunities are leaving great numbers of the marginalized stranded on the roadside" (71). Without appealing directly to Augustine's reading of the parable in *De Doctrina Christiana*, Pope Francis arrives at the same conclusion, saying that the parable "asks us not to decide who is close enough to be our neighbor, but rather that we ourselves become neighbors to all" (80).[32] This reading of the parable forms the biblical foundation of Pope Francis's plea for Christians and all people of good will to have the courage to transcend social, ethnic, religious, national, and economic borders to recapture a vision of solidarity and the common good.

Fratelli Tutti, as an encyclical should, begins with the current situation under analysis and then proceeds to offer the church's

[31] Pope Francis, *Fratelli Tutti* (Encyclical Letter on Fraternity and Social Friendship), October 3, 2020, https://www.vatican.va/content/francesco/en/encyclicals/documents/papa-francesco_20201003_enciclica-fratelli-tutti.html.

[32] Francis is echoing his predecessor, Benedict XVI, who, in his discussion of the parable, states that "anyone who needs me, and whom I can help, is my neighbor. The concept of 'neighbor' is now universalized, yet it remains concrete" (Pope Benedict XVI, *Deus Caritas Est* [Encyclical Letter on Christian Love] 15, December 25, 2005, https://www.vatican.va/content/benedict-xvi/en/encyclicals/documents/hf_ben-xvi_enc_20051225_deus-caritas-est.html).

response and call to action on the basis of Scripture, tradition, and magisterial teaching. Consequently, Pope Francis relies on the widespread interpretation of the parable that views the injured man on the side of the road as someone who is already an outsider and that consequently sees the fault of the priest and Levite—in contrast to the virtue of the Samaritan—as a failure to cross the boundary separating them from the injured stranger. This is similar to the approach of Aaron Wessman, whose book on polarization in the US church urges readers to imitate Jesus and "cross over" to have a genuine encounter with those on the opposite end of the polarized ecclesial community.[33] Wessman does not cite the parable of the Good Samaritan in his discussion of Jesus as an example of crossing over for Christians to imitate, but his book is an important discussion of polarization in the church that makes very good use of this image. That being said, I think it is important to underscore the way the image works in the parable as discussed above. The problem is not that the priest and the Levite do not dare to cross a boundary; it's that they create one where it didn't exist before. The love of neighbor that Jesus illustrates with the parable begins from the assumption that everyone is already a neighbor, and it is our actions that shrink the circle and put some people out.

This is more than a minor distinction or academic nicety. If we think of polarization as only a boundary that must be crossed to meet the other then we risk normalizing the state of polarization and viewing the work of repairing it as an effort to create something new. When looked at from the point of view of the parable, the state of polarization is viewed as an anomaly, something we have created and which we can undo. The act of dialogue is revealed to be the work of restoring the default state of reality—seen in the theological vision and interpretive approach of Jesus to the Bible as described by Augustine—in which every person is fundamentally encompassed within a single boundary that connects every individual with every other. Polarization is not the norm nor the ideal; it's the aberration that demands response and repair.

[33] Aaron Wessman, *The Church's Mission in a Polarized World* (Hyde Park, NY: New City Press, 2023), 174–87.

Restorative Interpretation

Augustine's rule of love demands that every biblical reading support either love of God or neighbor, no matter how much interpretive work that requires. Furthermore, love of God and of neighbor, although two separate commandments, are both realized in the love of other human beings, given that God is most clearly imaged in the human person by virtue of both creation and the incarnation of Jesus.[34] Love of neighbor entails the restoration of the fundamental human unity that has been broken by unjust social and economic structures, nationalism, racism, and religious intolerance. The Bible's fundamental moral call, according to the rule of love, is to respond to these instances of fragmentation and to seek a restoration of the wholeness insofar as we are able in our own historical milieu.

For the purposes of this book, reading the Bible according to the rule of love involves engaging with those who read the text differently with compassion and awareness of fundamental human solidarity. For Catholics, who affirm the unity of the church every Sunday when they recite the Nicene Creed, this is a challenge demanding an immediate response if the current polarization in the church is not to worsen or even break the ecclesial community. Briefly, I want to describe how people might go about this process, first within the Catholic Church, but also in dialogue with other US Christians for whom the Bible plays an important role in their views on pressing social and political issues.

While one can find a good number of books that deal with the importance of dialogue in contexts such as the workplace or education, I want to focus on some of the principles outlined by Pope Francis in *Fratelli Tutti*.[35] First is that the kind of dialogue the pope

[34] "Love of God and love of neighbor have become one: in the least of the brethren we find Jesus himself, and in Jesus we find God" (Benedict XVI, *Deus Caritas Est* 15).

[35] The United States Conference of Catholic Bishops, in response to *Fratelli Tutti*, has created a website with educational materials that "seek to encounter and to grow . . . identify common values . . . listen to understand . . . seek the truth together . . . jointly come up with creative solutions to the problems that face our world" (USCCB, A Better Kind of Politics, https://www.usccb.org/civilizeit).

advocates for happens on a small interpersonal scale and takes time. There are no quick fixes for problems that have developed over decades. Second is that consensus in pluralistic contexts can be reached by agreement on some commonly held values: "Once those fundamental values are acknowledged and adopted through dialogue and consensus, we realize that they rise above consensus; they transcend our concrete situations and remain non-negotiable. Our understanding of their meaning and scope can increase—and in that respect, consensus is a dynamic reality—but in themselves, they are held to be enduring by virtue of their inherent meaning" (*Fratelli Tutti* 211). Here we see a point of contact with Charles Cosgrove's observation that the values underlying biblical commands carry more moral force than the commands themselves because the values operate at a higher level of abstraction. People who disagree on an issue such as abortion can look at the biblical texts both sides cite for support, or that both sides see as important, and seek to determine the underlying values behind those texts. Those values, and not the texts themselves, would then be the starting point for a genuine dialogue that would seek consensus in the area of fundamental values from which further conversation about how best to enact those values can ensue.

It's important that such conversations happen face-to-face. Too often digital interaction, because it shields one person from the other person and masks the other's embodied humanity, encourages otherwise decent human beings to resort to vitriol, ridicule, or insult when disagreeing with others. A favorite tactic in these kinds of interactions is to cite laws from the Bible that are clearly untenable today in response to someone appealing to a biblical text to support a particular moral conviction or take a side on a social issue. The implicit criticism in this strategy is that the person appealing to the biblical text is "picking and choosing" which parts of the Bible to follow or ignore. Yet as this book has gone to great lengths to demonstrate, this is how everyone necessarily must read the Bible. We come to the biblical text with theological and ethical convictions that act as interpretive standards for our reading. It is unreasonable and impossible for any person to take the Bible whole and entire as authoritative without recourse to the interpretive strategies and external standards that have been developed over centuries. Rather than engage in a "gotcha" moment to earn fictitious points in some imaginary contest that views serious disagreement about an issue as a zero-sum game to be won at all costs, both parties in the conversation can explore which values and reading traditions underlie the selection of certain biblical passages rather than others. This can lead to a discussion of the issue on the level of values and how they're expressed in the texts which, as the citation from *Fratelli Tutti* states above, might allow for exploration of potential areas of consensus around certain values.

I'd like to return to the Great Commandment story one last time. Whereas Augustine read the text as an indication of how Jesus interpreted the Bible, I also want to look at how Jesus provides a positive model for the kind of dialogue that I envision. In Mark's version, quoted above, we notice that Jesus and the scribe mutually affirm each other's interpretation and, by extension, each other's character. The scribe affirms that Jesus is a true teacher and that his selection of the Great Commandment is correct. Jesus in turn affirms the scribe's character based on the latter's expansion of those two commandments ("You are not far from the kingdom of God"; Mark 12:34). In Luke's Gospel Jesus engages with the lawyer despite the fact that the latter appears to have less than noble motives for engaging Jesus (he "stood up to test Jesus"; Luke 10:25). In fact, by answering the lawyer's question with one of his own, Jesus invites the lawyer into a deeper conversation when, as is the case in Matthew's Gospel, Jesus could have simply answered the question himself and ended the encounter. Moreover, even though we are told that the lawyer's follow-up question is driven by his desire to "vindicate himself," there is no trace of impatience or rebuke in Jesus' response. He tells the lawyer the parable and then follows up with a question to make sure the lawyer has understood.

Finally, insights gleaned from interreligious dialogue can be modified and applied to the current situation of Christians disagreeing about biblical interpretation in regard to pressing moral questions. The Scriptural Reasoning Project at Cambridge University seeks to bring members of different faith communities together into groups that interact with the sacred texts of each particular community. The exercise "is not about seeking agreement but rather exploring the texts and their possible interpretations across faith boundaries and learning to 'disagree better.' The result is often a deeper understanding of others' and one's own scriptures, as well as the development of strong bonds across faith communities."[36] Here participants begin with a theme which they then identify in their respective sacred texts. This leads to an open, moderated discussion which seeks to honor each tradition and its text while at the same time acknowledging real differences.[37] Again, this is a gradual process, but the result of sustained engagement of this kind in interreligious dialogue is that participants develop both a new appreciation for the different religious traditions of others and a deepened appreciation for their own religion.[38]

I would be remiss if, in a book about hermeneutics, I were to overlook at this juncture the fact that reading is also a kind of dialogue (as discussed above in chapter 2). To that end, another way to address the separation that has come about among US Christians would be to read books on biblical interpretation by authors from different Christian groups. If we are embedded in our own culturally and historically determined vantage points from which we see the text, then we have an obligation to dialogue and listen with others who view the texts from different vantage points, and so widen our own horizons. As Pope Francis has stressed during his entire pontificate, the voices most in need of being engaged are those who have historically been on the margins. Fortunately, there is no shortage of important and engaging books about biblical interpretation practiced from a variety of social locations determined by ethnicity, race, gender, sexuality, and economic

[36] "What Is Scriptural Reasoning?," Cambridge Inter-faith Programme, http://www.scripturalreasoning.org/what-is-scriptural-reasoning.html.

[37] Pope Francis speaks of "a society where differences coexist, complementing, enriching and reciprocally illuminating one another, even amid disagreements and reservations. Each of us can learn something from others. . . . What is important is to create *processes* of encounter, processes that build a people that can accept differences" (*Fratelli Tutti* 215, 217).

[38] See the detailed study and analysis of one such group in Mara Brecht, *Virtue in Dialogue: Belief, Religious Diversity, and Women's Interreligious Encounter* (Eugene, OR: Pickwick Publications, 2014).

status.[39] Members of churches with governing bodies that produce documents on faith, doctrine, and ethics can read those documents with an eye to which biblical texts are cited in support of positions, how those biblical texts are being used (as communication or disclosure), and what underlying values the cited texts are pointing to. Catholics in particular should avail themselves of the easy accessibility of magisterial documents, not only from the Vatican but from the US Conference of Catholic Bishops and their own local bishop. I want to stress here that this kind of interaction involves slow, careful reading. There are no shortcuts. Social media accounts that try to condense nuanced and centuries-long reading traditions into memes, catchphrases, or soundbites are of little to no use in trying to expand one's horizons regarding how others read the Bible. On the contrary, the reductive nature of social media, combined with the disproportionate attention given to extreme or hostile positions, has contributed to the current state of polarization we find ourselves in today.[40]

Over forty years ago, Jonathan Z. Smith made an important analogy to describe how sacred texts both limit interpretation and foster creativity. Smith makes the distinction between diet—a limiting factor based on environmental and cultural factors that

[39] For a Jewish interpretation of the biblical text that is very similar to the rule of love, see Shai Held, *Judaism Is About Love: Recovering the Heart of Jewish Life* (New York: Farrar, Straus and Giroux, 2024). Among the wide array of books that approach the biblical text from the various standpoints discussed are: Shannon T. L. Kearns, *In the Margins: A Transgender Man's Journey with Scripture* (Grand Rapids, MI: Eerdmans, 2022); John H. Walton, *Wisdom for Faithful Reading: Principles and Practices for Old Testament Interpretation* (Downers Grove, IL: InterVarsity Press, 2023); Richard E. Averbeck, *The Old Testament Law for the Life of the Church: Reading the Torah in the Light of Christ* (Downers Grove, IL: InterVarsity Press, 2022); Munther Isaac, *The Other Side of the Wall: A Palestinian Christian Narrative of Lament and Hope* (Downers Grove, IL: InterVarsity Press, 2020); Mitri Raheb, *Faith in the Face of Empire: The Bible through Palestinian Eyes* (Maryknoll, NY: Orbis, 2014); Francisco Lozada Jr., *Toward a Latino/a Biblical Interpretation* (Atlanta: SBL Press, 2017); Cain Hope Felder, ed., *Stony the Road We Trod: African American Biblical Interpretation*, Thirtieth Anniversary Expanded Edition (Minneapolis: Fortress Press, 2021); Nyasha Junior, *An Introduction to Womanist Biblical Interpretation* (Louisville: Westminster John Knox, 2015); Sheri Faye Rosendahl, *Not Your White Jesus: Following a Radical, Refugee Messiah* (Louisville: Westminster John Knox, 2018).

[40] Wessman, *Church's Mission in a Polarized World*, 38–41.

dictate what may and may not be eaten—and cuisine—the cultivation of methods that take the elements of diet and seek to create as much variety as possible. He writes that "if food is a phenomenon characterized by limitation, cuisine is a phenomenon characterized by variegation."[41] The insight of Smith's analogy has been demonstrated again and again throughout this book, but here perhaps is its most important contribution. The limited multiplicity of all texts includes that of the Bible. While it means many things, it cannot mean anything. But among the many things it can mean are readings that are beyond our own determined historical horizon (to borrow Hans-Georg Gadamer's image discussed in chapter 2). While our horizons are a given, they are not a prison. They can be expanded by interaction with the textual cuisines of others and, in those encounters, lead to greater empathy and understanding.

[41] Jonathan Z. Smith, "Sacred Persistence: Toward a Redescription of Canon," in *Imagining Religion: From Babylon to Jonestown* (Chicago: University of Chicago Press, 1982), 40.

Conclusion

I invite you to consider the three following scenes:

In churches, homes and workplaces[1] across the country, a familiar event occurs: a group of people gather to discuss a book. The book in question is not a novel, nor a volume focused on workplace motivation, self-help, or how to have a fulfilling marriage. It's actually not even a single book, but an anthology of writings from over two thousand years ago, written over a span of almost a millennium, in languages that almost everyone in the gathering does not know, and from a part of the world that almost all of the readers will never have visited. These features, however, are either not known or not considered by the readers as they look over a passage together and takes turns commenting on it. Their interpretations involve thinking about how a passage speaks to them directly or what its deeper meaning is. Their interpretations will lead to meanings that reinforce the pre-existing assumptions of these readers that this anthology of ancient writings is rather a

[1] The "corporate effort to create a sense of belonging at work grew after the murder of George Floyd in May 2020, when many companies rushed to improve their diversity, equity and inclusion, or D.E.I., efforts. Employees from underrepresented groups were encouraged to bring their 'authentic' or 'whole' selves to work, and companies increased support for identity-based employee groups organized around gender, race, ethnicity and sexual orientation. Increasingly, faith is a part of this list. Human resources professionals, diversity consultants and scholars all say it's become more common for employees to share their religious identities at work and to request the same corporate recognition and support given to other identity groups. Most major tech companies now have official faith-based affinity groups" (Jennifer Miller, "What Happens When the Boss Invites You to Bible Study?," *New York Times*, September 22, 2023, https://www.nytimes.com/2023/09/22/business/religion-work-diversity-equity-inclusion.html).

single book from a single author with almost immediate applicability to modern readers' lives in much the same way that books about workplace motivation, self-help, or how to have a fulfilling marriage are, but with the added feature that this particular book has been and is still relied upon by millions upon millions of people for guidance and is believed to have a supernatural origin.[2]

Here is another oft-repeated scene: a person awakes in the morning and prepares for work or school. Before leaving the house (or perhaps on their commute) they open an app on their phone that selects for them a single verse or very brief passage of biblical text for the day chosen to inspire or comfort the reader. The app's developers have taken steps to select verses that meet a certain set of criteria: the selection must be uplifting or inspirational—most often connected to the mental and emotional stresses of living in a frenetic late capitalist society. It should be brief, easy to understand, and easy to apply directly to the life of an educated person—someone who can read, afford a phone, and use apps. To the user the daily phrase seems random at first (albeit not perhaps to the app's developers) and it's the randomness that adds to the supernatural quality of the daily passage. Here's something that, without knowing who I am, speaks directly to my current situation, or reveals to me something important that I need to know right now. In this way the app functions much like horoscopes producing a text with enough ambiguity and a basic positive tone and let the readers do the interpretive work of connecting it to themselves while giving the credit to the text's power.[3] Each time a "random" text lands a connection with a reader's life, the

[2] This is not simply a modern phenomenon. Recall the letter of Innocent III from the twelfth century discussed above in chapter 4 that criticized French Catholics for gathering in groups to read and discuss the Bible.

[3] Jeremiah 29:11 merits special mention, as it is one of the more popular Bible verses people cite as comforting or as a guide for their lives: "For surely I know the plans I have for you, says the LORD, plans for your welfare and not for harm, to give you a future with hope." What readers of English cannot know is that in the Hebrew text, this verse is addressed to the people of Israel and the pronouns are plural. In its biblical neighborhood, it's not a message of comfort directed to an individual as almost everyone reads it today, demonstrating the interpretive power of the reader to have this passage be a message of direct, individual comfort.

status of the text grows based on its seemingly inexplicable ability to be directly applicable.

Finally, picture a home with a cross on the wall, or a picture of Jesus, or both. Somewhere in the living room a family Bible sits in a place of honor. In that room, a young person tells their parents for the first time about their inborn attraction to people of the same sex. The young person is most likely afraid. In response, the parents tell their child that he or she is no longer welcome to live in the house or even to have any contact with them, because the parents view their child's sexual orientation as deviant or unnatural. This judgment is based upon the parents' religious belief and supported by appeal to the Bible.[4]

These scenes are not hypothetical or imaginary. Each one of them draws upon my actual experience with numerous US undergraduates in my thirty years of teaching. They attest to the ongoing, if invisible, influence of the Bible in the lives of many. While it's common for older Americans to lament the loss of Bible literacy in the US, and while some data bear that out in terms of content knowledge, the Bible continues to be engaged as a book that offers comfort and guidance to Americans from many walks of life.

Let's turn from these manifold private instances of encounter with the biblical text to singular public instances, all of which have happened in the last six months of this writing. In February 2024, the Alabama Supreme Court issued a ruling in response to an appeal from the Mobile, Alabama, circuit court. The case involved three couples who sued a fertility clinic for wrongful death of a minor after their frozen embryos were accidentally destroyed at the clinic. The Alabama Supreme Court found for the plaintiffs on the basis that embryos are human persons. Significantly, in his concurring opinion, Alabama Supreme Court Chief Justice Tom Parker based his reasoning in part on Genesis 1:27 (humanity is created in the image of God), Genesis 9:6 (the prohibition against killing with capital punishment as the consequence), and Exodus

[4] This scene is no outlier. According to research compiled at Lesley University, half of all teenagers who come out to their parents receive a negative reaction, and one in four are forced to leave their homes (Lesley University, "The Cost of Coming Out: LGBT Youth Homelessness," https://lesley.edu/article/the-cost-of-coming-out-lgbt-youth-homelessness).

30:12 (the commandment from the Decalogue that forbids murder). Parker writes:

> In summary, the theologically based view of the sanctity of life adopted by the People of Alabama encompasses the following: (1) God made every person in His image; (2) each person therefore has a value that far exceeds the ability of human beings to calculate; and (3) human life cannot be wrongfully destroyed without incurring the wrath of a holy God, who views the destruction of His image as an affront to Himself. Section 36.06 recognizes that this is true of unborn human life no less than it is of all other human life—that even before birth, all human beings bear the image of God, and their lives cannot be destroyed without effacing His glory.[5]

It's important to note that the chief justice's interpretation of the biblical text goes farther theologically than the passages' plain sense. Nowhere in Genesis 1, Genesis 6, or Exodus 20 is there any mention of God's holy wrath awaiting those who take a human life. The only penalty mentioned at all is in Genesis 6, and it is to be performed by other people, not an angry deity. Similarly, the biblical text does not explain exactly what it means to be made "in God's image," and interpreters have proposed many explanations. This leads to the second point. The chief justice's summary introduces language of value or worth that one doesn't find in the biblical text. What the summary text by the Alabama chief justice does is use the biblical text to point to binding values, the first

[5] James LePage and Emily LePage, individually and as parents and next friends of two deceased LePage embryos, Embryo A and Embryo B; and William Tripp Fonde and Caroline Fonde, individually and as parents and next friends of two deceased Fonde embryos, Embryo C and Embryo D v. The Center for Reproductive Medicine, P.C., and Mobile Infirmary Association d/b/a Mobile Infirmary Medical Center, SC- 2022-0515; and Felicia Burdick-Aysenne and Scott Aysenne, in their individual capacities and as parents and next friends of Baby Aysenne, deceased embryo/minor v. The Center for Reproductive Medicine, P.C., and Mobile Infirmary Association d/b/a Mobile Infirmary Medical Center, SC- 2022-0579 (Alabama Supreme Court, 2022), 37–38. In addition to the use of the Bible, Chief Justice Parker draws on the thought of Thomas Aquinas, John Calvin, and the lesser-known seventeenth-century Protestant theologian Petrus van Mastricht. The opinion also uses three different Bible translations and cites an explanatory note from the Geneva Bible (discussed in chap. 1) with the rationale that it was the "most popular book in colonial homes" (36).

being the inestimable worth of the human person and the second being the character of God as willing to judge with righteous wrath those who take human life. This creates a theological world where a God whose main characteristic is majesty commands obedience of people and sits ready to punish any failure of that obedience.

Second, on June 19, 2024, Louisiana Governor Jeff Landry signed into law Act 676, which requires that the Ten Commandments be posted in every public school classroom on the basis of their importance "in our state and national history, culture, and tradition."[6] Significantly, the text of the Ten Commandments mandated in the law is that of the King James Bible and they are numbered according to the Protestant biblical tradition.[7] The commandments are to be displayed along with the Mayflower Compact of 1620 and the Northwest Ordinance of 1787. If the meaning of texts is determined by their neighborhoods, as discussed in this book's introduction, then the placement of the Ten Commandments alongside these two other texts is meant to emphasize that, from the beginning of "America"—here understood to coincide only with the arrival of white, Protestant colonists—religious practice was meant to be part of civic life. In the words of Act 676, the Mayflower Compact was "America's first written constitution and made a Covenant with Almighty God . . . the first purely American document of self-government and affirmed the link between civil society and God." Similarly, the Northwest Ordinance is chosen as one of the required documents because it states that "religion, morality, and knowledge, being necessary to good government and the happiness of mankind, schools and the means of education shall forever be encouraged." It's clear from the text of the law that the importance of these documents is due to more than their witness to "our state and national history, culture, and tradition." Together they send the message that American public life should include religious—here understood to be European Protestant—values and that those values are encapsulated by the Ten Commandments.

[6] Text of the bill available at https://legis.la.gov/legis/BillInfo.aspx?i=245592&sbi=y.

[7] Jewish, Catholic, and Protestant numbering of the Ten Commandments differ, with the three different numberings agreeing only on the tenth commandment.

The neighborhood of the Mayflower Compact and the Northwest Ordinance serve to underscore the need for the Ten Commandments to be engaged by students as a religious text.

Finally, on June 27, 2024, Oklahoma state superintendent Ryan Walters ordered all public schools in the state to teach the Bible by virtue of the fact that it is "a necessary historical document to teach our kids about the history of this country, to have a complete understanding of Western civilization, to understand the basis of our legal system. . . . Every teacher, every classroom in the state will have a Bible in the classroom and will be teaching from the Bible in the classroom."[8] The need for the superintendent to emphasize that every classroom will have a Bible is curious, given that every classroom obviously has copies of all relevant material in its curriculum. It should go without saying that a classroom teaching the Bible would have a Bible in it, ideally multiple copies of it, as is the case with other books that students are taught. Walters's statement reveals a religious significance given to the mere presence of a Bible, apart from how it is used. It is reminiscent of the story of Nicolaus discussed in chapter 3, whose inadvertent carrying of a biblical text into a brothel demonstrated the inherent power of the text. Superintendent Walters's stipulation of a Bible in every classroom reflects the idea that the mere presence of a Bible is powerful, and views it as more than just a text that helps shed light on Western civilization, history, or US jurisprudence. As is the case with the Louisiana law requiring the posting of the Ten Commandments in public schools, there is a theological belief about the Bible as an inspired text whose power is such that any encounter with it allows for the possibility of religious effects on those who are exposed to it.

Readers will not be surprised that the states with these legislative and judicial uses of the Bible are all in the Southern US, and that all of the government officials involved are from the Republican Party, to which most White Evangelical Christians belong. As we saw in chapter 1, the view of the Bible as a book of commandments was dominant in the antebellum south in the debate over slavery

[8] Sarah Mervosh and Elizabeth Dias, "Oklahoma's State Superintendent Requires Public Schools to Teach the Bible," *New York Times*, June 27, 2024, https://www.nytimes.com/2024/06/27/us/oklahoma-public-schools-bible.html.

and the legacy of these readings have marked how we argue over the Bible in the US ever since. It's not my interest here to critique these decisions, although as I indicated in the introduction, I think the separation of church and state is essential to the health and survival of our republic. Nor do I want to examine the legality of these actions. I don't have the expertise, and it will take at least several months for any court actions to be undertaken and completed. Rather I want to point out a curious disconnect. The justifications provided for these introductions of the biblical text in public school classrooms rely on the Bible's historic or cultural importance. A such, they argue that the Bible merits inclusion in social studies or history in our public school curriculum. This is only part of the picture, however. As seen in the discussion of these justifications, there is also a not-so-subtle implicit belief that views the Bible as an inspired text whose supernatural presence or power is needed in the classroom as the content and justification for a particular set of moral beliefs.

We shouldn't be surprised that people view the Bible as a book with transcendent power and moral force. As we have seen, this is how biblical texts have been read for a very long time. If anything, our concern should lie with the fact that this rather common understanding of the Bible seems to have been put into the background in favor of a more anodyne view of the text as a resource for explaining nonreligious cultural traditions. In other words, the Bible is portrayed in the newly introduced Louisiana and Oklahoma directives as a cultural classic discussed above in chapter 2, but the underlying view of the Bible's necessity to be in the classroom is because of its status as a sacred text. In this regard I find it particularly interesting to notice the common understanding of the biblical text in both the Louisiana Ten Commandments law and the daily Bible verse app described above. Both see the Bible as a powerful text with a unified message that can be effectively conveyed using only a tiny portion of its content, whether that be a single biblical verse generated by computer program or a mere sixteen verses from the book of Exodus hung on a classroom wall.[9]

[9] I also find fascinating the fact that the view of the Bible as a single book with a single author justifies finding meaning in tiny snippets of text is similar to the tendency of much historical-critical study to isolate small units of text

This should give us pause. All texts have a surplus of meaning, sacred texts most of all. Disagreements among Christians and Jews about the meaning of the Bible are for the most part founded on the shared assumption of the text's special status. Biblical interpretation is argued over because all parties see it as important. When my students begin to read the Bible with the tools of biblical scholarship and the history of theological interpretation, they will unconsciously write in their papers and exams about the need to find the Bible's "true meaning." Four months of classroom work isn't enough to dent the ironclad hold of our culture's understanding of the Bible as a unified text with a single correct meaning.[10] This view leads to the bitter arguments among Christians when, inevitably, different interpretations emerge. After all, there can only be one "true meaning." In his novel, *The Name of the Rose*, Umberto Eco tells the story of the medieval Catholic Church ready to defend with violence any deviation from a narrow understanding of the truth seen as divinely authorized and practiced with a lack of charity. When this fixation on a single truth that cannot tolerate the existence of an alternative results in the predictable physical, mental, and spiritual devastation, the novel's protagonist, the Franciscan friar William of Baskerville, offers the story's lesson that "the only truth lies in learning to free ourselves from insane passion for the truth."[11] It's one we would also do well to take to heart.

---

based on the view that the Bible is an anthology made up of numerous earlier sources.

[10] See also Timothy Beal, *The Rise and Fall of the Bible: The Unexpected History of an Accidental Book* (New York: Houghton Mifflin, 2012), who describes and critiques the view of the Bible as a "book of answers."

[11] Umberto Eco, *The Name of the Rose* (New York: Harcourt and Brace, 1980), 491.

Bibliography

Adiele, Pius Onyemechi. *The Popes, the Catholic Church and the Transatlantic Enslavement of Black Africans 1418–1839*. Hildesheim: Georg Olms Verlag, 2017.

Agenzia Giornalistica Italia. "Perché Papa Francesco ha deciso di cambiare il Padre nostro." August 14, 2018. https://www.agi.it/blog-italia/idee/post/2018-08-14/padre_nostro_papa_francesco-4267420/.

Archambault, George, ed. *Dialogue avec Tryphon*. Paris: Librairie Alphones Picard, 1909.

Arndt, W., and B. Krusch, eds. *Gregorii Turonensis Opera*. Volume 1. Hanover: Impensis Bibliopolii Hahniani, 1884.

Averbeck, Richard E. *The Old Testament Law for the Life of the Church: Reading the Torah in the Light of Christ*. Downers Grove, IL: InterVarsity Press, 2022.

Babcock, William S., trans. *Tyconius: The Book of Rules*. Atlanta: Society of Biblical Literature, 1989.

Baker, Carlos, ed. *Ernest Hemingway: Selected Letters 1917–1961*. New York: Scribner, 2003.

Bakewell, Sarah. *At the Existentialist Café*. New York: Other Press, 2016.

Barton, John. *Ethics in Ancient Israel*. New York: Oxford University Press, 2014.

Barton, John. *The Nature of Biblical Criticism*. Louisville: Westminster John Knox, 2007.

Barton, John. *Oracles of God: Perceptions of Prophecy in Israel after the Exile*. New York: Oxford University Press, 1986.

Barton, John. *People of the Book? The Authority of the Bible in Christianity*. Louisville: Westminster John Knox, 1989.

Barzun, Jacques. *From Dawn to Decadence: 500 Years of Western Cultural Life*. San Francisco: HarperCollins, 2000.

Beal, Timothy K. *The Rise and Fall of the Bible: The Unexpected History of an Accidental Book*. New York: Houghton Mifflin, 2012.

Béchard, Dean P., trans. *The Scripture Documents: An Anthology of Official Catholic Teachings*. Collegeville, MN: Liturgical Press, 2002.

Beecher, Henry Ward. "Our Blameworthiness." In *Patriotic Addresses in America and England, From 1850 to 1885, on Slavery, the Civil War, and the Development of Civil Liberty in the United States*. New York: Fords, Howard, and Hulbert, 1887.

Beeke, Joel R. "The Perspicuity of Scripture." *Puritan Reformed Journal* 7, no. 2 (July 2015): 45–64.

Bellis, Alice Ogden. "The Bible in African American Perspectives." *Teaching Theology and Religion* 1 (1998): 161–70.

Ben Zvi, Ehud, ed. "Rereading Oracles of God: Twenty Years after John Barton, *Oracles of God: Perceptions of Prophecy in Israel after the Exile* (London: Darton, Longman and Todd, 1986)." *Journal of Hebrew Scriptures* 7 (2007), https://doi.org/10.5508/jhs.2007.v7.a14.

Benedict XVI, Pope. *Deus Caritas Est* (Encyclical Letter on Christian Love). The Holy See. December 25, 2005. https://www.vatican.va/content/benedict-xvi/en/encyclicals/documents/hf_ben-xvi_enc_20051225_deus-caritas-est.html.

Bolin, Thomas M. "The Biblical Commission's Instruction, *On the Historical Truth of the Gospels (Sancta Mater Ecclesia)* and Present Magisterial Attitudes Toward Biblical Exegesis." *Gregorianum* 93 (2012): 765–85.

Bolin, Thomas M. *Ecclesiastes and the Riddle of Authorship*. London: Routledge, 2017.

Bolin, Thomas M. *Ezra-Nehemiah*. Collegeville, MN: Liturgical Press, 2012.

Bolin, Thomas M. *Freedom Beyond Forgiveness: The Book of Jonah Re-Examined*. London: Bloomsbury, 1997.

Bolin, Thomas M. "Job, White Privilege, and the Case for Reparations." *Ancient Jew Review* (February 2019). https://www.ancientjewreview.com/articles/2018/12/9/job-white-privilege-and-the-case-for-reparations.

Bolin, Thomas M. "Out of the Wilderness? Some Suggestions for the Future of Pentateuchal Research." In *History, Archaeology and the Bible Forty Years after "Historicity,"* edited by Ingrid Hjelm and Thomas L. Thompson, 47–59. New York: Routledge, 2016.

Brecht, Mara. *Virtue in Dialogue: Belief, Religious Diversity, and Women's Interreligious Encounter*. Eugene, OR: Pickwick Publications, 2014.

Breed, Brennan W. *Nomadic Text: A Theory of Biblical Reception History*. Bloomington: Indiana University Press, 2014.

Brettler, Marc Zvi. "I Have a Dream: Martin Luther King Jr.'s Biblical Prophetic Speech." *The Torah* online. https://www.thetorah.com/article/i-have-a-dream-martin-luther-king-jrs-biblical-prophetic-speech.

Brown, Dan. *The Da Vinci Code: A Novel.* New York: Anchor Books, 2003.

Brown, Jeannine K., and Kazuhiko Yamazaki-Ransom. "The Parable of the Good Samaritan and the Narrative Portrayal of Samaritans in Luke-Acts." *Journal of Theological Interpretation* 15 (September 21, 2021): 233–46.

Brown, Peter. *Augustine of Hippo.* Berkeley: University of California Press, 1969.

Callahan, Allen Dwight. *The Talking Book: African Americans and the Bible.* New Haven: Yale University Press, 2006.

Calvin, John, and Jacopo Sadoleto. *A Reformation Debate.* Translated by Henry Beveridge and edited by John Olin. Grand Rapids, MI: Baker Books, 1966.

Carvalho, Corrine. *Primer on Biblical Methods.* Winona, MN: Anselm Publishing, 2009.

Catechism of the Catholic Church. 2nd ed. Washington, DC: United States Catholic Conference—Libreria Editrice Vaticana, 1997. https://www.vatican.va/archive/ENG0015/_INDEX.HTM.

Chalmers, Matthew. "Rethinking Luke 10: The Parable of the Good Samaritan Israelite." *Journal of Biblical Literature* 139, no. 3 (January 1, 2020): 543–66.

Chan, Yiu Sing Lúcás. "Biblical Ethics 3D." *Theological Studies* 76, no. 1 (2015): 112–128.

Chan, Yiu Sing Lúcás. *The Ten Commandments and the Beatitudes: Biblical Studies and Ethics for Real Life.* Lanham, MD: Rowman & Littlefield, 2012.

Chan, Yiu Sing Lúcás, James F. Keenan, and Ronaldo Zacharias, eds. *The Bible and Catholic Theological Ethics.* Maryknoll, NY: Orbis, 2017.

Chancey, Mark, Carol Meyers, and Eric Meyers, eds. *The Bible in the Public Square: Its Enduring Influence in American Life.* Atlanta: Society of Biblical Literature, 2014.

Coates, Ta-Nehisi. "The Case for Reparations." *The Atlantic* 313 (June 2014): 54–71.

Collins, John J. *What Are Biblical Values? What the Bible Says on Key Ethical Issues.* New Haven: Yale University Press, 2019.

Cone, James H. "God and Black Suffering: Calling the Oppressors to Account." *Anglican Theological Review* 90, no. 4 (Fall 2008): 701–12.

Cone, James H. *The Spirituals and the Blues*. Maryknoll, NY: Orbis, 1972. Repr., Maryknoll, NY: Orbis, 1991.

Congar, Yves. *Tradition and Traditions: An Historical and a Theological Essay*. Translated by Michael Naseby and Thomas Rainborough. London: Burnes and Oates, 1966.

Cosgrove, Charles. *Appealing to Scripture in Moral Debate: Five Hermeneutical Rules*. Grand Rapids, MI: Eerdmans, 2002.

Cox, Jillian E. "Martin Luther on the Living Word: Rethinking the Principle of *Sola Scriptura*." *Pacifica* 29, no. 1 (2016): 3–21.

Crouch, Carly L., ed. *The Cambridge Companion to the Hebrew Bible and Ethics*. Cambridge: Cambridge University Press, 2021.

Crystal, David. *Begat: The King James Bible and the English Language*. New York: Oxford University Press, 2010.

Cupich, Blase. "Statement of Cardinal Blase J. Cupich, Archbishop of Chicago, on the Administration's Family-Separation Policy." WTTW online, June 2018. https://chicagotonight.wttw.com/sites/default/files/article/file-attachments/Statement%20Version%20-%20English.pdf.

Cupples, Anna Jane. *Tappy's Chicks: And Other Links Between Nature and Human Nature*. London: Strahan, 1872.

D'Antonio, William V., Michele Dillon, and Mary L. Gautier. *American Catholics in Transition*. Boston: Rowman & Littlefield, 2013.

Davies, Philip. *Whose Bible Is It Anyway?* 2nd ed. London: T&T Clark, 2004.

Deleuze, Gilles. *Bergsonism*. Princeton, NJ: Princeton University Press, 1991.

Dell, Katherine. *Who Needs the Old Testament? Its Enduring Appeal and Why the New Atheists Don't Get It*. Eugene, OR: Wipf & Stock, 2017.

Dodge, Charles. *Systematic Theology, Volume 1*. New York: Charles Scribner's, 1871. Repr., Grand Rapids, MI: Eerdmans, 1940.

Douglass, Frederick. "The Dred Scott Decision: An Address Delivered in Part, In New York, New York." In *The Frederick Douglass Papers, Series 1, Vol. 3: Speeches, Debates, and Interviews, 1855–1863*, edited by John W. Blassingame, 181–83. New Haven: Yale University Press, 1979.

Douglass, Frederick. *The Life and Times of Frederick Douglass, Written By Himself*. London: Park Publishing, 1882.

Douglass, Frederick. *Narrative of the Life of Frederick Douglass, An American Slave*. Boston: Anti-Slavery Office, 1845.

Douglass, Frederick. "What to the Slave Is the Fourth of July?" July 5, 1852. Teaching American History website. https://teachingamerican history.org/library/document/what-to-the-slave-is-the-fourth-of -july/.

Eco, Umberto. *The Name of the Rose*. New York: Harcourt and Brace, 1980.

Ehrman, Bart D. *Truth and Fiction in The Da Vinci Code*. New York: Oxford University Press, 2004.

Evans, Rachel Held. "All Right Then, I'll Go to Hell." Blog post. May 23, 2012. https://rachelheldevans.com/blog/huck-finn-hell.

Evans, Rachel Held. *Inspired: Slaying Giants, Walking on Water, and Loving the Bible Again*. Nashville: Thomas Nelson, 2018.

Fea, John. *The Bible Cause: A History of the American Bible Society*. New York: Oxford University Press, 2016.

Flannery, Frances, and Rodney A. Werline, eds. *The Bible in Political Debate: What Does It Really Say?* London: Bloomsbury T&T Clark, 2016.

Fletcher, Jeannine Hill. *The Sin of White Supremacy: Christianity, Racism, and Religious Diversity in America*. Maryknoll, NY: Orbis, 2017.

Floyd-Thomas, Juan, Stacey Floyd-Thomas, and Mark Toulouse. *The Altars Where We Worship: The Religious Significance of Popular Culture*. Louisville: Westminster John Knox, 2016.

Francis, Pope. *Fratelli Tutti* (Encyclical Letter on Fraternity and Social Friendship). The Holy See. October 3, 2020. https://www.vatican .va/content/francesco/en/encyclicals/documents/papa-francesco _20201003_enciclica-fratelli-tutti.html.

François, Wim. "Vernacular Bible Reading in Late Medieval and Early Modern Europe: The 'Catholic' Position Revisited." *Catholic Historical Review* 104, no. 1 (2018): 23–56.

Fredriksen, Paula. *Augustine and the Jews: A Christian Defense of Jews and Judaism*. New Haven: Yale University Press, 2008.

Gadamer, Hans-Georg, *Truth and Method*. 2nd rev. ed. London: Continuum: 2004.

Gafney, Wilda. "Reading the Hebrew Bible Responsibly." In *The Africana Bible: Reading Israel's Scriptures from Africa and the African Diaspora*, edited by Hugh R. Page, Randall C. Bailey, Valerie Bridgeman, Stacy Davis, Nathaniel Samuel Murrell, Cheryl Kirk-Duggan, Madipoane Masenya, and Rodney Steven Sadler, 45–51. Minneapolis: Fortress Press, 2010.

Galilei, Galileo. "Letter to the Grand Duchess Christina." In *Discoveries and Opinions of Galileo*. Translated and edited by Stilman Drake, 173–216. New York: Anchor-Doubleday, 1957.

Gallagher Elkins, Kathleen. *Mary, Mother of Martyrs: How Motherhood Became Self-Sacrifice in Early Christianity*. Cambridge, MA: Feminist Studies in Religion Books, 2018.

Gates, Henry Louis, Jr.. *The Signifying Monkey: A Theory of African-American Literary Criticism*. New York: Oxford University Press, 2014. First published 1988.

Gates, Henry Louis, Jr., and William L. Andrews, eds. *Pioneers of the Black Atlantic: Five Slave Narratives from the Enlightenment, 1772–1815*. New York: Civitas, 1998.

Gavrilov, A. K. "Techniques of Reading in Classical Antiquity." *Classical Quarterly* 47 (1997): 65–73.

Gonzales, Richard. "Sessions Cites the Bible to Justify Immigrant Family Separations." *National Public Radio*. June 14, 2018. https://www.npr.org/2018/06/14/620181177/sessions-cites-the-bible-to-justify-immigrant-family-separations.

Goodman, Hananya, ed. *Between Jerusalem and Benares: Comparative Studies in Judaism and Hinduism*. Albany: SUNY Press, 1984.

Gould, Stephen Jay. *Rocks of Ages: Science and Religion in the Fullness of Life*. New York: Ballantine, 1999.

Grafton, Anthony, and Megan Williams. *Christianity and the Transformation of the Book: Origen, Eusebius, and the Library of Caesarea*. Cambridge: Harvard/Belknap, 2006.

Greenspahn, Frederick E. "Why Prophecy Ceased." *Journal of Biblical Literature* 108 (1989): 37–49.

Gronniosaw, James Albert Ukawsaw. *A Narrative of the Most Remarkable Particulars in the Life of James Albert Ukawsaw Gronniosaw, An African Prince as Related by Himself*. N.p.: W. Gye, 1772.

Gutjahr, Paul C. "Protestant English-Language Bible Publishing and Translation." In *The Oxford Handbook of the Bible in America*, edited by Paul C. Gutjahr, 45–51. New York: Oxford University Press, 2018.

Hains, Todd R. *Martin Luther and the Rule of Faith: Reading God's Word for God's People*. Downers Grove, IL: IVP Academic, 2022.

Halivni, David Weiss. *Peshat and Derash: Plain and Applied Meaning in Rabbinic Exegesis*. New York: Oxford University Press, 2018.

Hamori, Esther. *Women's Divination in Biblical Literature: Prophecy, Necromancy, and Other Arts of Knowledge*. New Haven: Yale University Press, 2015.

Hanegraaff, Hank, and Paul Maier. *Da Vinci Code: Fact or Fiction?* Carol Stream, IL: Tyndale House, 2004.

Hanson, Drew. *The Dream: Martin Luther King, Jr. and the Speech That Inspired a Nation*. New York: Ecco, 2003.

Harrill, J. Albert. "The Use of the New Testament in the American Slave Controversy: A Case History in the Hermeneutical Tension between Biblical Criticism and Christian Moral Debate." *Religion and American Culture* 10 (2000): 149–86.

Hayes, John H., and Frederick Prussner. *Old Testament Theology: Its History and Development*. Atlanta: John Knox, 1985.

Haynes, Stephen. *Noah's Curse: The Biblical Justification of American Slavery*. New York: Oxford University Press, 2002.

Hays, Richard B. *The Moral Vision of the New Testament*. San Francisco: HarperCollins, 1996.

Held, Shai. *Judaism Is About Love: Recovering the Heart of Jewish Life*. New York: Farrar, Strauss and Giroux, 2024.

Hequet, Suzanne. "The 1518 Proceedings at Augsburg." *Lutheran Quarterly* 32, no. 1 (2018): 60–70.

Hertzler-McCain, Aleja. "Survey: US Catholics More Polarized Than Ever over Pope Francis." *America*. April 12, 2024. https://www.americamagazine.org/politics-society/2024/04/12/pope-francis-polarization-us-catholics-247690.

Higton, Mike. "Boldness and Reserve: A Lesson from St. Augustine." *Anglican Theological Review* 85, no. 3 (2003): 447–56.

Hill, C. E. *Who Chose the Gospels? Probing the Great Gospel Conspiracy*. New York: Oxford University Press, 2010.

Hill, Edmund, OP, trans. *Saint Augustine: Homilies on the Gospel of John 1-40*. Hyde Park, NY: New City Press, 2009.

Hill, Edmund, OP, trans. *Saint Augustine: Teaching Christianity (De Doctrina Christiana)*. Hyde Park, NY: New City Press, 1996.

Hock, Ronald F. *The Chreia in Ancient Rhetoric, Vol. 3*. Atlanta: Society of Biblical Literature, 2012.

Hock, Ronald F., and Edward N. O'Neil. *The Chreia in Ancient Rhetoric, Vol. 1*. Atlanta: Scholars Press, 1986.

Hock, Ronald F., and Edward N. O'Neil. *The Chreia in Ancient Rhetoric, Vol. 2*. Atlanta: Society of Biblical Literature, 2002.

Hope Felder, Cain, ed. *Stony the Road We Trod: African American Biblical Interpretation*. Thirtieth Anniversary Expanded Edition. Minneapolis: Fortress Press, 2021.

Irenaeus. *The Demonstration of the Apostolic Preaching*. Translated by Armitage Robinson. New York: Macmillan, 1920.

Isaac, Munther. *The Other Side of the Wall: A Palestinian Christian Narrative of Lament and Hope*. Downers Grove, IL: InterVarsity Press, 2020.

Jensen, Alexander. *Theological Hermeneutics*. London: SCM Press, 2007.

Joalland, Michael. "Isaac Newton Reads the King James Version: The Marginal Notes and Reading Marks of a Natural Philosopher." *Proceedings of the Bibliographical Society of America* 113 (2019): 297–339.

John Paul II, Pope. *Veritatis Splendor* (Encyclical Letter Regarding Certain Fundamental Questions of the Church's Moral Teaching). The Holy See. August 6, 1993. https://www.vatican.va/content/john-paul-ii/en/encyclicals/documents/hf_jp-ii_enc_06081993_veritatis-splendor.html.

Junior, Nyasha. *An Introduction to Womanist Biblical Interpretation*. Louisville: Westminster John Knox, 2015.

Kallas, Endel. "Martin Luther as Expositor of the Song of Songs." *Lutheran Quarterly* 2 (1988): 323–41.

Kearns, Shannon T. L. *In the Margins: A Transgender Man's Journey with Scripture*. Grand Rapids, MI: Eerdmans, 2022.

Keddie, G. Anthony. "'Who Is My Neighbor?' Ethnic Boundaries and the Samaritan Other in Luke 10:25-37." *Biblical Interpretation* 28, no. 2 (March 2020): 246–71.

Knowles, Michael P. "What Was the Victim Wearing? Literary, Economic, and Social Contexts for the Parable of the Good Samaritan." *Biblical Interpretation* 12, no. 2 (April 2004): 145–74.

Kolb, Robert. "Current Perspectives on Luther's Biblical Interpretation." *Lutheran Quarterly* 36, no. 3 (2022): 249–67.

Konieczny, Mary Ellen, Charles C. Camosy, and Tricia C. Bruce, eds. *Polarization in the US Catholic Church: Naming the Wounds, Beginning to Heal*. Collegeville, MN: Liturgical Press, 2016.

Kozyra, Wojciech. "Kant on the Jews and Their Religion." *Diametros* 17, no. 65 (2020): 32–55.

Larsen, Matthew D. C. *Gospels Before the Book*. New York: Oxford University Press, 2018.

Legaspi, Michael C. *The Death of Scripture and the Rise of Biblical Studies*. New York: Oxford University Press, 2010.

Leim, Joshua Eugene. "To Inherit Eternal Life: Jesus, the Lawyer, and Luke's Soteriological Grammar." *Bulletin for Biblical Research* 31, no. 2 (July 7, 2021): 167–90.

LePage, James, and Emily LePage, individually and as parents and next friends of two deceased LePage embryos, Embryo A and Embryo B; and William Tripp Fonde and Caroline Fonde, individually and as parents and next friends of two deceased Fonde embryos, Embryo C and Embryo D v. The Center for Reproductive Medicine, P.C., and Mobile Infirmary Association d/b/a Mobile Infirmary Medical Center, SC- 2022-0515; and Felicia Burdick-Aysenne and Scott Aysenne, in their individual capacities and as parents and next friends of Baby Aysenne, deceased embryo/minor v. The Center for Reproductive Medicine, P.C., and Mobile Infirmary Association d/b/a Mobile Infirmary Medical Center, SC- 2022-0579 (Alabama Supreme Court, 2022).

Levine, Amy-Jill. *Short Stories by Jesus: The Enigmatic Parables of a Controversial Rabbi*. San Francisco: HarperCollins, 2014.

Levine, Amy-Jill, and Marc Zvi Brettler. *The Bible With and Without Jesus: How Jews and Christians Read the Same Story Differently*. New York: HarperOne, 2020.

Lieu, Judith. *Marcion and the Making of a Heretic: God and Scripture in the Second Century*. Cambridge, UK: Cambridge University Press, 2015.

Lindenberger, James M. *Ancient Aramaic and Hebrew Letters*. Atlanta: Scholars Press, 1994.

Lipka, Michael, and Gregory A. Smith. "Like Americans Overall, U.S. Catholics Are Sharply Divided by Party." Pew Research Center. January 24, 2019. https://www.pewresearch.org/fact-tank/2019/01/24/like-americans-overall-u-s-catholics-are-sharply-divided-by-party/.

Lischer, Richard. *The Preacher King: Martin Luther King, Jr. and the Word That Moved America*. New York: Oxford University Press, 1995.

Longman, Tremper. *The Bible and the Ballot: Using Scripture in Political Decisions*. Grand Rapids, MI: Eerdmans, 2020.

Lozada, Francisco, Jr. *Toward a Latino/a Biblical Interpretation*. Atlanta: SBL Press, 2017.

Lubin, Timothy. "The Virtuosic Exegesis of the Brahmavadin and the Rabbi." *Numen* 49, no. 4 (2002): 427–49.

Luijendijk, Anne Marie, and William E. Klingshirn, eds. *My Lots Are in Thy Hands: Sortilege and Its Practitioners in Late Antiquity*. Leiden: Brill, 2019.

Luther, Martin. "Answer to the Hyperchristian, Hyperspiritual and Hyperlearned Book by Goat Emser in Leipzig Including Some Thoughts Regarding His Companion, the Fool Murner." Translated by Eric Gritsch and Ruth Gritsch. In *Luther's Works* 39, edited by Eric Gritsch, 137–225. Philadelphia: Fortress Press, 1970.

MacCulloch, Diarmaid. *Silence: A Christian History*. New York: Penguin Books, 2013.

MacDonald, Dennis R. "Alexandria and Allegory." *Bible Odyssey*. https://www.bibleodyssey.org/places/related-articles/alexandria-and-allegory/.

Markham, Edwin. "Outwitted." *The Literary Digest* 49 (July–December, 1914): 801.

Marks, Jonathan. "Solving the Riddle of Race." *Studies in History and Philosophy of Biological and Biomedical Sciences* 59 (2016): 161–64.

Martín Hernández, Raquel. "Using Homer for Divination: Homeromanteia in Context." *CHS Research Bulletin* 2, no. 1 (2013). https://research-bulletin.chs.harvard.edu/2014/03/28/using-homer-for-divination-homeromanteia-in-context/.

Massingale, Bryan. "A Parallel That Limps: The Rhetoric of Slavery in the Pro-Life Discourse of U.S. Bishops." In *Voting and Holiness: Catholic Perspectives on Political Participation*, edited by Nicholas P. Cafardi, 158–77. Mahwah, NJ: Paulist, 2012.

Massingale, Bryan. *Racial Justice and the Catholic Church*. Maryknoll, NY: Orbis, 2010.

Mastnjak, Nathan. *Before the Scrolls: A Material Approach to Israel's Prophetic Library*. New York: Oxford University Press, 2023.

Matera, Frank J. *New Testament Ethics: The Legacies of Jesus and Paul*. Louisville: Westminster John Knox, 1996.

Matthews, Victor H. *The Hebrew Prophets and Their Social World*. Grand Rapids, MI: Baker, 2012.

McGrath, Alister. *In the Beginning: The Story of the King James Bible and How It Changed a Nation, a Language, and a Culture*. New York: Anchor Books, 2001.

Mencken, H. L. "Law and Freedom, Mencken Discovers, Yield Place to Holy Writ in Rhea County." *Baltimore Evening Sun*. July 15, 1925.

Mencken, H. L. "Yearning Mountaineers' Souls Need Reconversion Nightly, Mencken Finds." *Baltimore Evening Sun*. July 13, 1925.

Mervosh, Sarah, and Elizabeth Dias. "Oklahoma's State Superintendent Requires Public Schools to Teach the Bible. *New York Times*. June 27, 2024. https://www.nytimes.com/2024/06/27/us/oklahoma-public-schools-bible.html.

Miller, Jennifer. "What Happens When the Boss Invites You to Bible Study?" *New York Times*. September 22, 2023. https://www.nytimes.com/2023/09/22/business/religion-work-diversity-equity-inclusion.html.

Miller, Keith D. "City Called Freedom: Biblical Metaphor in Spirituals, Gospel Lyrics, and the Civil Rights Movement." In *African Americans and the Bible*, edited by Vincent Wimbush, 546–57. New York: Continuum, 2000.

Miller, Keith D. "Second Isaiah Lands in Washington, DC: Martin Luther King, Jr.'s 'I Have a Dream' as Biblical Narrative and Biblical Hermeneutic." *Rhetoric Review* 26, no. 4 (2007): 405–24.

Millies, Steven P. *Good Intentions: A History of Catholic Voters' Road from Roe to Trump*. Collegeville, MN: Liturgical Press, 2018.

Montague, George, SM. *Understanding the Bible: A Basic Introduction to Biblical Interpretation*. Rev. ed. Mahwah, NJ: Paulist, 2007.

Moran, Jeffrey P. *The Scopes Trial: A Brief History with Documents*. Boston: Bedford St. Martins, 2002.

Mørkøre Stigel Hansen, Bjarke. "Biblical Hermeneutics in Galileo's 'Letter to the Grand Duchess Christina': On the Issue of Negative Theology." *Studia Theologica: Nordic Journal of Theology* 74, no. 1 (2020): 67–93. https://doi.org/10.1080/0039338X.2020.1750477.

Moss, Candida R. *God's Ghostwriters: Enslaved Christians and the Making of the Bible*. New York: Little, Brown, 2024.

Mroczek, Eva. *The Literary Imagination in Jewish Antiquity*. New York: Oxford University Press, 2016.

Mueller-Vollmer, Kurt, ed. *The Hermeneutics Reader*. London: Continuum, 2006.

Mullen, Lincoln. "The Fight to Define Romans 13." *The Atlantic*. June 2018. https://www.theatlantic.com/politics/archive/2018/06/romans-13/562916/.

Newton, Isaac. *Observations upon the Prophecies of Daniel and the Apocalypse of St. John*. London: J. Darby and T. Browne, 1733.

Newton, Isaac. "Untitled Treatise on Revelation." The Newton Project. https://www.newtonproject.ox.ac.uk/view/texts/normalized/THEM00135.

Newton, Richard. "The African American Bible: Bound in a Christian Nation." *Journal of Biblical Literature* 136, no. 1 (2017): 221–28. https://doi.org/10.15699/jbl.1361.2017.1366.

Nickelsburg, George W. E., and James C. VanderKam. *1 Enoch: The Hermeneia Translation*. Minneapolis: Fortress Press, 2012.

Nissinen, Marti, C. L. Seow, and Robert K. Ritner. *Prophets and Prophecy in the Ancient Near East*. Expanded ed. Atlanta: Society of Biblical Literature Press, 2003.

Noll, Mark A. *America's God: From Jonathan Edwards to Abraham Lincoln*. New York: Oxford University Press, 2002.

Olson, Carl E., and Sandra Miesel. *The Da Vinci Hoax: Exposing the Errors in the Da Vinci Code*. San Francisco: Ignatius Press, 2004.

Paine, Thomas. *The Age of Reason*. 200th Anniversary Edition. N.p.: Wet Water Publications, 1992.

Painter, Nell Irvin. *The History of White People*. New York: W.W. Norton, 2010.

Pardes, Ilana. *The Song of Songs: A Biography*. Princeton: Princeton University Press, 2019.

Parpola, Simo. *Assyrian Prophecies*. Helsinki: Helsinki University Press, 1997.

Paul VI, Pope. *Dei Verbum* (Dogmatic Constitution on Divine Revelation). The Holy See. November 18, 1965. https://www.vatican.va/archive/hist_councils/ii_vatican_council/documents/vat-ii_const_19651118_dei-verbum_en.html.

Paul VI, Pope. *Gaudium et Spes* (Pastoral Constitution on the Church in the Modern World). The Holy See. December 7, 1965. https://www.vatican.va/archive/hist_councils/ii_vatican_council/documents/vat-ii_const_19651207_gaudium-et-spes_en.html.

Peerbolte, Bert Jan Lietaert. "Ending a Life That Has Not Begun: Abortion in the Bible." In *The Bible in Political Debate: What Does It Really Say?*, edited by Frances Flannery and Rodney A. Werline, 47–59. London: Bloomsbury T&T Clark, 2016.

Pelikan, Jaroslav. *Whose Bible Is It? A Short History of the Scriptures*. New York: Penguin, 2006.

Peng, K. W. "Inspiration, Authority, and Hermeneutics." *Melita Theologica* 57, no. 2 (2006): 23–54.

Pew Research Center. "Political Polarization in the American Public: How Increasing Ideological Uniformity and Partisan Antipathy Affect Politics, Compromise and Everyday Life." June 12, 2014.

https://www.pewresearch.org/politics/2014/06/12/political-polarization-in-the-american-public/.

Pew Research Center. "45% of Americans Say U.S. Should Be a 'Christian Nation.'" October 27, 2022. https://www.pewresearch.org/religion/2022/10/27/45-of-americans-say-u-s-should-be-a-christian-nation/.

Philo. *On the Creation: Allegorical Interpretation of Genesis 2 and 3*. Translated by F. H. Colson and G. H. Whitaker. Cambridge, MA: Harvard University Press, 1929.

Pius XII, Pope. *Divino Afflante Spiritu* (Encyclical Letter on Promoting Biblical Studies). The Holy See. September 30, 1943. https://www.vatican.va/content/pius-xii/en/encyclicals/documents/hf_p-xii_enc_30091943_divino-afflante-spiritu.html.

Plato. *Republic*. Translated by Paul Shorey. Cambridge, MA: Harvard University Press, 1969.

Plummer, Robert. "Contra Origen: Martin Luther on Allegorizing the Biblical Text." In *Always Reforming: Reflections on Martin Luther and Biblical Studies*, edited by Robert L. Plummer and Channing L. Crisler, 13–30. Bellingham, WA: Lexham Press, 2021.

Pontifical Biblical Commission. "The Bible and Morality: Biblical Roots of Christian Conduct." The Holy See. May 11, 2008. https://www.vatican.va/roman_curia/congregations/cfaith/pcb_documents/rc_con_cfaith_doc_20080511_bibbia-e-morale_en.html.

Powery, Emerson B. *The Good Samaritan: Luke 10 for the Life of the Church*. Grand Rapids, MI: Baker Academic, 2022.

Powery, Emerson B., and Rodney S. Sadler, Jr. *The Genesis of Liberation: Biblical Interpretation in the Antebellum Narratives of the Enslaved*. Louisville: Westminster John Knox, 2016.

Proctor, Mark A. "'Who Is My Neighbor?' Recontextualizing Luke's Good Samaritan (Luke 10:25-37)." *Journal of Biblical Literature* 138, no. 1 (2019): 203–19.

Raboteau, Albert J. *Slave Religion: The "Invisible Institution" in the Antebellum South*. Rev. ed. New York: Oxford University Press, 2004.

Raheb, Mitri. *Faith in the Face of Empire: The Bible through Palestinian Eyes*. Maryknoll, NY: Orbis, 2014.

Reasoner, Mark. *Five Models of Scripture*. Grand Rapids, MI: Eerdmans, 2021.

Retief, F. P., J. F. G. Cilliers, and S. P. J. K. Riekert. "Eunuchs in the Bible." *Acta Theologica Supplementum* 7 (2005): 247–58.

Richard, Carl J. *The Founders and the Bible*. Boston: Rowman & Littlefield, 2016.

Rodriguez-Galarza, Gerardo. "The Contribution of Bernhard Neuschäfer's *Origenes als Philologe*." In *The Oxford Handbook of Origen*, edited by Ronald E. Heine and Karen Jo Torjesen, 160–74. New York: Oxford University Press, 2022.

Rosendahl, Sheri Faye. *Not Your White Jesus: Following a Radical, Refugee Messiah*. Louisville: Westminster John Knox, 2018.

Roukema, Riemer. "The Good Samaritan in Ancient Christianity." *Vigiliae Christianae* 58, no. 1 (February 2004): 56–74.

Russell, Donald A., and David Konstan. *Heraclitus: Homeric Problems*. Atlanta: Society of Biblical Literature, 2005.

Sargent, Benjamin. "Biblical Hermeneutics and the Zurich Reformation." *Evangelical Quarterly* 86, no. 4 (2014): 325–42.

Sargent, Benjamin. "'Interpreting Homer From Homer': Aristarchus of Samothrace and the Notion of Scriptural Authorship in the New Testament." *Tyndale Bulletin* 65, no. 1 (2014): 125–39.

Schipper, Jeremy. *Denmark Vesey's Bible: The Thwarted Revolt That Put Slavery and Scripture on Trial*. Princeton: Princeton University Press, 2022.

Schlesinger, Kira. *Pro-Choice and Christian: Reconciling Faith, Justice, and Politics*. Louisville: Westminster John Knox, 2017.

Schneiders, Sandra. *The Revelatory Text: Interpreting the New Testament as Sacred Scripture*. 2nd ed. Collegeville, MN: Michael Glazier, 1999.

Schroeder, H. J. *The Canons and Decrees of the Council of Trent*. St. Louis: Herder, 1941.

Shalev, Eran. "'Written in the Style of Antiquity': Pseudo-Biblicism and the Early American Republic 1770–1830." *Church History* 79 (2010): 800–826.

Sharrow, Walter G. "John Hughes and a Catholic Response to Slavery in Antebellum America." *Journal of African American History* 57 (1972): 254–69.

Simkovich, Malka. *Discovering Second Temple Literature*. Melrose Park, PA: Jewish Publication Society, 2018.

Smith, Gregory, A. "8 Facts about Catholics and Politics in the U.S." Pew Research Center. September 15, 2020. https://www.pewresearch.org/fact-tank/2020/09/15/8-facts-about-catholics-and-politics-in-the-u-s/?amp=1.

Smith, Jonathan Z. "Sacred Persistence: Toward a Redescription of Canon." In *Imagining Religion: From Babylon to Jonestown*, 36–52. Chicago: University of Chicago Press, 1982.

Stavrianos, Kyriakos. "The Parable of the Good Samaritan in Patristic Thought." *Greek Orthodox Theological Review* 57, nos. 1–4 (2012): 29–48.

Stock, Brian. *Augustine the Reader: Meditation, Self-Knowledge, and the Ethics of Interpretation*. Cambridge, MA: Belknap, 1998.

Strine, Casey. "What the Bible's Romans 13 Says about Asylum—And What Jeff Sessions Omitted." *The Conversation*. June 2018. https://theconversation.com/what-the-bibles-romans-13-says-about-asylum-and-what-jeff-sessions-omitted-98483.

Suriano, Matthew J. *A History of Death in the Hebrew Bible*. New York: Oxford University Press, 2018.

Thompson, Mark D. "Biblical Interpretation in the Works of Martin Luther." In *A History of Biblical Interpretation, Vol. 2: The Medieval through the Reformation Periods*, edited by Alan Hauser and Duane Watson, 299–318. Grand Rapids, MI: Eerdmans, 2009.

Tolkien, J. R. R. *The Fellowship of the Ring*. Boston: Houghton Mifflin, 1954.

Troutner, Timothy. "Sowing Seeds of Progressive Revelation: Origen on the Knowledge of the Prophets." *Scottish Journal of Theology* 75, no. 2 (2022): 123–36.

Turner, James. *Philology: The Forgotten Origins of the Modern Humanities*. Princeton: Princeton University Press, 2014.

Twain, Mark. *The Adventures of Huckleberry Finn: The Only Comprehensive Edition*. New York: Random House, 1996.

Unger, Dominic. Introduction to *St. Irenaeus of Lyons: Against the Heresies Book 1*. New York: Newman Press, 1992.

United States Conference of Catholic Bishops. *Open Wide Our Hearts: A Pastoral Letter Against Racism*. Washington, DC: USCCB, 2018.

Urbano, Arthur P. "Difficulties in Writing the Life of Origen." In *The Oxford Handbook of Origen*, edited by Ronald E. Heine and Karen Jo Torjesen, 118–40. New York: Oxford University Press, 2022.

Vanderbilt Project on Unity and American Democracy. "Latest Vanderbilt Unity Index Shows the U.S. Continuing Its Trend toward Increased Political Polarization." February 14, 2024. https://news.vanderbilt.edu/2024/02/14/latest-vanderbilt-unity-index-shows-the-u-s-continuing-its-trend-toward-increased-political-polarization/.

Vann, Kevin, Timothy Freye, and Thanh Thai Nguyen. "On Taking Human Persons (and Holy Scripture) Out of Context." *Orange County Catholic*. June 20, 2018. https://occatholic.com/diocese-of-orange-bishops-on-taking-human-persons-and-holy-scripture-out-of-context-2/.

Various. "An Appeal to the Cardinals of the Catholic Church." *First Things*. August 15, 2018. https://www.firstthings.com/web-exclusives/2018/08/an-appeal-to-the-cardinals-of-the-catholic-church.

Vermeulen, Karolien, and Elizabeth R. Hayes. *How We Read the Bible: A Guide to Scripture's Style and Meaning*. Grand Rapids, MI: Eerdmans, 2022.

Vosté, James M. "The Vulgate at the Council of Trent." *Catholic Biblical Quarterly* 9 (1947): 9–25.

Walton, John H. *Wisdom for Faithful Reading: Principles and Practices for Old Testament Interpretation*. Downers Grove, IL: InterVarsity Press, 2023.

Walton, Jonathan L. *A Lens of Love: Reading the Bible in Its World for Our World*. Louisville: Westminster John Knox, 2018.

Walvoord, Barbara E. *Teaching and Learning in College Introductory Religion Courses*. Oxford: Blackwell, 2008.

Warren, E. W. *Nellie Norton, Or, Southern Slavery and the Bible: A Scriptural Refutation of the Principal Arguments Upon Which the Abolitionists Rely*. Macon, GA: Burke, Boykin, 1864.

Wessman, Aaron. *The Church's Mission in a Polarized World*. Hyde Park, NY: New City Press, 2023.

Wicks, Jared, SJ. "Vatican II on Revelation—From Behind the Scenes." *Theological Studies* 71 (2010): 637–50.

Williams, Thomas, trans. *Augustine: Confessions*. Indianapolis: Hackett, 2019.

Witherup, Ronald. *Biblical Fundamentalism: What Every Catholic Should Know*. Collegeville, MN: Liturgical Press, 2001.

Witherup, Ronald. *Scripture: Dei Verbum*. Mahwah, NJ: Paulist, 2006.

Zimmermann, Ruben. "The Good Samaritan (Luke 10:30–35) and the Parables in Luke." In *Puzzling the Parables of Jesus: Methods and Interpretations*, 293–332. Minneapolis: Augsburg Fortress, 2015.

Zuckerberg, Donna. *Not All Dead White Men: Classics and Misogyny in the Digital Age*. Cambridge, MA: Harvard University Press, 2018.